JOINING HANDS

Other books by Roger S. Gottlieb

History and Subjectivity: The Transformation of Marxist Theory

Marxism 1844–1990: Origins, Betrayal, Rebirth

A Spirituality of Resistance: Finding a Peaceful Heart and Protecting the Earth

Edited by Roger S. Gottlieb

*An Anthology of Western Marxism:
From Lukacs and Gramsci to Socialist-Feminism*

A New Creation: America's Contemporary Spiritual Voices

Thinking the Unthinkable: Meanings of the Holocaust

Radical Philosophy: Tradition, Counter-Tradition, Politics

This Sacred Earth: Religion, Nature, Environment

The Ecological Community

*Deep Ecology and World Religions:
New Essays on Common Ground (with David L. Barnhill)*

JOINING HANDS

Politics and Religion Together for Social Change

Roger S. Gottlieb

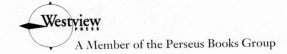

A Member of the Perseus Books Group

A Cataloging-in-Publication record is available from the Library of Congress.
0-8133-6554-6 (hardcover)   0-8133-4188-4 (paperback)

Westview Press is a member of the Perseus Books Group.
Find us on the World Wide Web at http://www.westviewpress.com

Westview Press books are available at special discounts for bulk purchases in
the U.S. by corporations, institutions, and other organizations. For more
information, please contact the Special Markets Department at the Perseus
Books Group, 11 Cambridge Center, Cambridge, MA 02142, or call (800)
255-1514 or (617) 252-5298, or e-mail specialmarkets@perseusbooks.com.

Text design by *Trish Wilkinson*
Set in 10.5-point Janson

1 2 3 4 5 6 7 8 9 10

To Life

Let Justice roll down like the waters,
Righteousness like a never ending stream.
Amos 5:24

From each according to his ability
to each according to his needs.
Karl Marx

Contents

Preface and Acknowledgements

In an old Jewish joke, two rabbis are engaged in an animated argument over the interpretation of a complicated bit of scripture. A third, seeking to make peace, reassures them, "You're both right."

"But how can that be; they say opposite things?" an onlooker asks.

"Ahh," says the peacemaker, "You . . . you're also right!"

In a nutshell, that is what *Joining Hands* says about religion and politics. There are many religious people who believe that faith enables them to live more fully, joyously, and compassionately and that it makes their communities more likely to value and sustain life. There are, likewise, many people in the tradition of progressive politics—a tradition that runs from the Declaration of Independence to struggles for women's equality, from the New Deal to environmentalist criticisms of globalization—who believe a political response to the human condition is not just about satisfying some particular interest group but is vital to the happiness of the entire human community.

I say: You are both right.

But that, of course, is not the end of the story, for at the same time there are many religious thinkers who tell us that political activism is foreign to religion, or that a religious understanding of the meaning of life does not need the insights of progressive social criticism. There are also many activists who think that religion should be private, that it can, at best, only cooperate with political movements in working on problems understood in purely political terms.

At this point, I say to them: You are both wrong. That is why I wrote this book.

I believe that although religious ethics and progressive political movements share a common vision of a transformed world, it is also true that neither can fulfill that vision without the other's help. They urgently need each other's strengths and insights. Religion and politics can—and must—cooperate to make *society* more just, environmentally sustainable, and humanly fulfilling and *religious life* more authentic and holy.

The details of these rather broad claims will be provided in the following pages.

———————

Although writing this book took eighteen months, it has actually been in preparation for more than three decades. It was during my coming of age, in the exhilarating and troubled 1960s, that I first saw how politics and religion could challenge what seemed to be a boring, complacent, and in many ways morally empty American culture and liberal capitalist economy. Resisting America's dirty war in Southeast Asia and experiencing hallucinogenic altered states, coming to grips with criticisms of corporate power and discovering spiritual alternatives to the vacuous Reform Judaism in which I'd been raised, it always seemed—during those exciting, naive and pretentious early years of the counterculture—that these new ways of seeing and living in the world should be working together.

A few years later, the counterculture split: The politicos emphasized Serious Political Work, Organizing the Masses, and Revolution. The hippies and spiritual seekers Went Back to the Land, Got Their Heads Together (or not), and sought Inner Peace.

Although I spent much more time with the politicos, the spiritual awakening I'd experienced in the 1960s never left me. I taught courses in Oriental philosophy as well as seminars on Western Marxism; I practiced yoga and helped edit a Democratic Socialist newspaper. Returning in a very different way to a very different Judaism, I helped lead Freedom Seders for Passover and joined with others to be a Jewish voice on the left and a leftist voice among Jews. I came to believe, as in a lecture I gave in 1976, that "Bodhisattvas [Buddhist saints] Belong on the Barricades" and that political life, which had become increasingly sectarian, bitter, and boring, needed a healthy dose of spiritual wisdom.

I had been teaching along these lines for some time, but it was only after the death of my first child—when I saw how inadequate purely political perspectives were to personal tragedies of this sort—that I decided to write about the spiritual contribution to politics. Because I wasn't sure exactly how these ideas needed to be expressed, and because I wanted first to be clear on my intellectual assessment of the radical tradition, it took me a while to get there. My first written efforts at synthesizing the two appeared in 1990 as the essay "Heaven on Earth: A Dialogue Between a Political Radical and a Spiritual

Seeker" and in the last chapter of my *Marxism 1844–1990: Origins, Betrayal, Rebirth,* which offered a spiritual critique of the limitations of the socialist tradition. Individual essays and edited volumes followed. Since 1994, I have focused on how a global ecological crisis is transforming traditional religion, personal spiritual life, and politics worldwide.

Now I am ready (I hope) to tackle these connections once again, this time with a comprehensive understanding that enables me to put many of the issues in wider historical and political context. My focus here includes traditional religion as well as more individually oriented forms of spirituality, the whole range of political issues as well as environmental questions, a more broadly conceived domain of politics and not just the socialist tradition. My goal throughout is to offer a fresh perspective on the relations between religion and politics. If I am successful, people will think twice (at least) before presuming that religious life and progressive political movements have different goals. More important, speakers who are rooted in either religion or politics will no longer take for granted that they can accomplish their own objectives without the help of the other side. If nothing else, I hope to propose a viewpoint in which humility, self-examination, and openness to insights from hitherto distant sources can become more of the norm for religious believers and political activists alike.

———————

If no man is an island, no author—and certainly not this one—writes without the help, inspiration, and support of many other people.

To begin with, I am grateful to Worcester Polytechnic Institute for some release time to begin the project and to students in my seminars there who read early versions of chapters and responded to the book's overall theme with intelligence and openness.

Colleagues, friends, and a few strangers interrupted their own busy lives to offer helpful comments. What they said enabled me to avoid many errors and see the big picture more clearly. My thanks to Bland Addison, Bill Baller, David Barnhill, Seamus Carey, Danny Faber, David Gottlieb, Michael Lerner, Lisa Lebduska, Mordechai Liebling, Bill Martin, reviewers for Westview Press, Richard Schmitt, and Shelley Tennebaum.

My friend and colleague Thomas Shannon gave expert critical comments on the entire project and provided helpful answers to my confused questions about Christian theology and history.

My friend and student Nick Baker provided remarkably astute comments on the entire first draft, showing that youth and inexperience are no barrier to penetrating and enormously valuable editorial help.

My specific treatments of disability, Reinhold Niebuhr, religious peace-making, and pluralism—as well as my ability to think of myself as a national commentator on religious issues—arose partly through my "Reading Spirit" column in *Tikkun* magazine. I am grateful to *Tikkun*'s editor, Michael Lerner, and its managing editor, Jo Ellen Green Kaiser.

My Westview editor, Sarah Warner, was always a treasure. She offered supportive critical encouragement, astute encouraging criticism, and some great lunches at conventions. Westview's production team—including Project Editor Katharine Chandler and Copy Editor Michele Wynn—did great work at their end.

The comments of my wife, Miriam Greenspan, helped make the book clearer and wiser. I thank all the Good Spirits for her intellectual companionship, her reassuring words during my moments of author's panic, and for the life and love we've shared for thirty years.

Most important, I owe a debt of inspiration to the brave souls who have refused to accept the world as it is. Drawing strength from contemporary communities and traditional wisdom, offering insights from religious scripture and social critique, resisting the destruction of the earth and the oppression of human beings, their moral courage and vision are the true meaning of this book.

Introduction

To the surprise of many of the last century's most respected philosophers, sociologists, historians, and freelance forecasters, religion remains a vital part of contemporary society. Whether in the striking number of Americans who believe in God and attend religious services at over 300,000 local congregations or in the appeal of a more diffuse "spirituality" in everything from twelve-step programs to mind-body medicine, it is clear that a purely secular form of life is unacceptable to a great many people. Science, technology, democracy, and large malls are not enough.

When this continuing religious sensibility moves beyond personal experience or small communities of faith and enters the wider world of politics, what then? In recent years religious voices in the political arena have been predominantly conservative. The religious right has opposed reproductive freedom and homosexuality, criticized the welfare state and affirmative action, rarely focused on racism or violence against women, and often dismissed environmentalists as pagan tree-huggers. Internationally, fundamentalists of various faiths have repressed women, suppressed democracy, and used religious appeals to justify terrorism. These forms of religion have yet to assimilate the accomplishments of modernity and certainly are not open to the insights of secular progressive politics. Explanation, analysis, and critique of such fundamentalisms are not my purpose here.

Yet for all their self-proclaimed ownership of the "true faith," the fundamentalists' violent, premodern form of devotion is not the only game in town. Religious values have taken other forms, adopting democratic, liberal, progressive, or even radical ways of thinking about and seeking to change some of society's most basic features. Groups defined by religious faith have supported women's equality, called on the broader society to protect God's creation, sought reconciliation in the midst of ethnic violence, and resisted the human costs of the triumphant global economy. And they have done so not only in support of secular justice but as an expression of God's will and spiritual wisdom. It is this aspect of contemporary religions that is my focus.

There are two main roots of progressive religious social activism. The first is the traditional ethical teaching at the core of every religious tradition. The Torah frequently admonishes us to care for the powerless and choose justice rather than siding "with the mighty to do wrong" (Exodus 22:2). In Mahayana Buddhism, the true sage seeks not a personal enlightenment but the end of suffering for all sentient beings. Christianity's focus on the poor signals the importance it accords to equality and community. Second, in modern times many people have realized that to be meaningful for the wider community, religious ethics cannot confine itself to personal relationships or charity. Rather, religion must engage in the pursuit of justice. And justice, in the modern world, has to do with politics.

At the same time, a wide range of historical developments has opened political movements to the presence of religious ideas and spiritual practices. Some liberals and radicals have realized that in struggles over poverty, peace, the environment, and social justice, they can make common cause with those motivated by religious values rather than class analysis or the interests of a particular oppressed group. Also, the track record of progressive forces has included failures, reversals, betrayals, and recurring political irrelevance. As a result, leftists have become more modest about their own accomplishments and more willing to learn from other sources. Finally, political activists have seen that religions have deep resources for dealing with the ineluctable human experiences of birth, raising children, aging, and death and that religions are adept at developing the virtues of gratitude, compassion, and joy.

Thus, from Gandhi and Martin Luther King Jr. to feminist peaceniks and Green defenders of the rain forest, from Jewish Renewal and Catholic liberation theology to the Quaker Peace Fellowship and Engaged Buddhism, people have sought to synthesize political and religious goals and values. They have claimed that authentic religion requires an activist, transforming presence in the political world and that the moral and psychological insights of religion are of enormous value for those engaged in political struggle. Many who identify primarily as "religious" or "political" have seen the virtues of each other's knowledge; and for some, the cooperation of religion and progressive politics is taken for granted.

Joining Hands examines the philosophical basis of religion and radical politics as two "ways of world making," investigating their similar capacities as critical alternatives to conventional social life and arguing that the most vital parts of each cannot be fulfilled without the critical help of the other. Both religion and radical politics claim universal and extrasocietal sources of values and knowledge, but the tendency of each to inauthentic forms of self-interest, violence, or oppressiveness needs to be checked by its counterpart. Properly understood, they are not enemies, but comrades.

In Part 1 of the book, I establish this position through extensive discussion of the essential values, successes, and failures of both traditional religions and progressive political movements. In the first few chapters, I pay more attention to religion than to politics. This imbalance stems from the simple fact that although it is reasonably clear that politics is in the business of changing the world, it is less obvious that religion, especially in modern times, should have a similar vocation. Once my reasons for believing why it does so are clear, a rough equality of attention returns. In Part 2, I offer interpretations of the achievements and limitations of nonviolent Christianity in the civil rights movement, of the feminist transformation of contemporary religion, of the remarkable fellowship of religion and politics in global environmental politics, and of how the personal sorrows of breast cancer and disability call for both spiritual wisdom and political action.

First, however, it is necessary to indicate in a little more detail why the book is necessary. "After all," you might be saying, "do we really need *another* book on religion and politics?" Not surprisingly, I think we do. To put it simply: The full openness of religion and politics to each other's insights is far from complete. It is accepted by a modest percentage of theorists and activists; and in many cases it is held only incompletely. In particular, many are willing to recommend a distressingly one-sided openness: Religious thinkers will tell us how social struggles can benefit from religious values, but they ignore the beneficial effects of politics on religion. Secular liberals describe how political values need to circumscribe religion into an appropriately "private" sphere, but they are blind to religion's creative contributions to social ethics and community.

To take one example, consider *God's Name in Vain: The Wrongs and Rights of Religion in Politics*, by Yale law professor and cultural critic Stephen L. Carter. Rarely has support for religion's contributions to social life—and an argument *against* restricting those contributions because of some imagined wall between church and state—been so clearly spelled out. That is why an account of some of the limitations of Carter's lucid and thoughtful book is important.

For Carter, precisely to the extent that America is committed to religious freedom, it must not only allow but welcome religiously inspired voices in public debates. Religion offers, Carter tells us, a "prophetic voice" that is an alternative to the immorally pragmatic, narcissistic, and power-for-power's-sake tendencies of the state and popular culture. To ask religious people to engage in public life without their religious values is as unfair and nonsensical as asking a Democrat, a CEO, or a union leader to jettison the values and beliefs that command their allegiance.

As an indication that Carter's concern is warranted, consider two stories from today's morning newspaper.[1] First, there is liberal columnist Joan Vennochi's condemnation of local Catholic leader Bernard Cardinal Law. His mistake, she tells us, is mixing "politics with religion," in a "very unsubtle way" by supporting Massachusetts Republican governor Jane Swift. Swift had been criticized by some Massachusetts Democrats for conducting business by phone and fax from a hospital room while awaiting the birth of twins. Law had rallied to her defense. It's not clear whether the Democrat Vennochi was more upset about the cardinal's lack of subtlety in supporting a Republican or the fact that he is politically conservative, not much of a feminist, and pro-life. In any case, though my political views are much closer to Vennochi's than Law's, I do not see why it might be legitimate to express views inspired by John Locke, John Stuart Mill, or Betty Friedan but not those emanating from whatever sources a Catholic cardinal uses. If it is Law's positions that bother Vennochi, let her criticize them without suggesting there is something suspect about Law expressing himself—on whatever topic—in a sermon. If it is the tacit idea that religion somehow lowers itself by participating in the corruptions of politics, then Vennochi should realize two things: First, religious figures can be as corrupt and self-serving as any politician; and, second, our task is therefore to support political and religious figures who are not corrupt, whether they are commenting on the governor, administering church funds, or passing laws.

On the same day, the *Boston Globe* also reported that Attorney General John Ashcroft had been criticized for holding Bible-study sessions, among other reasons because some observers feared he might punish those who didn't attend. Little would have been said, I imagine, if Ashcroft had been studying secular ethicists like John Rawls or Alasdair MacIntyre. It's all right to study moral ideas, these critics seem to be saying, as long as they are not religious ones! From my point of view, it would certainly be wrong for Ashcroft to force attendance or to demote those who prefer Plato to the Gospels. But so would it be a problem if someone penalized subordinates who preferred Kant to Aristotle, for liberal feminists to punish radical feminists, or for Democrats to be antagonistic to Republicans. Is religion, after all, the only topic on which elected officials can be narrow, sectarian, and punitive? The key point is not which books are being read, but how superiors' beliefs of any kind are forced on subordinates.

The kind of narrow-mindedness expressed in the *Globe* articles is thus something quite properly rejected by Carter. But he goes much further than defending believers' right to be heard in the public square by claiming that American religion has manifested uniquely prophetic gifts. From the abolition of slavery and struggles against the excesses of industrial capitalism to the civil rights movement, he tells us, religion has been at the forefront of movements for social justice. The real danger for the broader society is that excluding religion from public debate will allow the state to dominate social life without a competing and corrective voice. The political pursuit of domination and power will reign supreme, as will, sadly, a secular culture oriented to psychologically and spiritually debilitating consumption. The only cautionary note Carter sounds is to warn religion not to become invested in actually wielding political power. The pursuit of power leads to compromise, accommodation, and, not to put to fine a point on it, selling out to the highest bidder for popular acceptance. The way of the prophet is to witness, to call, to instruct—not to win elections! In an image Carter adapts from colonial religious leader Roger Williams, the religious spirit must tend its own garden, and not become overwhelmed by the wilderness of politics.

Although I respect Carter's intelligence and passion, I think his position has some serious problems. The most important of these is his presumption that politics is the realm of power, compromise, and expedience, and religion's is that of moral values and timeless spiritual truths. Little serious attention is devoted to the way religion can contain narrow, sectarian, violent, and oppressive values and practices, to the way religion itself is, in a broad sense, *political*—or, at least, to the way religion might benefit from the moral insights of secular politics.

> Religion is, *at its best*, subversive of the society in which it exists. Religion's subversive power flows from its tendency to focus the attention, and ultimately the values of its adherents on a set of understandings often quite different from the understanding of the dominant forces in the culture. The larger culture ... will always try to impose a set of meanings on all of its subcultures; of all the subcultures in a society, religion is almost always the one best able to resist.[2]

I agree that religion "at its best" can do these things—and I offer an account of why it can in Chapter 1 and throughout the book.

But what about religion "at its worst" or even at its "less than best"? Does it fail *only* when it is seduced by the lust for political power? Or could it be that religion has always included within itself many of the conventional values of the society in which it functions, values in need of serious reform or transformation? Carter is at pains to show how Christians contributed to the abolition of slavery, but while he points out that there were preachers on both sides of the issue, he doesn't seem to think the religious support of slavery tells us very much about the true nature of religion. Religion's resistance to slavery is essential; its support, it seems, is insignificant. Similarly, Carter stresses the role of Christianity in the civil rights movement—a role I'll examine in some detail in Chapter 5—without stressing its part in supporting segregation. Martin Luther King Jr. used to say that the most segregated hour in American life is 10 A.M. Sunday morning, when everyone goes to church. And we might remember that what might be his most famous piece of writing, the "Letter from the Birmingham Jail," was a response to eight clergymen telling him to go slow, be patient, and obey the law. As historian of the times Charles Marsh observes: "[B]oth the civil rights and the anti-civil rights movements were saturated with religion; in every mass meeting, church service and Klan rally, God's name was invoked and His power claimed."[3]

It will not do to applaud religion for inspiring the civil rights movement without also criticizing it for legitimizing segregation. In regard to race relations, religion has reinforced the status quo as much as resisted it. Senator Joseph Lieberman made the same error as Carter in a widely publicized vice-presidential campaign speech. "The core of those original values [of American democracy and culture]—faith, family, and freedom; equal opportunity, respect for the basic dignity of human life; and tolerance for individual differences—clearly had their roots in the Judeo-Christian ethic of the Founders." One can only ask, which versions of the "Judeo-Christian ethic" are these? The ones that sanctioned slavery? Disenfranchised women? Justified the genocide against Native Americans?[4]

It is not only past religious errors that are at stake. Carter (and other commentators like him) tells us that in contemporary America, religious communities are distinct alternatives to liberal, secular modernity. And of course believers' attitudes about sexuality, drug use, the nuclear family, pornography, and abortion typically present such an alternative. On the other hand, the religious right's attachment to patriarchy, hierarchy, violence, capitalism, militaristic patriotism, and homophobia (to name a few) exhibits the ways in which it very much resembles, and hardly serves as an alternative to, the wider culture. This is because the religious right, like every other religious group, is a complicated mixture of transcendence and self-interest, authentic moral values and the perpetuation of unjust privilege—and because, as I'll argue in the following pages, the most sincere life of faith is liable to make some real moral errors if it does not learn from progressive political movements.

Carter ignores these issues because, I suspect, he sees "politics" as pretty much exclusively the realm of government. What other people would call "political movements"—such as the civil rights movement or the women's movement—he terms "social movements." (Except, that is, when he wants to use the religious presence in those movements as proof of religion's contribution to American "politics.") However, limiting "politics" to the state is a mistake. As large, impersonal, and powerful as our government may be, in a democracy its policies and principles are still an outgrowth of, and dependent on, "civil society." The government is deeply affected by the powers and preferences of corporations and media, by mass movements of class, gender, race, religion, and ethnicity, by communities and citizen initiatives, by what folks learn in school, teach their children, and talk about at work. Further, as the women's movement taught—and Carter seems not to have learned—our most personal relationships and our most prized cultural traditions are shot through with "politics"; that is, with beliefs and practices that justify how power is acquired and held and how social roles are distributed. Any statement of values is potentially political; any social movement is political; all moral values that govern human relations have a political dimension.

As dismaying as it may be, even the very notion of what a religion is has political overtones. To ask for "freedom of religion"—along with enviable exemptions from taxes and from laws against discrimination in hiring—is to presuppose that we know how to pick out "religions" from other sorts of social groups. But this matter has always been political, decided by laws and courts. These tell us that Catholics' swallowing the Eucharist is a religious ritual, but Native Americans' swallowing peyote is something else—no matter what is claimed by Native Americans. The synagogue I attend gets its tax exemption; a gathering of radical feminist followers of Wicca attended by a friend of mine does not.[5]

For most of Carter's narrative, prophetic religious voices confront an overweening state bureaucracy; vacillating believers get seduced by the trappings of power; and secular intellectuals make fun of sincere devotion and faith. Left out (among other things) are the positive effects political movements have had on religion. He laments the political irrelevance of the mainstream churches while failing to acknowledge how many of them, under the tutelage of secular feminists and environmentalists, have taken truly radical stands about gender justice and about humanity's relation to nature. Conversely, when Carter attributes the successes of the civil rights movement to its religious ideals, he does not consider that its failures or limitations might be the result of its inability to join those religious ideals with a political understanding of racism as a complicated social structure. Such an understanding might have enabled the civil rights movement to accomplish deeper, and less easily co-opted, goals.

All these points will be developed in Part 2; and I offer throughout the book many other examples of how secular political ideas and movements have—or could have—helped religion become what Carter calls "its best." Of course the view that religions are improved when they accept democracy, the equal value of women, and environmentalism is one view among many. If

I am asked what gives me the right to define religion's proper course, my answer is that arguments about what religion should be are part of what religion is, just as arguments about justice, beauty, knowledge, and objectivity
have been essential to law, art, education, and science.[6] Debates about God,
faith, the true church, and the nature of authentic devotion permeate the history of all religious traditions. Consequently, there is just as much—probably
more—deep disagreement about religion among believers themselves than
there is criticism of religion from secularists.

Missing this point, Carter, like too many other believers, confuses the seriousness of religion—its binding call, its claim to know us best and speak to the
best within us—with its literal truth.[7] Yet one can take religion seriously—believe, for instance, that the Bible is the word of God—without necessarily taking it literally, for literal statements are not the only ones we take seriously.
We know that poetry must be interpreted, that myths may be enormously
powerful without being factual in the same way store inventories or newspaper stories are, and that dreams, while important, carry hard-to-decipher
meanings. There is no reason we cannot be deeply religious, even biblical, and
see sacred scriptures in these ways. And there is simply no unambiguous truth
to be found in any case. Religious life always requires selection and interpretation. The Bible is an instructive example here, since it is part of Carter's claim
that believing Christians are those who follow it literally. Yet how many of the
Christian fundamentalists who, for instance, appeal to the Bible in defense of
their disdain for homosexuality, refuse to eat shrimp or pork because "holy
scripture" forbids it? How many follow prescriptions about bringing animal
sacrifices to the temple in Jerusalem three times a year? Or are ready to stone
someone to death for working on the Sabbath? These commands are stated as
unequivocally as is the condemnation of homosexuality.

For all these reasons, we cannot simply agree or disagree with Carter's
claims that religions make society better, any more than we can unequivocally say that politicians, movies, or public education do the same. It all depends, really, on which ones you have in mind.

The task, as I argue throughout this book, is to take religion seriously in
the face of ever-increasing state power and an ever more manipulative and immoral popular culture, and also to bring a religious consciousness into the
public square in a manner free from violence and absolutism. Believers should
certainly avoid the spiritless relativism of popular culture, but they can hardly
be a "light unto the nations" if they forget their own limitations.

———————

Not surprisingly, comparable mistakes are made on the other side of the
fence. For instance, aggressively secular feminist Ellen Willis—writing in

America's premier left publication, *The Nation*—presumes that religious believers cannot be passionate without being intolerant. Whereas Carter (for reasons that are not exactly clear) thinks believers should accept religious pluralism even while they "know" that their religion is absolutely true, Willis has deep suspicions about the role of religion in public life altogether.[8] Further, she explicitly rejects an increasingly "pro-church" stand by the left. Democracy, she believes, absolutely requires a secular culture. And though her passion for secular values might seem to put her at odds with Carter, their beliefs are similar in at least one respect: Just as Carter does not realize that religious life has a great deal to learn from politics, so Willis cannot see progressive politics learning much from religion. In this position she echoes a familiar secular refrain: that religion is too irrational to be taken seriously and too volatile to be allowed a public presence.

Willis's immediate focus is the controversy over "charitable choice," the provision, first passed into law in the 1996 Welfare Reform Act, of allowing religious institutions to receive federal funds to administer welfare services. In the early days of his administration, George W. Bush sought to expand faith-based welfare services, even establishing a government office of "faith-based and community initiatives" to make policy suggestions about how religious organizations could help with the nation's welfare services.

Critics have raised many questions about charitable choice, and Bush's proposed expansion—which included broadening the religious exemption from antidiscrimination laws in hiring—provoked the wrath of much of the liberal establishment, as well as that of some religious groups concerned that the government regulations accompanying financial support might lessen religious autonomy.[9] Charitable choice has been opposed by "Christian establishmentarians" fearful that minority religions might get governmental recognition and supports, by "strict separatists" who believe in the importance of an inviolable wall between church and state, and by liberals who see charitable choice as a ruse to allow government to abandon responsibility for the poor. By contrast, some "constructive pluralists" "recognize that American religious diversity is here to stay" and are "apt to see the constructive rather than destructive potential of permitting a space in public life for adherents of the various faiths."[10] Willis's article arises in this context.

Just like Carter, Willis believes that religion cannot avoid maintaining the literal and absolute quality of its claims.

[A]s many devout believers will admit, there is *an inherent tension between religion and democracy*. The authority of the biblical religions—which are the main subject of this debate—is embedded in sacred texts, religious laws and ecclesiastical hierarchies that claim to transmit absolute truth and serve the

will of a Supreme Being. Democracy, in contrast, depends on the Enlightenment values of freedom and equality, which are essential to genuine self-
government. In a democracy, truths are provisional and subject to debate—
which doesn't mean arbitrary, only arguable. A society grounded in
democratic principles can neither restrict people's choices because they
don't conform to religious truths nor give them privileged treatment because they do.[11]

Generalizing from religious totalitarians, Willis believes that religions *as such*
must be restrained in order to protect democratic society and secular culture.
The proper place for religion, she tells us, is as a "matter of personal conscience and identity." Only when it is in fundamental agreement with—and,
as it were, takes direction from—secular political movements can it legitimately join public debates and struggles: "[C]hurches have played a significant role in left movements for peace, civil rights and abolition of the death
penalty. But for the most part, religious liberals and leftists have allied with
their secular counterparts on matters of common concern, rather than working to promote the power of religion itself or taking issue with the secular left
on specifically religious grounds."
   Willis's position contains many errors. For example, she explicitly resists
Carter's "religious" appropriation of the civil rights movement by asking
"What about A. Philip Randolph, Rosa Parks, Ella Baker, Bob Moses, John
Lewis, Julian Bond, Jim Forman—secular activists all—and such nonchurch-
run organizations as the NAACP, CORE and SNCC?" One wonders first if
the historical errors here reveal a desire to downplay religion's positive contributions. For instance, John Lewis was deeply molded by religious faith and
was a seminary student when he joined the movement. The founding statement of the Student Nonviolent Coordinating Committee (SNCC), written
by key movement organizer James Lawson, stated: "We affirm the philosophical or religious ideal of nonviolence as the foundation of our purpose,
the presupposition of our faith, and the manner of our action. Nonviolence
as it grows from the Judaic-Christian tradition seeks a social order of justice
permeated by love."[12]
   More important than these clearly religious influences on activists Willis
lists as secular is the fact that even secular advocates of civil disobedience were
employing a perspective on social change that had extremely strong roots in religious or spiritually oriented philosophies. The major sources of nonviolence
are Thoreau, Tolstoy, and Gandhi—thinkers whose understanding of social life
was hardly limited to secular "individual rights." These men rejected the notion that spiritual ideals—for example, religiously inspired use of nonviolence

to pursue social justice—could be limited to Willis's "personal identity and conscience."[13] They sought to make very definite social changes, at times by using the power of the state. (The civil rights movement, for instance, gave great support to the Voting Rights Act of 1964.) Yet they did so in a way that was at least as compatible with democracy and religious pluralism as principled secular political movements from organized labor to radical feminism.

As Carter has little use for the insights of politics, so Willis sees no place for the particular strengths of religion. Yet some religious values might assist her own political agenda. For instance, as theologian Francis Schussler Fiorenza argues, government welfare policy is typically about the use of laws and money. To the extent that other resources are needed to help individuals or communities confront personal or collective problems, religiously oriented values of compassion, valuing each person, forgiveness, and self-transformation may be critical for success.[14] Similarly, a prominent Protestant leader argues that faith-based agencies

> seek spiritual transformation in their clients not only as a worthy goal in itself, but also as fundamental to their ability to achieve the secular social goals desired by government and foundations. The faith-based approach of these agencies is grounded in an understanding of persons as free body-soul unities created in the image of God. In this worldview, no area of a person's life can be adequately considered in isolation from the spiritual, and spiritual well-being has a profound effect on the psychological, physical, social and economic dimensions of a person's life as well. A vibrant personal faith, it is claimed, endows life with meaning and purpose, overcoming the grip of nihilism and despair; brings a new sense of dignity and worth, countering the stigmatizing effects of poverty; and offers hope for the future, motivating positive steps toward change . . . Further, the community of believers offers a network of caring friends who provide emotional, spiritual and material support.[15]

Although the overall effectiveness of such an orientation remains open to question, it seems probable that—like different types of psychotherapy or dress styles—it will work wonderfully for some people and poorly for others. What is disappointing is that Willis hardly considers the prospect that the secular progressives' goal of improving the life of the poor might be furthered by religious values. Instead, she seems to think, we all need to be protected from those values.

Most generally, Willis seems unaware of how varied religion is and of the way many forms of religion have sought to integrate themselves into democratic modernity without becoming secular. She ignores the ecumenism of Vatican II in the 1960s, Buddhist-Christian dialogue, and African-American Baptist churches and Jewish groups creating "Freedom Seders" together. In fact, finding ways to live with and learn from other religions and from secular thought has been on some people's religious agenda for centuries.

Unfortunately, advocates on both sides of the religion-politics divide have a tendency to err in these ways. When Christian thinkers John Milbank and Stanley Hauerwas tell us that liberal secular society is oriented toward domination and control ("necessarily implicated in an ontology of violence") they—like Willis—are simply painting the other side with a broad and distorting brush.[16]

If history has taught us anything, it is that secular values, just like religious ones, can be held violently or nonviolently, with mutual respect and openness or with dogmatism and hate. Thus, religious social activism—over poverty or abortion or peace—is not *in principle* different from that of feminists who seek to outlaw wife beating and sexual harassment in the workplace or environmentalists who seek to restrict the ecologically destructive use of private property. These are all expressions of strongly held beliefs that *in principle* cannot be kept private and that while not necessarily leading to direct violence call on society to accept certain actions and forbid others.

That is why Willis's claims that political values are subject to discussion but religious ones are not, and that therefore religion is incompatible with democracy, are wrong. Are we to suppose that *she* is particularly open-minded about her feminism? That the leftist editors of *The Nation* are seriously examining the possibility of becoming Republicans? When human beings have religious *or* political beliefs that they take seriously, they rarely (if ever) seriously examine the foundations of those beliefs. Further, could Willis have forgotten that in the history of the "secular left" there are countless occasions when the pursuit of political values led to repressive political behavior, intolerance of alternative views and—in many of the tragic histories of socialism and communism—to massive state violence against dissidents? If religion should be restricted because of the sins of religious fundamentalists, should political movements be privatized because of the sins of political fundamentalists?

Contrary to Willis, there are now voices within virtually all religions calling for universal respect, compassion, and care. Thich Nhat Hanh claims it is *religiously* wrong ever to try to impose one's views on another. Protestant theologian John Cobb says that openness to change and to learning from other faiths is *essential* to Christianity.

Gandhi read from the scriptures of several religions before his mass meetings and Martin Luther King Jr. found no conflict between the highest ideals of democracy and religious truth. In Boston, a quiet group of pro-life Catholics and pro-choice secularists has been meeting, talking, and finding at least some common ground for several years. Dialogue among different religions and between religious and secular ethicists is everyday stuff. These ideals do not settle all disputes or remove all differences, any more than ideals of secular justice eliminate all conflicts over rights or property. But placing a premium on virtues of universal compassion and concern means that hatred, violence, and self-righteousness are devalued and the search for understanding, appreciation, and common ground are given greater respect.

If we applied the same kind of sloppy generalizations to "secular" political thinkers that secular critics do to religion, we might lump Strom Thurmond with Robert Kennedy, Barry Goldwater with Ralph Nader, and perhaps Stalin with Franklin Delano Roosevelt. Further, when we see how Catholic priest Daniel Berrigan and the secular Daniel Ellsberg joined in antiwar civil disobedience while "religious" Catholic bishops and the secular Robert MacNamara supported the war, we realize that the distinction between "religion" and "secular" is perhaps not so enlightening. Those who would persecute and exploit others can use religion to justify their ends, but they can also appeal to the free market, nationalism, or "globalization." In our tortured age, religion has not cornered the market on sectarian violence and dogmatism.

Of course, passionate religious souls might well upset our liberal applecart, but so have the union movement, Students for a Democratic Society (SDS), and Greenpeace. At times, some upset is just what we need. By now the "best" of the religious spirit has learned its lessons and the worst is no more threatening than secular fanatics, totalitarians, and exploiters. In fact, the history of socialist governments, movements for social equality, contemporary debates about political correctness, and murderous ethnic conflicts teaches us that political movements would do well to seek some religious instruction about listening, compassion, and valuing other human beings.

From my own standpoint, which is (as the reader may have guessed) somewhat to the left of center, it seems downright silly to criticize conservative or fundamentalist religion on the grounds that religion should be excluded from public life, or in the name of some abstract, universal objectivity. Rather, we should criticize right-wing fundamentalists not because they are *religious* but because they are *wrong:* because they have an uncaring attitude toward the earth, suppress the rights of women, and accept government repression or unfettered capitalism. In this criticism, our most effective ally may well be forms of religion that have already been touched by the insights of modern progressive politics but nevertheless also hold fast to their connections with tradition. Argumentative strategies are generally more effective the more of the opposing position they accept. One is more likely to be heard if one says, "I too worship Jesus, but I don't think Jesus would support the murder of abortion providers" than if one says, "All you religious crackpots ought to be excluded from the public realm." The choice is no longer between "secular reason" and "faith," but between different meanings of faith itself.

Passionate sincerity and repressive intolerance—is it really surprising that these are found in *both* religions and politics? As Carter points out repeatedly in regard to religion: Deeply held beliefs are only that to the extent that they shape the way we live, thus molding not only our personal lives but the norms and goals we want for our communities. When Carter dismisses politics as a realm without principle and Willis paints religion as too explosive to be let out of the private realm, they make similar—though opposite—errors. Both want to downplay their tradition's historically obvious failings and exaggerate those of the other side!

Given the inadequacy of both approaches, what shall we conclude? Well, we might be tempted to declare "a plague on both your houses." This response, however, would leave us with little alternative to the status quo: from MTV and the existing political parties to the current state of public education and our treatment of the environment. Anyone who thinks these things are acceptable, sustainable, or rational probably doesn't need to read any further—for the religion and politics of which I write here are not so tolerant, and the best of today's religion and politics simply cannot accept the status quo. They deny that unending economic development without moral purpose, theocratic tyrannies, ever larger supplies of Prozac, and the prospect of the Internet in every village are the best humanity can do in the way of justice and human fulfillment. For them, the prophetic voice of religion and the secular left's historical struggles remain the best hopes of changing—and perhaps of saving—the world.

Whatever their errors or excesses, it is to these two traditions we must turn. But we must do so, I believe, with eyes open to their failures as well as their successes, their weaknesses as well as their strengths. And as I will try to show, it is precisely in each other's strengths that the resources to help overcome each other's weaknesses may well be found.

Part ONE

1

Two Ways of
World Making

*This is the fast I desire: To unlock the fetters of wickedness,
and untie the cords of the yoke. To let the oppressed go free;
to break off every yoke.
It is to share your bread with the hungry
And to take the wretched into your home;
When you see the naked, to clothe him,
And not to ignore your own kin.*

—Isaiah 58:6–7

*Life is beautiful. Let the future generations cleanse it of all
evil, oppression, and violence, and enjoy it to the full.*

—Leon Trotsky[1]

As we grow up, we learn that the physical world has limits that can be
transgressed only at our peril—the sharp edges of the stones by the river, the
wasp's sting, taxis speeding down the street. In the same way, we discover that
the human world has its limits as well. We find out what is allowed and what
forbidden, who lives in luxury while others serve, and who has the last word
around the house, in the village, in the global economy. We take into ourselves the shape of the social world, conforming to its division of labor, hierarchy of power, distribution of worth and dishonor. Our very selves are
formed by our acceptance of social life as it is. After all, we did not create

these things; to grow up at all we must learn that "this is the way things are." As Martin Heidegger put it, we are "thrown" into a world we did not make.

Others have made the world. And it is our task, like it or not, to conform.

Throughout history this kind of acceptance has been the norm, yet another response has also existed. Along with acquiescence, conformity, and fitting in, there have been attempts to challenge existing values and forms of power and to make the world anew. In the same way the development of technology has allowed us over the centuries to change our experience of nature, so there are historical forms of thought and collective action that offer us the possibility of fundamental social change.

I will call these forms of thought and collective action "ways of world making." They invite us to view the contours and confines of social life as a human creation subject to human judgment and transformation. They instruct us not to accept but to evaluate critically, not to fit in but to break the mold, not to play the game but to change the rules.

As the sources of our most comprehensive understandings of human existence, religion and politics are our two most important ways of world making. Paradoxically, their ideals serve as the building blocks of the social reality we find—and also offer hope and courage that society can be changed for the better. At their best they offer a way out of stultifying habits, unjust norms, oppressive social relationships, and collective irrationality. At their worst they mimic, reinforce, or even make up the social world as it is. What I seek to show in this book is that their shared identity as ways of world making give religion and politics a shared purpose and that both religion and politics stand a much better chance of succeeding at that shared purpose if they mutually reinforce, teach, and aid each other.

Of course this claim may sound somewhat peculiar. How can religion, which has for much of human history been the main buttress of conventional social reality, be considered a critical alternative *to* that reality? The major task of religious authorities has been, many will say, to reinforce existing values and institutions or offer an escape from them, not to rebel. Similarly, it might be asked, doesn't "politics" define the existing distribution of social power rather than some hoped-for alternative? Most important, haven't religion and politics always been antagonistic adversaries?

These questions are valid. Religion and politics have been (at least) two-sided in their relation to society: at once supportive and critical, defining the norms and overthrowing them, counseling obedience to standard values, and teaching new ones. Yet their world-making capacity clearly emerges when we consider some of their basic features. For example, religions claim that what they believe is based on the word of God or on the teachings of sages who have comprehended the essential meaning of the human condition. It is on this basis that they offer a counterweight to the conventional wisdom that would respect norms simply because of their wide acceptance or obey secular authorities simply because they have the most power. Liberal, radical, or revolutionary politics, relying on different forms of justification, have a similar interest in rejecting the oppressive logic of "prevailing conditions" and "common sense." Political visions assert that the present social reality is not the best we can hope for, that it can be decisively changed, and that the end result will be both morally better and more humanly fulfilling than what we have now.

Similarly, both religion and politics claim sources of knowledge, value, and authority that escape the limitations of conventional ways of thinking and acting. Religions draw on inspiration, revelation, and inner knowledge; radical politics draw on a reasoned critique, a creative vision of what is possible, and the emotionally charged understanding of the social sources of one's most personal suffering. Both ways of world making, that is, find truths that transcend the self-limiting acceptance of existing forms of power and belief.

Also, we find that in many ways a common ethical core motivates both activist religion and progressive politics. Every religion, however imperfectly its adherents may practice them, has detailed ethical teachings that instruct us to love, respect, and care for one another. Similarly, a common thread of the pursuit of ever wider social justice runs from the American Bill of Rights to the platform of the early-twentieth-century Socialist Party, from Martin Luther King Jr. to the National Organization of Women, from Greenpeace to Peace Now. Marx's vision of a socialist utopia clearly carries some of the elements of the Judeo-Christian concept of the messianic age. Progressive attempts to mitigate the lot of the poor resonate with the Sermon on the Mount. The Engaged Buddhist concern with community echoes the feminist stress on connection rather than autonomy.

Further, in rare cases both religion and politics can inspire a similar transcendence of the self, a joyous dissolution of our private concerns into the holy camaraderie of the struggle for justice, peace, and community. In this light, consider a tale of the Chinese revolution. It happened during the Long March, when the Communists were escaping encirclement by repressive forces of the conservative central government by making a several-thousand-mile journey from southern China to the North. Proceeding along a mountain trail, they needed to traverse a narrow bridge spanning a deep chasm. Warplanes strafed them from the sky; on the other side of the bridge, a machine gun threatened anyone who dared to cross. Volunteers were needed to charge the machine gun, the first twenty or thirty of whom would surely die before it could be overrun. After officers called for volunteers, more than a hundred men stepped forward without hesitation. In a very different setting, we find the monks who burned themselves to death to protest the violence of the Vietnam War. With principled dedication to nonviolence, they rejected all military options. With calm courage, they set themselves on fire in order to awaken others to the full horror of the war.[2] However we might judge these particular movements or the actions taken on their behalf, we nevertheless see in both examples a dedication to a new world, which moves people far beyond the limits of ordinary human capabilities.

Sadly, however, along with their similar goals and the selfless passions they can inspire, religion and radical politics also share a common tendency to fall short of what they could be—and in fact of their own self-proclaimed goals. History offers us many dismal examples of claims to spiritual virtue or revolutionary purity that mask self-interest and oppression.

How religion and politics can redress some of these failures by making use of the insights and practices of the other is described throughout this book. In the rest of this chapter, I explain more clearly what I mean by "religion" and "politics" and continue to develop my account of how they can remake the world.

————————

Definitions of religion abound, but few carry as much weight as the term itself. Long before we try to figure out what the word means, we pray or we see people pray; we enter churches or synagogues, see crosses hanging from people's necks, and listen to actresses thank God for their Academy Award; we hear politicians invoke God's blessing on their country (and political party) or see a minister at a wedding.

When we try to define the concept in detail, we find that it needs to be understood not as some fixed set of attributes held by each and every religion but rather as a cluster of related, overlapping, but distinct characteristics. Every religion will have some of these characteristics, and perhaps no religion will have them all.

If, for example, we identify religion with belief in a Supreme Being, we exclude Buddhism, which is rooted in the teaching of a wise person rather than a God. If we emphasize the ethical teachings that are in fact central to religion, we include many secular moralities that pride themselves on being virtuous without accepting holy texts or divinities. If we think of religion as centering on the supernatural, we leave out the kind of nature worship that finds divinity in nature.

One response to these difficulties is to emphasize the adverb and adjective derivatives rather than the noun. A "religion," we might say, is what we believe or follow "religiously"—with dedication, passion, and commitment. A ceremony is "religious" when it is performed with a certain gravity or intensity. A "religious" view of the world is one that tries to understand the whole of things, to relate personal and social destiny to the fundamental nature of the universe. But if this is our strategy for understanding religion, we end up saying that passion, devotion, seriousness, and a philosophical view of life are necessarily religious. In that case, the orthodox Communist would be as religious as the Orthodox Jew; and we would have no way to distinguish a secular devotion or a worldly passion from a spiritual one. I suspect that this outcome would ultimately be unsatisfying. Even though a number of thinkers have shown the psychological similarity between fervent political activists and fanatical religious devotees, it is still a stretch to talk about purely secular involvements as religion—no matter how much passion is shown at college football games or rock concerts.

So, at the risk of adding to the confusion or violating the reader's intuitions, I will sketch how the concept is used here. For me, religions are systems of belief, ritual, institutional life, spiritual aspiration, and ethical orientation that view human beings as more than simply their social or physical selves. Teachings are "religious" when they assert (as in Judaism, Christianity, and Islam) that there exists a Supreme Being whose moral commands and ultimate power supersedes even the grandest of earthly political authorities. Alternatively, even without a Supreme Being, Buddhism offers a religious insight when it teaches that we can achieve a state of consciousness that transcends the attachments and passions of our ordinary social egos. To be religious, in this sense, is to be aware that some things have "ultimate significance"—in the sense of being fundamental, important, long-lasting, and supremely fitting to who we really are.[3]

Yet whatever our essential religious identity, we must live in and with the world. As religious beings we move between the holy and the secular, our spiritual aspirations and our conventional lives, reaching toward God or Ultimate Truth and just hanging out. In this complex and demanding dance, religions prescribe norms of conduct to shape the familiar settings of family and community. These teachings are meant to root our everyday relationships in spiritual truths about our essential identity. God, or Truth, or our Buddha Nature can be expressed in the way we marry, do business, raise our children, or deal with rush-hour traffic. To make these ideas a vital presence in the world, church schools teach the young and buildings are maintained for collective gatherings. Special holidays provide concentrated arenas of religious energy. Ritual acts of prayerful worship, meditation, collective contrition, or celebration awaken and reinforce personal and communal connections to Ultimate Truth(s), train the personality to reflect certain values in daily life, and provide emotional outlets during life-cycle events such as marriage, birth, and death.

Finally, religions invite us to cultivate a sense of awe and mystery. This need not be a blind attachment to a confusing creed or a dogmatic attachment to making endless moral judgments about others. It can reflect, as in the title of a book by Abraham Joshua Heschel, simply a desire for wonder: a sense, that is, that the universe as a whole and human existence within it are more beautiful and profound than we can ever fully realize.[4]

What then of the concept of the "spiritual," often used to suggest something different from—but closely related to—religion? "I'm not religious at all," people will frequently say, "but I do have a pretty active spiritual life." Spiritual aspirations, I believe, are in fact a kind of religious perspective, sharing the emphasis on a reality distinct from one's conventional social position and on values that dissent from the social order. Yet it is a kind of religiosity that accentuates personal experience, theological tolerance, and lifelong pursuit of spiritual development rather than contentment with religious normality. People who say they are "spiritual" but not "religious" often mean that they pick and choose among different traditions and practices, that they are not part of a formal religious congregation, that they are more concerned with their own spiritual development than with judging the religious orthodoxy of anyone else. For my purposes, then, the term "spirituality" is not opposed to religion but simply emphasizes a certain way of being religious.[5] Although the widespread use of the term is recent, there have been, after all, many voices in the history of religion that resisted institutional authority, accepted that other faiths had value, and pursued a lifetime of searching rather than a settled certainty. Such seekers, like those who call themselves spiritual today, may also engage in world-making activities. A lack of institutional affiliation or rigid orthodoxy need not entail a lack of social concern.

Just because the hallmark of religion is the transcendence of the ordinary, religions can offer something beyond conventional self-interest and oppression. In ordinary usage, the very notion of a "religious" value or a "spiritual" response to a difficult situation can suggest hidden strengths, positive moral character, or an unconventional (and valuable) way of settling a dispute or responding to a loss. Insofar as religion appeals to us in the name of some facet of our identity that is somehow distinct from our social role, physical body, or usual sense of self, its moral demands or teachings about true self-fulfillment may imply a different set of norms for human relationships and even a new set of social institutions to make those norms live in history.

What is essential to this definition is my claim that religions are—or can be—ways of world making. Clearly, this view of religion runs counter to a good deal of what has been said by secular critics. Ever since Marx, it is not hard to see how religious teachings, for all their pretensions to Ultimate Truth, reflect the social world to which they claim to provide an alternative. For Marx, religion was the "opium of the masses," serving to dull the pain of inequality and exploitation.[6] Denied access to a decent life, the poor and downtrodden turned to fantasies of a happier realm and of an Ultimate Power who would assuage the pain they could not escape on earth. Because human beings actually had it in their own power to create that better realm on earth, religion was a form of alienation: a loss of our collective human capabilities through a projection of them onto some other Being. The truth of religion was thus its ability to imagine a realm of human satisfaction. Yet by deferring that realm to a time after death and typically endorsing existing social arrangements in the meantime, religion actually reinforced the unjust powers that ruled on earth. When we think of the Catholic Church's sanctioning of monarchy during the Middle Ages, or bishops blessing armies for colonial conquest, or Hindu endorsement of a rigid caste system that kept millions locked into abject poverty and social humiliation, we see the truth of Marx's position.

But Marx's critique is incomplete. If religion were only a fantasy of escape combined with an endorsement of existing social power, it would contain no basis for social criticism. But in fact it does. In theology, in the spiritual lives of heroic individuals and in activist social movements, religious sensibilities have confronted entrenched inequalities and injustices. The Hebrew prophets laid out God's wrath on the rich and powerful of Jewish society. There was (as Carter insisted) a vital religious presence in the abolition of slavery. Adherents of Catholic liberation theology have, sometimes at great personal cost, supported the rural poor in Latin America. Buddhists have criticized the ecologically and culturally devastating effects of modernization and militarism.

Although I do not completely agree with Marx, neither am I suggesting that the world-making, socially critical aspect of religion is religion's "essence," its "truth." A casual glance at today's headlines shows us the conservative side of religious life: religious sanctioning of women's oppression in Afghanistan, religiously inflamed violence in the Middle East, the religious right's homophobia. If religion has any essence at all, it is two-sided. However conservative or repressive it may be at a given time, religion also contains the seeds of radical, dramatic, critical evaluation of and action against an unjust social order. This is of course no news to those who have used religion in the struggle for civil rights or against militaristic foreign policies. But we cannot pretend that this is the *only* meaning of religion.

There is, to use Scott Appleby's apt phrase, an "ambivalence of the sacred."[7] Religion is conservative and revolutionary, passive and active, escapist and vigorously involving. These two tendencies are described when theologian David Tracy asserts: "*When* not domesticated as sacred canopies for the status quo, *nor* wasted by their own self-contradictory grasps at power, the religions live by resisting. . . . Above all, religions are exercises in resistance."[8] It is, as we shall see, just because of its ethical *ambivalence* that religion needs politics.

Of course it might be suggested that the whole idea of religion as politically transformative is only possible after ideas of political transformation have been created; that is, when religion is seen through the lens of activist social movements. This lens, it is sometimes argued, distorts religion beyond recognition. I agree that religious sensibilities will be changed by political theories. Yet I also believe that if the political implications of religion were not there to begin with, no radical perspective could put them there.

————

In fact, the political implications of religious teachings are not hard to find even in the most traditional of religious teachings. We do not have to limit our sources to liberation theologians influenced by Marxism or radical feminist ministers. The story of Exodus, the image of the crucifixion, and the Buddhist theory of consciousness are universally accepted by their respective traditions. They also provide a basis for the criticism of society and an alternative framework of meaning for communal life.

Exodus is among the most important mythical narratives of Western civilization. It is absolutely central to Judaism—mentioned repeatedly in daily prayers, appealed to as the basis of Jewish ethics, celebrated explicitly each Passover. It also carries great weight in Christianity.

The bare outlines of the story are familiar. Faced with a devastating famine, a small tribe relocates to the jurisdiction of the world's greatest power, their way paved for them by one of their members (Joseph) who had risen to a high position in the government. Time passes, the tribe increases in number, and "A new King arose over Egypt, who did not know Joseph" (Exodus 1:8). The tribe is enslaved. Conditions steadily worsen until their cries, it is said, reach all the way to God (Exodus 2:23). God decides to liberate the Hebrews, choosing Moses as his instrument. Like Joseph, Moses was a Hebrew who had risen to prominence in the host country. Abandoned to the river by his mother as an infant to escape Pharaoh's genocidal edict to have all male Hebrew children killed, Moses was adopted by the queen and raised as a prince. Learning that he himself is of Hebrew blood, he kills an Egyptian overseer who is beating a Hebrew and then flees to another land to begin life anew. He is working for his father-in-law as a shepherd when God tells him to return to Egypt and confront Pharaoh. He demurs, scared of confronting the most powerful man on earth and embarrassed at what seems to be a speech defect ("I am slow of speech and slow of tongue" Exodus 3:10). But God is relentless, and Moses (with his brother's help) convinces Pharaoh that it is better to let the Jews go than to continue to suffer the plagues God is using as punishment. Pharaoh frees the Jews, who then escape from the pursuing Egyptian army across a Red Sea parted for them at God's command. Years of struggle in the wilderness follow, as the Jews receive God's moral and religious teachings, but frequently yearn for the comparative comfort and security of Egypt, turn to other gods, and then must be transformed as a people before they are ready to enter the Promised Land.

My concern with this compelling tale lies in its potential meaning for the development of religion as a way of world making, as providing a critical alternative to dominant forms of political power and social value. In using the story this way, I am building on a widely held tradition. African-American slaves and Socialist Jews, black liberation theologian James Cone, and Catholic liberation theologian Gustavo Gutiérrez, among countless others, have used the story to explore political contexts of oppression and freedom.[9]

The story's most obvious meaning describes one nation's escape from injustice. (Insofar as the Jews had not been bought or won in a war, even in the context of the times there was no justification for their slavery.)[10] Since the triumph was only possible with God's help, it establishes Jews as chosen by God to receive special aid, a continuation of the initial covenant made between God and Abraham. The story can also be used by non-Jews who put themselves in the Jews' place and use Exodus to legitimate their own struggle for liberation. In James Cone's work, for instance, African-Americans become the Jews and white Americans are the Egyptians.[11]

However inspiring the story may be for a particular group, there is a lesson in it that is even more profound: a lesson both particularly Jewish and expansively universal. As Reinhold Niebuhr trenchantly argued, the power of biblical ethics is not that God is on the side of any *particular* people. It is, rather, that there are universal standards of justice commanded by God, standards that we violate at our peril. These standards take precedence over the command of any earthly ruler and remain valid for the previously subject people even after they have won their freedom.

Justification for this more general interpretation can be found in a direct line that runs from the Exodus experience to the Torah's ethical teachings to the self-criticism of the Jewish people that emanates from the Prophets. In each case, the Jews are taught that their status as the "chosen people" is not a divine gift that belongs to them by some cosmic chance but depends on their fulfillment of ethical commands rooted in the experience of slavery.

> You shall not abuse a needy and destitute laborer, whether a fellow coun-tryman or a stranger in one of the communities of your land. You must pay him his wages on the same day, before the sun sets, for he is needy and ur-gently depends on it; else he will cry to the Lord against you and you will incur guilt . . . You shall not subvert the rights of the stranger or the father-less; you shall not take a widow's garment in pawn. Remember that you were a slave in Egypt and that the Lord your God redeemed you from there . . . When you reap the harvest in your field and overlook a sheaf in the field, do not turn back to get it; it shall go to the stranger, the fatherless, and the widow—in order that the Lord your God may bless you in all your undertakings. When you beat down the fruit of your olive trees, do not go over them again; that shall go to the stranger, the fatherless, and the widow. When you gather the grapes of your vineyard, do not pick it over again; that shall go to the stranger, the fatherless, and the widow. *Always remember that you were a slave in the land of Egypt; therefore do I enjoin you to observe this commandment.* (Deut. 24:14–15, 17–18, 20–22)[12]

Two themes from these passages are critical. First, as Gunther Plaut ob-serves, "God himself demands justice for the disadvantaged." Their claims are not a request for charity but a divinely sanctioned attempt to receive what God tells them they deserve.[13] Second, God's instructions are justified by ref-erence to the Jews' historical experience. Why should the Jews be concerned with justice to the laborer, the widow, and the stranger? *Because they know what it is like to have been slaves.* Ultimately, the Egyptians and the Jews are to some extent *interchangeable.* It is purposeful moral conduct that makes one a Jew or an Egyptian, and not simply the vagaries of birth. That is why the same adverb used to describe the Egyptian treatment of the Jews ("The Egyptians *ruthlessly* imposed upon the Israelites" [Exodus 1:13]) is employed in laws instructing Jews how to treat poverty-stricken Jewish workers ("You shall not rule over him *ruthlessly*" [Leviticus 25:43]). In other words, *anyone* can be ruthless, and to receive God's favor it is necessary to realize this fact and act accordingly. How is one to maintain that realization? By remember-ing an experience in which one was downtrodden. The Exodus narrative de-fines two fundamental ethical roles—that of slave and that of master. But once the yoke has been removed from a person's neck, *anyone* can then act like a master; and once people give up the master role, they must be treated fairly. "You shall not abhor an Egyptian, for you were a stranger in his land." (Deut. 23:8).

It is no secret that the Torah contains norms—such as strict gender hierarchy—that are morally objectionable to many in the present. What is remarkable, however, is that the Exodus narrative and its actual use in biblical ethics is a method of *self*-criticism, of seeing beyond any particular laws—even those of the Torah itself—by asking: In any particular relationship, who is the master and who the slave? Such a permanent possibility of criticism is the most *any* system of ethics can do to overcome the inevitable partiality and historically rooted character of its content. Whatever world we are thrown into—slavery in Egypt or a new life in the Promised Land—we can see that the slaves should be freed, that today's slaves might become tomorrow's masters.[14]

As a supporting theme, let us note that before Moses can confront Pharaoh he must leave Egypt entirely and build a new life, a life that must be abruptly terminated if he is to fulfill God's will. The struggle for liberation, in other words, requires that we abandon both our participation in the immoral powers and privileges of rulers and also the safety of the bystander. The narrative is that much more powerful just because Moses returns to his people after having left them. He is the key leader, and he knows what life is like both on the morally wrong side and outside the struggle completely.

At the same time that the Torah constantly stresses the uniqueness and chosenness of the Jewish people, therefore, it *also* provides images of the ways in which the social and ethical boundaries between Jews and non-Jews can be porous. This fluidity of identity provides continuing moral instruction in what I am taking as the fundamental political message of Exodus: that norms of justice are superior to accidents of birth and social affiliation; that Egyptian and Hebrew, like injustice and justice, are concepts that define a moral position as much as national identity. Instead of a "divine right" to God's favor, the Jews must "do and hear" God's commands for worship *and* justice.

This point is continued by the Prophets. While many of their complaints concern failures of ritual (pining after the Gods of the surrounding peoples), others focus on failures of social ethics. In many crucial passages, God's message is that Jews are living unjustly, that in effect they have now become masters. And, further: Without justice in the community, there can be no holiness. For example:

Wash yourselves clean; Put away your evil doings Away from My sight. Cease to do evil; Learn to do good. Devote yourselves to justice; Aid the wronged. Uphold the rights of the orphan, Defend the cause of the widow . . . Your rulers are rogues and cronies of thieves, Every one avid for presents and greedy for gifts; They do not judge the case of the orphan, and the widow's cause never reaches them. (Isaiah 1:16–17, 23)

This prophetic message has powerfully resonated in religiously guided political movements, both Jewish and non-Jewish. It was generalized by Abraham Heschel: "The prophet was an individual who said No to his society, condemning its habits and assumptions, its complacency, waywardness and syncretism."[15] Or as Desmond Tutu, South African Episcopalian bishop and leader in the nonviolent struggle against apartheid, writes: "How anyone having read the prophets could say, 'Do not mix religion with politics' is quite baffling. Which Bible had they read? In situations of injustice nothing could be so revolutionary and so subversive of that *status quo* than the Bible and its prophets."[16]

———————

The story of Christ's life, like the Exodus narrative, is a concrete image that contains a universal ethical model. For instance, the image of Jesus' sacrifice has been identified with victims of war, poverty, or child abuse. Rebecca Chopp uses the "broken body" of Jesus to identify God with those who suffer from disabilities.[17] Just as in the Torah we have the roles of master and slave, so in the Christian tradition we have the aggressive, crucifying force and the innocent victim. Just as the Exodus story teaches freedom, so the crucifixion instructs people to be in solidarity with those who suffer—including and perhaps especially those who suffer because of injustice. In this way, the fundamental element of the Exodus-Prophetic tradition is continued; and Christianity, like Judaism, carries (among other things) an implicit standard by which to judge both society and itself. If Christianity has often been lax in using that standard, that gives more support to the point, which I will argue later at length, that religions often need the stimulus of a progressive political tradition to remember their world-making vocation.

But the sources of that vocation remain constant. It is always possible, from *within* Christianity, to claim that the religion has lost its way and forgotten its essential message. The moral roots of the tradition allow any critic or reformer to say: "We are not living up to the teachings of Jesus. A true Christian cannot tolerate (for example) slavery, or nuclear weapons, or the poisoning of our rivers, or discrimination against lesbians." One can always call on believers themselves to be *more*, or *more authentically*, religious, and to do so in a way that shapes participation in public life. Thus, Christians who turn to politics can proclaim that the real meaning of the Gospel has to do with response to poverty and oppression, that as Pharaoh "stands" for any oppressor, Jesus "stands" for all who suffer. As Benedictine nun Joan Chittister remembers, in describing her early years as a novice:

> When Pope John XXIII talked about "the signs of the times"—poverty, nuclearism, sexism—I began to read these signs with a new conscience and with a new sense of religious life in mind. Most of all, I began to read the Scriptures through another lens. Who was this Jesus who "consorted with sinners" and cured on the Sabbath? Most of all, who was I who purported to be following him while police dogs snarled at black children and I made sure not to be late for prayer . . . What was the "prophetic dimension" of the church supposed to be about if not the concerns of the prophets?—the widows, the orphans, the foreigners, and the broken, vulnerable of every society.[18]

When Judaism and Christianity forget this self-critical element, they cause great suffering. Within Exodus itself we have the wresting of the land from the Canaanites, their expulsion, and in some cases extermination. We also have a constant assumption of male superiority.[19] Christianity has had an extremely violent history of expansion and persecution. Typically justified by claims about being the sole repository of God's will, Christianity's power has often eroded the possibility of self-criticism to the vanishing point. In particular, much of Christian history shows an inability to maintain ethical standards or compassion for the poor while being state-sanctioned and the religion of the majority.[20] As one small example of the Janus-faced quality of even the most politically potent religious imagery, we might remember that the Exodus narrative was used by the Boers in South Africa as a way to describe and justify their ever-wider rule and their wars against England and the natives. Ultimately, their identification with biblical history was a "vital element" of the Afrikaner's sense of divine mission: "a chosen people who had been persecuted and tested in the fire but delivered and given the Promised Land because they had been true to the Lord."[21]

———————

The political gift of the Judeo-Christian tradition is its moral imperative to sanctify the world. The great danger is that its ethical activism can turn into fanaticism and violence against those who disagree. Buddhism's gifts and dangers are rather different. Examining some of its central insights, comparable in their way to the centrality of the Exodus narrative for Judaism or the crucifixion for Christianity, reveals the powerful world-making resources of a non-Western and non-theistic tradition.

If ethical fervor and social criticism are the keys to Jewish and Christian world making, awareness is the essence of Buddhism. If the biblical prophets teach us to rail against injustice, Buddhism suggests that we should first be aware of our own passions and calm our minds. Then, perhaps, we might pray that all beings be free of suffering. This emphasis on self-awareness and universal compassion derives from the fact that Buddhism contains no sense of sin. For Buddhism, personal pain and ethical wrongdoing stem from ignorance about the ultimate nature of the self, the effects of our attachments, and the true sources of contentment. Human existence is suffering, taught the Buddha, precisely because we grasp after that which cannot be controlled. This includes both things in the world—such as money, power, sensual pleasure, social position, or personal relationships—and states of the self, such as contentment or pride. When something attracts us we pursue it; when something gives us pain, we try to escape. But it is precisely in this frantic dance that our greatest suffering lies. If we can fully relinquish our desperate clinging and avoidance, a calm, impersonal joy will arise. We will achieve a profound calm, a consciousness in which we no longer think, "I am this, this is mine, this is myself." Such a state of consciousness is not a gift from God but the fruit of moral and spiritual discipline, including a meditation practice that trains us to recognize how our grasping makes us (and often those around us) miserable. The gradual and profound process of awakening is the natural fruit of spiritual work: an essentially human process that can belong to any individual, community, or nation.[22]

If the Exodus narrative begins with a judgment on an Other that can then be transferred to a judgment on oneself (or one's own community), the Buddhist framework begins with an understanding of oneself that can be applied to society at large. The conditions that create unhappiness in the individual—for example, greed or violence—are both learned from the wider society and reproduced by individual action. If they need to be rooted out in the individual, so do they need to be eliminated in society as a whole. Whereas certain forms of Buddhism place the emphasis solely on personal transformation in the direction of enlightenment, the Mahayana school emphasizes a collective process in which everyone is "saved" together. The Bodhisattva, the Mahayana spiritual hero, is distinguished by her vow: "As many innumerable beings as there are, I vow to save them all."[23] As another text puts it: "Doers of what is hard are the Bodhisattvas . . . They do not wish to attain their own private Nirvana . . . They have set out for the benefit of the world, for the ease of the world, out of pity for the world."[24]

But how does one save a whole world of beings? By seeing, first, the essential interconnectedness of all aspects of existence. One representation of this interconnectedness is the "jewel net of Indra." Infinitely large, the net is composed of tiny, brilliant strands. Where the strands cross, there is a perfect jewel. *Each* jewel's facets reflect *all* the other jewels. The moral of the image is that the nature of each separate life, each particular existence, conditions and reflects all of the rest. Realizing this interconnectedness, the Bodhisattva utilizes a calmly persistent *upaya*, or "skillful means" to seek to undo the collective ignorance that is responsible for collective human misery. This would require politically structured changes in education, culture, and the economy—for a start!

Another Buddhist teaching that can lead in this direction concerns the manner in which "right livelihood"—defined as one without violence, theft, or the production or sale of poisons—is thought to be essential to spiritual development. With the exception of the most simple tribal or peasant economy, the moral character of one's livelihood depends on the organized structure of society as a whole. In an interconnected economy, it can at times be extremely hard to find work that meets the conditions of right livelihood, for a great deal of the available work is devoted to producing weapons, environmental toxins, or cultural junk. Only a global change can alter this fact, and thus the spiritual quality of one's work is a social, not just a personal, fact.[25]

Finally, just as the Torah teaches the potential interchangeability of Egyptian and Jew, Buddhism contains a similar message.

> Why do the Bodhisattvas . . . take such a long time to obtain [supreme enlightenment]? Because the supreme enlightenment is very difficult to obtain: one needs vast accumulation of knowledge and merit, innumerable heroic deeds . . . Why then do they undertake such infinite labor? For the good of others, because they want to become capable of pulling others out of this great flood of suffering. But what personal benefit do they find in the benefit of others? *The benefit of others is their own benefit, because they desire it.*[26]

This desire is embodied in the Mahayana ideal of the four "Unlimited" social emotions—friendliness, compassion, sympathetic joy, and even-mindedness. Here, concern for others joins with dissolution of rigid ego boundaries. Each person's sorrow or joy is as important as anyone else's.

Commitment to global enlightenment, recognition of global interdependence, the unlimited social emotions—these provide a basis for Buddhism, like Judaism and Christianity, to be a way of world making. To turn the Bodhisattva into a revolutionary, or at least a radical reformer, all that is required is recognition of how the distribution of wealth, the norms of gender or race, and economic imperatives are all contributing to our collective misery. Given the Buddhist stress on equanimity, nonviolence, and the eradication of anger, Buddhist revolutionaries are likely to conduct themselves peacefully, lovingly, and with a gentle smile. Their manner might well balance the passionate out- cries of the prophetic tradition; but their goals will be deeply transformative nevertheless. And like those who invoke Exodus or the crucifixion to justify their concern with the liberation of the oppressed, those who invoke Bud- dhist teachings will be calling on an authentic element of the tradition.

Of course Buddhism, no less than Christianity or Judaism, has often been quietly accommodating to the status quo. When a Buddhist ruler came to power in India in 135 B.C.E., he instructed his subjects in righteousness, gen- tleness, kindness, and nonviolence to animals; he built wells and planted trees to shade the roads. But he gave no thought to overturning a class structure divided between nobility and peasants or the caste system of inherited social privilege. For King Ashoka to be able to think that spiritual living required such massive political change, he would have needed the insights of another tradition, one that did not really flower until almost 2,000 years later.

——— ———

The framework that Ashoka lacked, that of secular justice pursued through systematic political change, finds its beginnings in Greek philosophy. Of course, the Greek concept of justice was in some ways very different from the biblical one. Rather than emphasizing divine commands and moral treatment of the weak, the Greeks stressed the idea of a rational social order that would be most appropriate to and make the best use of human beings' distinct na- ture. Emerging from a society in which slavery was not just tolerated (as it was in the Bible) but essential, Greek thought was much more likely to worry about the happiness of its leading citizens than fair treatment for its slaves. For the Greeks, justice had more to do with balance, proper order, and long- lasting human fulfillment than it did with moral fairness and equality. They saw justice, we might say, as reason incarnated in the social order.

When the Greek emphasis on reason and human fulfillment and the bibli- cal emphasis on fairness and concern for the weak combine with the belief that fundamental social change is possible, we get world-making politics. These politics are expressed in organized social movements that have, since the French Revolution, sought fundamental political, economic, and cultural reforms—and at times even revolutions. They began with struggles for basic democracy and have been followed by varieties of socialism; anarchism; fem- inism; gay/lesbian liberation; ecological movements; radical labor move- ments; and antiracist, anti-imperialist, and national liberation movements. They share the goal of sweeping social change in the direction of increased political rights, greater distributive justice, widespread democratization of power, and a commitment to recognizing and respecting the previously marginalized and oppressed. They call both for individual freedoms and for a more compassionate and rewarding life for the community.

Although religious authorities before the nineteenth century were capable of criticizing secular authorities for mistreatment of the poor, they were not able to envisage dramatic changes in social relations. They could call for different laws or social policies, but not for a new system. This latter demand, and the notion that the changes in question should be brought about by the people most involved, was the distinct contribution of world-making politics.

Instead of the ideas of divinity or of perennial wisdom that are found in traditional religions, liberal, progressive, and radical world-making political movements are rooted in three important myths of modernity: reason, freedom, and democracy. I call these ideas myths because like all the great animating ideals of culture, they are not susceptible to proof. Rather, it is their function to support and inspire the more particular ideals, theories, and policies that political movements pursue. We accept them by committing ourselves to living by them and to seeing what kind of life we get as a result.

The myth of reason is the belief that human beings are capable of accumulating increasing amounts of increasingly accurate knowledge about themselves and the world, knowledge that is relevant to collective human fulfillment. To believe in reason is to believe that we can know what we need to know—and give reasons for why we think we know it—and that therefore our social policies should be guided by knowledge rather than tradition, blind faith, or force. To believe that social life should be guided by reason is to hold that any social policy can be questioned and that every form of authority must justify itself by offering reasons potentially understandable by everyone. When these traditions speak of "reason," it should be emphasized, they do not mean the limited, and often individualistic, attempt to realize a single person's interests; nor do they mean a purely technical capacity to control nature. They have in mind, rather, a kind of deep comprehension of collective human needs, capacities, and paths to fulfillment. In precisely this sense, Marxists criticize capitalism for the irrationality of business cycles that create needless poverty; and antiglobalization activists in undeveloped countries criticize World Bank policies that lead to community-destroying unemployment and ecological damage.

The myth of freedom tells us that we are free to use the knowledge we have gained to make ourselves better and happier as individuals and as a society. It asserts that humans can remake the world and themselves, that limits are few. Reason will provide the knowledge we need. Temporary obstacles, ignorance, or entrenched bad habits will be overcome, and we will use knowledge to create a (practically and morally) better life. Further, what cannot be justified by reason is left up to individual choice. Tradition and convention can suggest how we should live; but without reason, they cannot impose on the unwilling or the eccentric.

Finally, the myth of democracy tells us that in the rational exercise of human freedom to create a just society, everyone's beliefs and desires need to be consulted. As humans we "begin," says the myth of democracy, in a condition of equal political status in which no one has more rights than anyone else. Any variation from that original situation is either something we accept because it benefits us (like designating special powers to the police) *or* is the fruit of injustice that can and should be overturned.[27] What we deserve, what we want, what we need—all these should be decided upon from an initial condition in which no one has special privileges or powers. And the "we" in question refers to communities defined by nationality, gender, race, religion (and so forth), as much as it does to individuals. Rights and justice pertain not only to particular persons but also to groups.

It should be stressed that the initial focus of world-making politics in the West was once individual freedom, the ultimate aim now is a collective life that certainly includes, but cannot be limited to, personal rights. When contemporary philosophers known as "communitarians" emphasize how moral virtues and group well-being depend on living ties within local communities and not just individual freedoms or governmental policies, they reinforce this insight.[28] In doing so, I believe, they continue rather than contradict many of the dominant strains of world-making politics: from the French Revolution's call for "fraternity" to socialist visions of a self-governing community without a formal government, from feminist emphasis on reciprocity and care to the rainbow politics of human connection within diversity.[29]

When the three myths of world-making politics are applied to issues of legal rights, national independence, economic organization, gender, ethnic and racial relations, sexual preference, and our connections to animals and the rest of nature, we get the different movements that make up the political spectrum of liberal, progressive, or radical politics. In this context, groups may vary in the arena of social life on which they focus, the range of human freedom they seek to exercise, or the subjects whose democratic equality they seek to realize. Some, proceeding from countries in which individualism is less culturally central than the West, may put a good deal more emphasis on sustaining community than on individual freedom and fulfillment. Their guiding value might be responsibility as much as rights.[30] Other groups will seek to free individual political prisoners in dictatorial regimes. But in each case they seek to use reason and freedom to increase human happiness, and to do so in a way that continually expands democratic access to social power and respect. When these movements are successful, more groups are included into the arena of social decisionmaking, more traditional areas of social life receive critical scrutiny. Yesterday's despised group becomes tomorrow's citizens; last year's colonies have their own governments; accepted roles of husband and wife are challenged; the taken-for-granted exploitation of nature is questioned by movements championing the inherent value of nature.

Another guiding thread among disparate groups can be found in their shared belief that human fulfillment and fairness for the weak or oppressed go hand in hand. Ultimately, Marxism teaches, an end to the exploitation and irrational business cycles endemic to capitalism will make a better life for everyone. Ultimately, many feminists believe, a world of gender fairness will not only dismantle male privilege but also sustain more loving and satisfying human relationships. Certain oppressive social positions need to be eliminated—the slave master, the corporate kingpin, the patriarchal husband—but the overall human experience will be deeply improved when freedom, reason, and democracy increase.

Are such changes possible? As the religious soul is guided by faith in God or the possibility of enlightenment, so the political activist is moved by what is in some ways a comparable faith in the human capacity for collective betterment. Although it may not take such faith to recognize what democracy or women's liberation have already accomplished, it may be required to believe that we can go further.

——— ———

Yet not everyone might want to go any further than we have already. Some will say that neither religion nor world-making politics provide solid reasons to believe that they can make the world a better place.

Consider, first, the often dismal history of world-making politics in the twentieth century: the murderous oppressiveness of Stalinism, the rhetorical excesses of political correctness, the economic inefficiency of communism, the dissolution of national liberation into ethnic cleansing and terrorism. Don't these make us wonder whether political attempts at sweeping social change deserve our respect at all? Is what some of us have now—the global marketplace, formal democracy, supposed equality under the law in some places—the best any of us can do? Karl Popper argued over four decades ago that social problems and political injustice require not a "revolution" but "piecemeal social engineering." Responding to the horrors of Nazism and Soviet communism, Popper admonished us to give up our utopian dreams of dramatic change.[31] So, perhaps the world does not need to be remade by politics. Perhaps it never did. Or perhaps all the work has been done. As Francis Fukuyama said in a celebrated article claiming that there simply is not and could not be an alternative to international "liberal" capitalism, perhaps we have in fact reached "the end of history."[32]

More than anything else, one's assessment of these possibilities defines one's political position. The perspective that animates this book, as the reader will probably already have guessed, rejects the notion that what we have now is pretty much the best we can hope for or that only a continual small tinkering will get us anything better. I believe that the vital tradition of political world making is still possible and still needed and that the scope of human injustice and human suffering requires sweeping, and not just piecemeal, social change. Although I agree that the list of radical political failures and errors is very long, it is also necessary to remember its achievements. The developed world as we know it is in great measure the product of struggles to transform the social order according to political standards of justice and care. Voting rights, racial and ethnic equality, workers' rights, women's rights, the social safety net, awareness of the environmental crisis, freedom for colonized nations—all these came to pass because groups of people believed that the world needed to be made anew. They rejected prevailing standards, conventional wisdom, and existing forms of power.

To be content with what we have, or to think that only slow, small and moderate changes are warranted, is to assert that either the movements of the past had little essential value or that they have all been pretty much successful. But who among us would deny the accomplishments of the struggles for democracy, or women's equality, or for a sane relation to nature? These ways of world making have given us much of what is most precious in our world. But have they all succeeded? Again, I think not. Gender equality has been struggled for but not achieved; racism continues; the power of the wealthy to control social life has increased and turned global; repressive governments torture and execute dissidents. Further, new forms of irrationality have arisen, as a toxic culture of consumption and electronic speed detaches us from each other, the earth, and our selves. Finally, looming above all our heads, the environmental crisis threatens our physical health, our ability to feel at home on earth, and our confidence that our children can expect a future worth having. Struggles over these issues are the critical facts of our time. Succeeding and failing throughout the world, movements in the service of human rights, social equality, and environmental sanity are the latest manifestations of a long and noble tradition. They are our greatest hope against those who would remake the world in the image of global capitalism.

Just as we question the history of political movements, so we can seriously wonder about the rising tide of politically conservative religion: the violence of the anti-abortion protesters who shoot doctors with one hand and finger rosary beads with the other, the Islamic fundamentalists who condemn women to social slavery and choose rigid hierarchy over democracy, the religious endorsement of ethnic conflict and ethnic cleansing. If progressive politics too often turned to sectarian tyranny or narrow group interest, doesn't activist religion signal the spiritual sanctioning of the social and political status quo—if not something worse?

As in the case of world-making politics, these complaints are indeed true—but do not tell the whole truth. Just as others have struggled over the authentic meaning of democracy or science, so leaders and movements have contested the authentic social and ethical meaning of religion. Throughout the world, there is a religious "left" as well as a religious "right." In Burma's Aung San Suu Kyi and South Africa's Desmond Tutu, in the religious presence in Mexico's Zapatistas and Poland's Solidarity, we've seen religious figures join—and even lead—broad struggles for social justice. Thich Nhat Hanh helped create a "socially engaged Buddhism." Publications such as *Sojourners* speak to those who would join the values of Evangelical Christianity with the healing and improvement of the social world. Writers speak of "emancipatory spirituality," a "spirituality of resistance," and "liberation theology" for peasants, African-Americans, women, homosexuals, the poor, indigenous peoples, and animals. Grassroots movements in India invoke Hindu gods in defense of their forests and freelance deep ecologists speak of the spiritual value of nature.[33]

The millions of people who pursue these kindred paths have no need to prove that theirs is the "one true religion." They only have to be clear—both in their own hearts and in what they say to the world—what it is they believe and why: to describe what a world would be like if people accepted their proposals and to live that passion in their own lives as best they can. "By their fruits ye shall know them" may be the best way to judge religion and politics alike, at least when it comes to making the world anew.

2

The Time Is Ripe

Is America ready to allow, even welcome, into the public arena a form of argument about public policy drawn from those moral traditions based on religious worldviews?
        —*Harvey Cox, "Citizens and Believers: Always Strangers?"[1]*

True religion is compassionate, respectful and devoid of hatred.
        —*Kofi Annan, secretary-general of the United Nations, after the September 11, 2001, terrorist attacks in the U.S.[2]*

These days, liberals and leftists want to maintain political and governmental activism on behalf of social justice, but without explicit religious underpinnings for calls to moral activism and renewal. It is not clear, however, that this can be done. . . . Fearing religion as "divisive" or as inherently tied to conservative activism, liberals fall back on secular arguments about individual or group economic self-interest. Such arguments, however, may be too anemic to serve as a basis for a bold new movement for social justice in America.
        —*Theda Skocpol, "Religion, Civil Society, and Social Provision in the U.S."[3]*

Two fundamental problems face any attempt to join religion and politics in remaking the world. First, there is widespread agreement in most developed countries that political life should be secular. Along with technology, the rise of the nation-state, urbanization, and the spread of fast food, becoming "modern" just means that religion turns into an essentially personal matter that we don't expect to constrain the law, economics, public education, or governmental policy. When religions claim absolute truth and demand absolute obedience, they contradict a social order based in political rights and social pluralism. They therefore must be exiled to the realm of each person's private business. This is, as it were, Ellen Willis's position writ large.

If this perspective is correct, then the religious spirit will have to content itself with personal growth, congregational piety, and being at best a social "interest group." Like owners of off-road vehicles, dentists or any other one-issue interest group, the faithful can petition the government for certain advantages (such as tax-free status for churches). Anything else can produce only fanaticism, tyranny, and the suppression of differences.

Second, there is the historic antagonism between religion and politics. Activist political movements have long criticized religions for supporting the social status quo and counseling political passivity among the downtrodden. And religious spokesmen often dismissed secular radicals as being sources of troublesome social unrest and disrespect for established values.

These points are legitimate, but they do not tell the whole story. Profound shifts in economics, popular culture, technology, and political life are creating the prospect of religion and politics remaking the world together. Despite certain appearances and protestations to the contrary, a good deal of modernity is reaching toward religious values and resources; but the religion to which it is reaching—and which is reaching back—has itself been transformed by modernity.

Can religion flourish in a world of technological development, scientific knowledge, secular democracy, and extreme individualism? And can it do so without undoing modernity's accomplishments?

RELIGION AND MODERNITY

To begin, let us note that like the fabled author who complained that news of his death had been greatly exaggerated, religious values and institutions have escaped a demise loudly predicted by leading social theorists for well over a century. The rise of the religious right, the religious aspect of ethnic conflict and anti-Western modernization, the spiritual dimension of feminism and the environmental movements, and the religious challenge to the government in nations from China to Egypt—all these testify that, contra Nietzsche, God is far from dead. Who would have thought that Russian Christianity would outlive the Stalinist secret police, that some of the most powerful postcolonial regimes would define themselves in terms of their religious piety? Or that in the last decade before the millennium, perhaps the single most powerful unified ideological group in the United States (that bastion of democracy, progress, and research grants) would be fundamentalist Christians?

All these developments seem to contradict religious historians' widely held "secularization thesis," which argues that modernization—especially individualism, scientific progress, and mass, pluralistic societies—necessarily makes religion less socially influential and personally meaningful.[4] This thesis seemed for many years to be the simple common sense of twentieth-century life.[5] Yet as we consider the last twenty years or so, it might seem that not only is God not dead, but He (or She) is not even sick.

Yet the whole matter of the social position of religion is quite complex, and there is some truth to the idea that we live in a profoundly secular age. However many of us in America or Western Europe go to church and say we believe in God,[6] we don't have religious wars or religious laws; religious intermarriage is common; and when people have questions about emotional health, nature, or social welfare, they are more likely to turn to psychotherapists, scientists, or sociologists than to priests or sacred texts. The political agenda of the American religious right, for all its fanfare, has not succeeded. And even its leaders have had to play on the terrain of secular democracy, making alliances with secular conservatives and being careful not to suggest that they seek to displace democracy. Even in countries such as Iran, theocracy faces a constant pressure toward democratic secularization.[7] In any case, the cultures I am concerned with in this book—those that have achieved a modicum of agreement over the political values of democracy and human rights—are witnessing a long-term lessening of traditional forms of religious influence.[8]

If religion is not disappearing, then, as the secularization theorists predicted, it is not staying the same either. To survive modernization, it has had to change. This change has been shaped by religion's response to four basic historical developments.

First, religion confronts the increasing ability of intricate scientific theories to explain natural phenomena and create technical knowledge that is essential to the lives of religious devotees themselves. Every fundamentalist, with the possible exception of some of the Amish, has his fax machine, Internet address, color TV, and cell phone! Or, at least, all of his leaders do. We all pray at the church of science and technology, wherever else we pray as well, because all of us depend on machines that only a few of us understand. We need the stuff and we use it, but very few of us have a clue about how it works. This combination of ignorance and dependence gives those who create the technology a powerful mix of political power and ideological authority. Our lives endorse this power no matter how much we may complain about it. As a consequence, the long-term social authority of religion is lessened.

Second, there now exist aggressive and self-confident secular philosophies that offer nonreligious visions of human fulfillment. Despite the excesses of Stalin or Hitler, the *Wall Street Journal* or *Playboy*, secularists believe that their views are as meaningful, moral, and psychologically healthy as anything coming out of religious traditions. Even with the rise of religious feeling in recent decades, these secular viewpoints are not going to go away. Religions are thus in competition with other broad perspectives on human experience and the cosmos. They are not the only game in town, and they know it.

Further, in a global society of shared media, accessible travel, and common intellectual culture, all religious believers know—in a way they never did before—that they are surrounded by countless other religions. The great texts are available in every language, and there are countless comparative studies showing what religions share. Some fundamentalists meet the challenge by proclaiming, endlessly, that they alone have The Truth. But their very insistence shows that there is something they quite desperately need to prove—to themselves as well as to outsiders. Many religious thinkers have taken another tack. Acknowledging both the success of science and the inability of *any* religion to "prove" its superiority in terms that other religions might ever accept, these voices now express an uncharacteristic and refreshing modesty.

> In the religious life of the Western world, the big change—from serial dogmatism to promiscuous liberalism—comes around the start of this century when the degree of social and cultural pluralism forces the denominational attitude to become common. Each major religious organization revised its self-perception from claiming an exclusive relationship with the divinity to supposing that it represented simply one of the many roads to God.[9]

Modesty is even more essential to the fourth historical development: religions' awareness of their own past sins. If not particularly widespread among the fundamentalists, this awareness is shared by virtually everyone else. Religious teachers and groups know all too well that in many instances the "Word of God" has been used to justify violence and suppression. Progressive Christians usually have some awareness of the shameful history of Christian anti-Semitism. Reform, Reconstructionist, and Jewish Renewal groups, even as they may be calling for more traditional forms of observance, take stands against traditional Judaism's sexism. Most of the faithful in the United States and Europe, outside of ethnic conflicts where nationalism is more at stake than theology, do not want such behavior repeated.

Thus, in the developed world at least, contemporary religion lacks innocence about its own history, limits, and powers. For people who don't want a return to fundamentalist violence, being religious now requires that we learn how to combine commitment to our faith with a very different understanding of what our faith requires of us.

FEAR OF FAITH

If religion is modest, must it therefore also be private? And can it refuse to be private without violating the bounds of pluralism and human rights? What follows here is an argument designed to show that religion, as such, poses no more threat to a liberal social order than anything else.

Historically, the secular liberal response to this dilemma was to separate church and state while replacing religion's authority with that of science and democracy. Part of the liberal view was that human nature provides us with a rational faculty enabling us to evaluate all beliefs according to universal standards. Public policy would be shaped by this universal reason, while religion, inherently irrational, was to be as personal as our tastes in food or literature.

However, thirty years of critical philosophy of science has shown that science is often deeply shaped by cultural bias and the political interests of those who fund it. Comparable criticisms of every humanistic discipline reveal the widespread effects of sexism and racism. A shared awareness of other cultures and of history makes us all realize that what we believe is historically and socially molded. Therefore, a liberal view of the separation of religion and political life faces a new problem. If a Pristine Reason does not keep religion in check, how is the line between public politics and private faith to be maintained?

The attempt—and lack of success—of one of the world's leading political philosophers to answer this question is instructive. John Rawls has designed his recent version of political liberalism to answer a "fundamental question": "How is it possible for those affirming a religious doctrine that is based on religious authority, for example, the church or the *Bible*, to also hold a reasonable political conception that supports a just democratic regime?"[10] In other words: What is the rational way to construct the boundaries of church and state? Or, more to the point: How do we keep those nutty religious folks from disrupting secular democracy? Rawls's answer is to try to provide political rules that must be accepted by anyone who wants a democratic society and to distinguish those rules from religious (or philosophical) perspectives that will necessarily manifest wide differences. The former will be public and universal, the latter private and particular. This version of liberalism, Rawls thinks, will specify the things we must agree on if we are to live together democratically at all, and not try to impose beliefs or values about human nature or the meaning of life that we can't. It will depend only upon the shared and necessary assumptions that everyone in our society is "free and equal" and that whatever we believe, we could be wrong. If we assume that public policy should be shaped by the views of Plato, Jesus, Buddha, or Ayn Rand, Rawls tells us, that's our private business. We can try to follow what they say, but we should not appeal to them in public forums, for if we are "reasonable," we know that we live in a diverse society in which only some people will agree with us. Therefore, when we discuss our common business we should offer only the kinds of reasons "everyone" must accept.

Although these might seem unobjectionable premises, they really don't give Rawls his desired result, which is a way to keep people from forcing their grand religious or philosophical views on unbelievers. To begin with, he is not really—as he claims—neutral between competing worldviews. To be considered reasonable, believers must think about politics without consulting their faith. If they can't disconnect from their religious beliefs, then they will have severed themselves from what Rawls takes to be the modern liberal consensus. Yet to expect religious people to think about politics in a secular way is simply to deny them a fundamental aspect of their identity. Furthermore, to expect them to voice their political beliefs while hiding or ignoring their faith—on the grounds that somehow this will preserve everyone's freedom—makes little sense. Rawls's idea of the "reasonable" excludes anyone who is zealous about religion, while he treats his own commitments as basic and essential to a rational society.

Also, his second essential condition of liberal democracy—that to be reasonable is to accept that we could always be wrong—really tells us little. As I argued in the case of Willis, secular liberals are no more likely to question their really fundamental premises than anyone else. One can no more imagine Rawls, who seems to think religion is a public menace, seriously considering the possibility that the Torah is true than one can imagine the pope trading in the Bible for the *Communist Manifesto*.

Most important, when Rawls tells us that we can settle basic issues of justice simply by accepting the principle that all of us are "free and equal," his premises are simply inadequate to the task. In the case of abortion rights, animal rights, and welfare entitlements, to name just three areas, it is not at all clear who "we" are and what equal treatment consists of. To debate these matters, we will necessarily refer to or presume a comprehensive perspective of one kind or another. Grand religious or philosophical views will be at stake in our sense of personhood and obligations to mother and fetus, to nonhuman animals, and to the poor. To say that a liberal idea of the self, or freedom, or goodness is permissible here but a Buddhist or Islamic or Lutheran one is not reveals the sheerest prejudice.[11]

Just as the liberal notions of freedom and equality are not sufficient for a just and democratic society, neither are they necessary. A religious perspective centered on compassion and humility might serve just as well. Certainly, thinking of individuals as being children of God or of infinite spiritual worth because they are an expression of the Ultimate is a pretty good basis for the kind of mutual respect and nonviolence one wants in a diverse society. To make matters more complicated, some thinkers even argue that you cannot make sense of human rights *without* a religious basis and that "secular human rights" ultimately derive from religious teachings such as the Golden Rule or the obligation to respect the needs of the stranger and the weak.[12]

Religious views, I believe, have as much place in the public world as any other. Rather than exclude some positions from the start, what is needed is a broad "deliberative democracy" in which *everything* is up for grabs, including the rules of the discussion and the topics on the table. If someone wants to argue that abortion is immoral because the Catholic Church forbids it, let them do so, but have them offer an account of the church's moral reasoning, its models of virtue, and its track record as a moral exemplar. I agree with the current pope on very little, but he does not simply lay down a rule—"No abortions"—and leave it at that. Rather, he offers reasons. His arguments may ultimately rest on faith, but so what? Before we hit that resting point, we will find a complex and articulate account of human nature, the meaning of life, and the effects of moral choices. In the end, all any of us can do— whether we are the pope or John Rawls—is tell other people what we believe and what we think will happen to the community if our beliefs are accepted. Perhaps people will listen. Perhaps they won't. We should not try to specify beforehand how "reasonable people" will think. As ethicist Jeffrey Stout argues, there is in place a broadly modern tradition of democracy partly defined by openness to dialogue among radically different worldviews: "When a people is diverse in upbringing, in religion, or in other ways likely to make its members think and speak differently, democracy involves discoursing with one another despite these differences."[13]

How about those fanatics who choose to fight rather than talk? Or those who would impose what they believe by force? Given the history of the twentieth century, we should know that such people are as likely to be secular as religious. For every authoritarian Bible-thumper using Jesus as an excuse to hate homosexuals, there is a cold-blooded technocrat who masks exploitation and imperialism as "democracy" and "development." We should no more keep religion out of politics because some believers are fanatics than we should outlaw calls for socialized medicine because Stalin was a tyrannical thug. If certain religious people are violent and dogmatic, their problem is not religiosity but violence and dogmatism. In our tortured time, religion has not cornered the market on sin.

A NEW FORM OF FAITH

Writers like Willis and Rawls, so afraid that dogmatic religion will disrupt civil society, seem to have missed the fact that theologians have been wrestling with these problems for centuries. As a result, religion, or at least an important part of it, has assimilated many of the accomplishments of modern political thought without abandoning its religious identity. Although this new form of faith is not universal and is opposed by persistent forms of fundamentalism, it is held broadly enough to be an essential part of contemporary religious life.

This change begins with an acceptance of the essentially historical nature of religious life itself—that whatever their original inspiration, religions are partly human creations and therefore are as changeable as anything else in human history. What we think we know now may be mistaken, or at least require significant alteration, addition, and reinterpretation. Once we accept the limited character of our understanding of religious truth, we cannot legitimately impose our beliefs on other people. As a number of Protestant theologians have argued, for example, there is a difference between the essence of Christianity and the form it takes in a particular culture. Christians must always be on guard, therefore, against self-aggrandizement and arrogance. Further, if much of our knowledge is partial and tentative, perhaps we can learn something from other people.[14] Thus, dialogue on "spiritual" matters with other religions and with the secular world becomes a commonplace rather than a threat. Interestingly, the very term "spirituality" entered contemporary religious discourse as a way for Christians of different denominations to refer to what they had in common with each other.[15] When discussing the effect on Christianity of political movements, encounters with Eastern meditation, and other "new ways of thinking," John Cobb remarks: "The Christianity that emerges will be different from anything we have known before, but that does not mean that it will be less Christian."[16]

The widespread recognition of limits and the embrace of religious plural-ism are accompanied by—and probably to some degree even *require*—the widespread redefinition of religious grace as tied to psychological intensity and ethical discipline rather than objective doctrine. One early version of this was mid-nineteenth-century Protestant theologian Søren Kierkegaard's claim that "truth is subjectivity," i.e., a passionate inward attachment to God. For Kierkegaard, the notion that God could be known directly, "as the obvi-ously extraordinary to the astonished observer," was always mistaken. It was passion, not doctrine, that was the key to Christianity, and thus for Kierke-gaard, a devoted pagan might well be more "Christian" than a self-satisfied and unenthusiastic Lutheran.[17]

When theology takes this turn, the goal is no longer to meet demands promulgated by an unquestioned authority but—in a continuation of a fun-damental move toward individualism that was the hallmark of the Protestant Reformation—for individuals to find their own way to God and to know that they have done so through their own inner knowledge. The rejection of the institutional authority of the Catholic Church was simultaneously an open-ing toward a kind of religious relativism, in which each person (or commu-nity or sect) could find its own truth.[18] But once we are willing to live with a variety of forms of Christianity, it is not that big a jump to peaceful coexis-tence with different religions altogether. In the post–World War II period, this development means that psychological and moral values of compassion, self-acceptance, joy, "finding your true self," and love take their place along-side, and sometimes supplant, "obedience to orthodox belief" and "hope for salvation after death."

As a result, theology's literal claims—for example, that Jesus is God, that the Talmud was given to Moses—radically diminish in importance. More at-tention is paid to the degree to which the individual or the congregation is living out its faith, as opposed to inflicting it on others. As twelve-step groups put it, the essential point is not to take "the inventory of others" but to con-centrate on oneself. We end up with devotion rather than dogma, purity of heart rather than orthodoxy, humility in the face of the complexity of reli-gious life rather than certainty that God's wishes are as easy to know as those of the corner grocer. I can orient my devotion to my beliefs, and allow you the same privilege. The foundation of all these virtues lies in the deep sense they make rather than in a "provable" set of statements about the nature of the cosmos. At least, believers become much more liable to allow for a dra-matic range of descriptions of that nature, believing that differences in detail are acceptable variations.

To develop this point, since it is at times hard for both the religious and the secular to take it in, consider what is perhaps an odd analogy. I can be passionately devoted to my wife, even think that loving her is the most important thing in my life, without expecting you to love her as well, or even without believing that you too should be married. I need not demand that other people agree that my wife is the best in the world, for in my own experience of our love, I have all the proof I need. Further, a good marriage will require me to be energetic, devoted, and disciplined. Laziness, vacillation, or unfaithfulness will ruin it. But my dedication need not interfere with anyone else's union, and indeed I will probably respect people who are devoted to each other. In the end, there is no reason I cannot learn something from their relationships that might improve my own. A person's religious identity can be formed around a similarly subjective, passionate, thoughtful, and dedicated relationship.

Since our doctrines must be held with some modesty, and since holding doctrines is no proof of religious validity in any case, the new public religion will treat everyone with moral respect, regardless of the church to which they do (or do not) belong. The creation of an economic and cultural global community gives rise to the notion of a world human family that is the object of religious concern. We may well judge certain *social roles* (for example, child pornographer, manufacturer of nuclear weapons) quite harshly, but attempts to eliminate these roles will also be tempered by a fundamental respect for human beings whoever they are and whatever they do. The spiritual platitude of "hating the sin but loving the sinner" has real weight here. Of course the "sinner" who makes his living selling child pornography or nuclear weapons may not see or appreciate the difference so much, but the difference is crucial nevertheless.

THE PROMISE OF SPIRITUALITY

If religion has become modest in its theology and more personal in its sense of grace, it might well be more compatible with democracy. But how then can it be help remake the world? How can a personal "spirituality" be relevant to politics?

Consider the following description of a particular Christian community:

The notion of an atoning ordeal and sacrifice and the age-old and dominant problem of sin and redemption is disappearing. The contemporary emphasis on the close personal relationship with God as a source of fulfillment and on the riches of relationships with others, is shifting parochial

Catholics towards "transcendent humanism," offering an "ethico-affective" and predominately this-worldly conception of salvation.[19]

Surprisingly, this is not a description of New Age types in California but of rural French Catholics! In California, as in virtually all of the urban centers in the developed world, the same tendencies are far stronger. Religion has been affected by, and often tends to shade into, psychotherapy, community activism, or the "development of the self."

The concept of the spiritual helps us understand that while religion has shifted in form and lessened in political authority, at the same time it remains significant in people's lives.[20] It can be personally meaningful without being like the authoritarian and orthodox religion of the Middle Ages—or today's fundamentalism. As Robert Wuthnow has convincingly argued, a shift in this direction has been occurring in American religion, one that may have analogues in other places in the developed world. For Wuthnow, religious values remain central to many people's understanding of selfhood, morality, and the cosmos. The much-heralded diminution of religion is actually a change of form rather than elimination.[21] Many people are moving away from clearly defined religious institutions and denominations and toward an often eclectic spiritual life of varied experiences, practices, and resources.

This change may well be good news for those who fear religion's pernicious influence on politics. When people say, as many do, "I'm not really religious, but I am very spiritual," they imply that they are on a path that is not universalizable to some larger group, that is clearly not the kind of thing for which one proselytizes, or which (God forbid) one might try to "enforce" in some way. The new version of religious life, which has this "nonreligious spirituality" as its most extreme expression, is nondogmatic and tolerant. It is often akin to psychotherapy—self-help with prayer, meditation, and hymns instead of a couch! Yet isn't the changed form described by commentators like Wuthnow another confirmation of the irrelevance of religion to world-making politics? How could it ever escape its own narcissism? How could it ever become relevant to the pursuit of social justice? And to the extent that established churches move in the same direction, won't they suffer the same fate?

The answer is, in part, that modern religion often does sink into narcissism and that apolitical self-absorption is certainly no basis for any kind of political life, let alone remaking the world.

I believe, however, that endless self-concern is ultimately *spiritually* self-defeating, that a kind of natural spiritual dialectic leads from concern with individual experiential fulfillment to concern with social life. Clearly a large number of contemporary spiritual teachers have offered the same message.[22]

If, as Wuthnow puts it, much of contemporary spiritual sensibility is a way of locating the self, the engagement of spiritual values in social life can be a way of realizing that *in crucial ways the self is collective as well as individual.*

> As American religion is transformed into an increasingly individualist spiri-
> tuality, one might expect a less focused, organized, and unified impact on
> political life . . . On the other hand, this is not self-evident. After all, if spir-
> ituality becomes more important and more deeply valued among more
> Americans, it is bound to affect their political outlooks and behavior, possi-
> bly more intensely—and more widely—than ever before.[23]

Clearly, religions that forbid nothing and assert nothing—because they are doubtful about everything—cannot remake either the world or the self. (And they also offer little in the way of meaningful religious experience, ei-ther.)[24] But this is not what has happened, at least not everywhere. Rather, in a strikingly important development, we find the ability to combine modesty about *metaphysical assertions* (the nature of God, the content of revelation, the attributes of the soul) and the particular habits of a *particular tradition* (liturgy, holy days, special foods) with an unflinchingly principled stand about *morality.* On the one hand, we try to coherently assert that there are many paths to The Truth. On the other hand, however, religions influenced by the achievements of modern politics and new interpretations of their own ethical teachings can be quite clear that these paths do not include sexism, racism, or ethnic hatred. The foundation of these moral and political values may be a sense that the ultimate nature of the universe supports them, but such a sense is compatible with a wide range of theologies. As an obvious ex-ample: Even a partisan supporter of the public importance of Christianity like Stephen Carter would, one imagines, accept the crucial difference be-tween *disagreeing* with someone about whether or not Jesus is God and *jailing* them for robbery or rape. Religions allied with world-making politics make comparable distinctions about ethical issues such as the oppression of women, militarism, and the fate of the earth. Further, as we will see through-out the rest of this book, such an ethically and politically oriented religion need not be simply another version of secular politics. Religious traditions have their own distinct genius to bring to social struggles and personal life.

Of course, one person's "theology" or "metaphysics" might be consid-ered a matter of morality to someone else. There are no neat dividing lines. My point is that in the debates over what differences we can and cannot ac-cept, the dividing line will be what might (roughly) be called the distinction between theology and ethics. Our newfound respect for the values of different religions will encourage us to draw that line with humility—but without wishy-washiness! As long ago as the mid-seventeenth century, responding to religious wars and suppression, Hugo Grotius faced this problem by arguing that Christianity had a common core in the pursuit of peace. This moral core was the basis for solidarity among all Christians, whereas differences in abstract theology could safely be ignored.[25] A similar affiliation is today a commonplace among a wide range of liberal religious groups. Contemporary Evangelical Christian leader Jim Wallis describes a convergence among different Christian denominations as one that is "biblical without being fundamentalist . . . spiritual without being withdrawn from the world . . . rooted in action without losing its reflective power . . . evangelical without being sectarian or self-righteous . . . [and] political without being ideological."[26] Believers from all faiths actively join with each other and with secular political forces on issues of peace, the environment, homelessness, and women's rights, while being totally untroubled by differences in the names of God or the titles of holy books. Surprisingly, cooperation based not on theology but on attitudes toward politics and the ethics of everyday life can also be found among some conservatives.[27] "A kind of cultural alliance has formed between conservative evangelicals and fundamentalists, some Catholics, and a few ultra-orthodox Jews. Activists call this alliance 'an ecumenism of orthodoxy.'"[28]

FROM MORALITY TO POLITICS

Religions place great emphasis on ethical teachings, yet even the simplest and most familiar of those teachings is deeply affected by the development of the global economy and the nation-state, for these have created a world in which people are physically, socially, and hence *morally* interdependent. In this world, social relations often determine the ethical character of individual action. That is why religions cannot actualize their own *moral* teachings without a *political* understanding of the world in which moral action arises. Being religious requires morality, and morality leads to politics.

As Reinhold Niebuhr put it seventy years ago:

The tendencies of an industrial era are in a definite direction. They tend to aggravate the injustices from which men have perennially suffered; and they tend to unite the whole of humanity in a system of economic interdependence. They make us more conscious of the relations of human communities to each other . . . [As a result] we can no longer buy the highest satisfactions of the individual life at the expense of social injustice. We cannot build our individual ladders to heaven and leave the total human enterprise unredeemed of its excesses and corruptions.[29]

Consider, as a simple example, the Golden Rule. Appearing first in Leviticus (19:18), it was repeated by Jesus and has become an essential element of Christian ethics.[30] But who *is* my neighbor? When acid rain caused by emissions from the power plants that provide my electricity kill forests a thousand miles away or when a government supported by my tax dollars provides money and military resources to a repressive dictator, the whole idea of a "neighbor" has been altered. If my farming methods poison the well of the family who lives down the road a piece, I have a clear moral obligation to change the way I farm. And it should be morally obvious that this obligation doesn't evaporate just because "a piece" is hundreds or thousands of miles. Technology confers an ethical complexity on the most mundane of routine daily activities. It is like a magical connecting rod, creating moral bonds where none existed before.

Just like the powers of physical machines, the large bureaucratic "machines" we call governments also extend the moral reach of our actions. Global systems of production and consumption enmesh us in global moral relations, but so do the connections forged by taxation and national allegiance. This is especially true for a nation such as the United States, which is both a democracy and a world power. As a democracy, it contains the political space for citizens to register dissent from policies they consider immoral. As a world power, its actions can seriously affect people's lives throughout the world. When our government supports a World Bank loan that will uproot indigenous tribes and flood rain forest containing endangered species, some of the moral responsibility belongs to those who pay taxes.[31]

Amid this complexity, we cannot rightly determine our proper allegiance to political parties or social policies without relying on fairly sophisticated theoretical accounts of how they affect the world. To determine the proper ethical response to globalization—or whether we should join the massive antiglobalization demonstrations in Seattle, Quebec City, or Genoa—we will need theories about the consequences of the global market, the relation between governmental policy and corporate interests, the effects of export agriculture on village life, the possibilities of renewable energy sources, and so on. Such theories are no more part of traditional religious teachings than are modern physics or instructions on how to build a computer.

Indeed, all ethics requires knowledge. It would be impossible to love our neighbors without knowing that smacking someone in the face causes physical pain or that screaming racial epithets causes emotional distress. If we are to be compassionate, we must empathize. And to empathize, we must have some real knowledge of what other people's lives are like and how they have suffered. It is political theories that tell us—and collective political actions that seek to redress—sources of unjust pain on a national or global scale. As Latin American theologian Gustavo Gutiérrez observes: "[T]he neighbor is not only a person viewed individually. The term refers also refers to a person considered in the fabric of social relationships, to a person situated in economic, social, cultural, and racial coordinates."[32]

Traditional religions or more contemporary forms of individualistic spirituality tend to concentrate on situations where people have pretty much total control over the moral character of their actions. We are told, as individuals, not to steal, lie, or kill. Now, however, a host of everyday actions—from paying taxes to using air conditioners—have consequences that are not chosen by us personally and cannot be changed by anything we do by ourselves. Hannah Arendt coined the chilling phrase "the banality of evil" to refer to the "ordinary" person who fulfills ordinary bureaucratic tasks that contribute to genocide. In less dramatic ways, all of us who pursue "normal" lives in advanced industrial society contribute to various kinds of ecological ruin.[33]

For instance, the large social structures that connect *our* electricity use to the death of *someone else's* forests are only occasionally, or to a limited extent, a matter of anyone's conscious ill will. We certainly bear no malice to the forests themselves or to those who live by or in them. And certainly it is not the goal of the Mega-Mega Power Company to hurt anyone's forests: It simply wants to make a profit and is burning oil or coal to do so. Instead of immediate forms of violence, calculated attempts to hurt or rob, we find that "[v]iolence today is white-collar violence, systematically organized bureaucratic and technological destruction . . . abstract, corporate, businesslike, cool, free of guilt-feelings and therefore a thousand times more deadly than the eruption of violence out of individual hate."[34] In the case of acid rain, there is a national energy policy, campaign contributions made in the hope of getting a break on emissions regulations, personal dependence on too much power use, psychological addiction to power-draining gadgets, and the threat of economic slumps if we don't have constant, high-energy economic "growth."

As a result of this complexity, seemingly endless questions arise. Should we pay taxes to a militaristic government? Should we abandon our cars and use public transportation to lessen our contribution to global warming, knowing that such a move would put a deep strain on our ability to fulfill *other* moral responsibilities? Do we have to alter our lives dramatically to consider ourselves decent people? The bleak truth is that unless we totally withdraw from society, we will be participating in morally questionable collective forms of life, forms that can be made more moral *only* by political change.

To quote Niebuhr again: "[A]n adequate Christian social ethic must avail itself of non-biblical instruments of calculation, chiefly a rational calculation of competing rights and interests and an empirical analysis of the structures of nature, the configurations of history and the complexities of a given situation in which decision must be made."[35] Christians, in other words, must think politically—socially, economically, ecologically—*if they are to be moral.* Clearly, the point applies to any religion whatsoever.

Just as in historic times Christianity was deeply affected by Greek philosophy, so over the last century, and especially over the last three decades, religion in general has been deeply affected by socialist and Marxist ideas (often in Latin America and Asia) and (in Europe and North America) by the "the new social movements"—feminism, racial liberation, gay/lesbian liberation, and environmentalism. These movements have created fresh models of transformative politics, challenged the socially conservative aspects of established religion, and brought political ideas and struggles inside existing religious institutions. Once the lessons of modernity are appropriated—including openness to religious pluralism, commitment to human rights and democracy, and principled political understanding of the role of spiritual values in social life—there is every reason to expect religion to be an active player on the political stage without devolving into sectarian violence.

It might be objected, of course, that the majority of people in advanced industrial democracies are deeply secular, hold their religious lives privately, or embrace a premodern fundamentalism. Even if the kinds of changes I describe do actually exist, how many people are involved in them? How many people, after all, are both passionate believers and open to the value of other religions? Or have tried to integrate progressive political values into their faith?

The simple answer is, I don't know! And I doubt that anyone does. However, I'm not sure that I *need* to know. Quite often in history a passionate, activist minority brings about profound historical changes. Of all the college students of the 1960s, it was only a minority that ever went on a demonstration. Despite the striking effects of black activism in the civil rights movement, the same was true for that community. I am not saying that the *majority* of religious believers have become political activists and spiritually ecumenical, only that *enough* of them have done so to have already had an impact on the very meaning of religious identity and on social life. I believe that this trend will continue and holds within itself a very real promise that the world will be made anew.[36]

NONVIOLENCE

But how can the passions of religious ethics be expressed without repeating the terrible errors of the Christian past or the Islamic present? A preliminary answer to this question may be found in the religiously inspired movements for political change led by King and Gandhi or the attitudes toward social change long espoused by Quakers. These examples offer lessons not only for political activists who want to change society without bloodshed but also for religious thinkers who want to know how to be both devout and socially engaged.

The moral example of nonviolent civil disobedience appeals to the heart of the Other and makes us vulnerable even while we are opposing social evil. That is why activist nonviolence seems to avoid the twin dangers of moral arrogance and moral passivity. Of course, people whose jobs, habits, or local culture are being contested might well experience nonviolent interference with the workings of the world as quite aggressive. Any serious movement of noncooperation with industrial civilization would probably throw people out of work, or at least disrupt the morning commute. Yet the challenges are rendered less threatening because those engaged in civil disobedience are sufficiently respectful of those they oppose to be willing to accept the civic penalties for their acts. And in proceeding nonviolently, mistakes are a lot less likely to produce disastrous, uncorrectable consequences.

In attempting to be politically active without being repressive, a socially engaged religion once again finds common ground with the progressive political tradition, for both these traditions must confront not only the world's evil or injustice but *their own*. They must be aware of all the times their predecessors sought to make the world better and actually made it worse. Every political radical speaks under the shadow of Stalin and Tiananmen Square, the jailed homosexuals in Cuba and the lockstep mindlessness of the American Communist Party, the self-indulgent narcissism of the New Left and the rigid arrogance of particular struggles against racism or sexism. Passionate religious believers must separate themselves from the Inquisition, Osama Bin Laden, the "people in each religion who hold their beliefs in a tightfisted way as if it were the only thing that could be true,"[37] and those who pursue anti-abortion and anti-gay politics to the point of violence. In too many heartbreaking contexts, religions and political movements have revealed violent and oppressive dark sides. Neither can be unhesitatingly identified with honesty, justice, peacefulness, or moral progress. The newfound religious modesty described above

should also be found in political circles. This modesty would be another motivation for secular activists to learn from religious ones, and vice versa. Since
neither politics nor religions have an unblemished moral track record, perhaps
the principled modesty of nonviolence might be the most reasonable course for
them both.[38]

SCIENCE AND SOUL

The last historical development that allows religion to reenter public life has
to do with the social status of science. Science's power is no threat to the vi-
tality of religion, because a religion shaped by metaphysical modesty will
have no trouble coexisting with lasers, the Internet, or the big bang theory.
Further, some achievements of science and technology have been overwhelming, while in other respects they have clearly failed to live up to their
advance billing. For nearly 300 years, we were told that technical control of
nature and professionalized planning of social life would make for collective
human progress. In the twentieth century, however, a dark shadow has fallen
over the optimistic Enlightenment prediction that science, democracy, and
the free market would give us freedom and happiness.

For a start, as the servant of government, business, and individual careers,
science and technology have proved a mixed blessing. It has become increasingly clear that the direction of scientific research and the effects of technical
breakthroughs are not always directed to some collective well-being but are
shaped by the interests of those who pay for the research, whether they be
corporate interests or governments seeking military power. We seek to know,
and we end up knowing, how to make things that will sell or will make our
armies more formidable. These constraints sometimes lead to widespread
human betterment, but often do not, or often lead to temporary satisfactions
at the cost of long-term pain.

As the early Western Marxist Georg Lukacs observed nearly eighty years
ago, the modern age is marked by a combination of increasingly sophisticated
parts integrated into an increasingly irrational whole.[39] One need only think
of the technological prerequisites for and the real-life consequences of traffic
gridlock, urban sprawl, or the way the overuse of antibiotics has led to new
and virulent strains of bacteria. In concrete settings, things don't work as well
as we thought—and as we'd been told—they would. Too many health problems seem impervious to a strictly detached, seemingly objective, medical expertise that clings to mind-body dualism. The war on cancer has not been
won. "Scientific management" often proves to be an oxymoron. Our nifty air-
planes drop horrible bombs; our air-conditioned cars cause skin cancer by

eroding the ozone layer; a pesticide is transmuted into a gas that kills people (Zyklon B, the gas used in concentration camps, was first used to eradicate insects from old buildings). Later, we discover that pesticides kill people even when they are aimed at bugs. The whole notion that scientific knowledge can replace real democracy and real self-knowledge—that experts can step back from reality and in so stepping back understand all they need to understand to "manage" it—has become for many increasingly doubtful. Thus, emerging areas of the scientific transformation of everyday life, such as the claim that genetically modified foods are safe and healthy, are met with deep skepticism. That skepticism has its roots partly in straightforward health concerns but also partly in a quasi-spiritual—or at least value-oriented—attitude that "nature" deserves a certain kind of respect both for its own good and ours.

In the absence of science as a guiding authority for social life, people have rediscovered or sought to create other kinds of knowledge: the kind that comes from awareness of one's own needs and social situation[40] and from spiritual practices such as meditation, mind-body medicine, and visualizations. The distinction between technical expertise and wisdom, obscured by an Enlightenment mentality in which everything that is not science is written off as literature,[41] becomes operative once again. In all these developments, space is made for both traditional religion and the new forms of spirituality.

If religion is impelled toward politics for ethical reasons, politics is impelled toward religion for political reasons. Also, both political life and modernized religion need to retain their spirit. The religious temperament has a distinct contribution to social life and should not be reduced to the ethical. I will address this topic in detail in Chapter 4, but I will begin the discussion here.

SPIRIT MATTERS

In a number of books and in the national Jewish magazine *Tikkun*, Michael Lerner has convincingly argued that leftist theorists and movements that ignore "spiritual" needs do so at their peril, condemning themselves to increasing irrelevance in a world in which people hunger for meaning alongside bread. Lerner's personal credentials are relevant, since he is both a rabbi and someone who has been active in leftist political movements from the 1960s to the present. His writings abound with lessons from Jewish religious teachings and forceful political criticisms of social institutions.

Lerner's basic argument is that "spirit matters": People's needs for meaning, connection, love, awe, mystery, rest, and joy are essential to their happiness and, when absent, are a source of profound personal *and* collective malaise.[42] He invites us to question the instrumental rationality that allows us to think carefully only about means and never ends and to adopt a "new bottom line" that would evaluate institutions and social policies in terms of their ethical and ecological content rather than only their monetary success. A society without spiritual values, he argues, produces environmental and moral devastation, professional technique that lacks both heart and real effectiveness, and an economy of unrestrained corporate greed. The religious right has a point, he tells us, in appealing to moral values and community over social engineering, state bureaucracies, and an anything-goes pop culture. Yet it is wrong when it does so in a way that ignores 200 years of liberal, socialist, feminist, and antiracist analysis of structural social injustice.

We need, says Lerner, a politics of meaning alongside a politics of living standards, individual rights, and group entitlements. Progressive movements should work for close relations with our neighbors and not just freedom to do what we want, appreciation of nature and not just control over it, celebration of life as well as consumption, producing something of value rather than simply producing something that someone can be convinced to buy. If progressive political movements cannot at least espouse these values, they will go nowhere. As French socialist André Gorz said bluntly more than three decades ago, "The working class will not unite politically or man the barricades for the sake of a 10 percent wage increase or an extra 50,000 dwellings."[43] What is at stake is a fundamentally different kind of social order, animated by different kinds of values, and these values include those of "spirit": wonder, awe, peace, compassion. These matters are not simply individual, though they are deeply personal. In a time when government on all levels is deeply implicated in our lives, when production is so extensively social, taking spiritual values seriously is necessarily a large-scale political question.

Lerner's position does not rest purely on naive hope. Rather, his claim that "spirit matters" is borne out by an impressive quantity of survey information, much of which is summarized in Ronald Inglehart's widely read *Culture Shift in Advanced Industrial Society*.[44] Inglehart's position is that the post–World War II rise in comparative economic security has led to a slow but basic shift in cultural values: away from stress on material goods, national military security, and economic development and toward concern with aesthetic, moral, psychological, and spiritual fulfillment. In this shift, religious concerns do not fade, as the secularization thesis would have it, but they do change form, becoming more "spiritual." They may be passionately held, but the passion is private, subjective, and ultimately apolitical.

Yet it may be a mistake to think that holding "spiritual values" must remove a person from the social realm. The opposite idea is suggested by the idea of "cultural creatives," a designation proposed by Paul Kay and Sherry Anderson to describe as many as 50 million Americans who, they claim, possess a significant new sensibility about personal and social life. This sensibility includes concern with environmental destruction and global problems, suspicion of unrestrained technological development and economic growth, spiritual involvement that is ecumenical rather than fundamentalist, support for women's equality and community needs, and a rejection of the notion that happiness can be founded in individualistic consumerism. Kay and Anderson share Inglehart's notion of a culture shift, yet see it as having significantly more political impact than he does. (It is interesting that Kay and Anderson were recent speakers at a conference hosted by the secular leftist journal *Mother Jones*.[45]) As Sociologist Philip Wexler suggests, using "mystical" where I might use "religious" or "spiritual":

> [A] new society is being created within and against the current society . . . It is a *mystical* society because the search for deeper and more authentic experience, which has strongly characterized the underlife of corporate modern society, leads to a resurgence of religion . . . Against the disorientation, decathexis [lack of emotional connection], and desensitization that . . . characterize modernity and postmodernity, the emerging form of life in a mystical society is characterized by unification . . . holistic relationality . . . faith . . . and joy.[46]

None of these considerations offer any certainty about where we are heading. Rather, what we see is that Lerner's call for a strong spiritual presence in politics does not occur in a vacuum. Secularization plus a culture shift, besides privatizing religions, *also* helps open the door to a politics in which some key social issues are understood spiritually as well as politically. Although this may sound pretty mushy in the abstract, we should remember that Lerner's call for the entry of spiritual values into politics follows in the footsteps of thinkers as socially significant as Martin Luther King Jr., Gandhi, Abraham Joshua Heschel, Dorothy Day, the Dalai Lama, and Desmond Tutu and of contemporary commentators from Jim Wallis and Dorothy Soelle to Joanna Macy and Riane Eisler. In the present, as we shall see in Chapter 7, vibrant social movements focused on environmentalism and globalization integrate religious inspiration and spiritual values with little hesitation.

To take but one small example where this happened, consider that in Prague, in September 2000, collective resistance to an international meeting of the International Monetary Fund was led by a group calling itself "Jubilee 2000." The term "Jubilee" did not refer to individual or group rights, to Marxist-derived concepts of exploitation, or to the idea of oppression as it emerged from black liberation or feminism. Rather, it hearkens back to God's commands in the Torah that periodically all unpaid debts should simply be forgiven.[47] Use of this term does not mean that resistance to the IMF is led by traditional Jews. However, it does suggest that people can understand struggles against dominant social powers in terms of ideas that have a religious connotation or formulation.

LIMITATIONS OF THE LEFT

To understand in a preliminary way why religious ideas can be extremely useful for progressive movements, let us briefly describe some of those movements' central values.

The typical message of world-making political groups has fallen into three categories. There is the pursuit of individual rights, the call for greater economic equality or power, and the liberation of particular groups (including colonized nations) from oppression or exclusion. Both the liberal and the radical versions of these languages have usually concentrated on issues such as basic political rights (voting, self-government, union membership), the aims of government programs (welfare, public education, public health), cultural respect for a group, economic rights, and—ultimately—social control of the economy.

The problem is that to some extent all such demands tend to focus on the fulfillment or happiness of the conventional social ego. Like secular psychotherapy, the goal has been to bring the benefits and privileges of the social order to an increasingly wider circle of recipients and to criticize those in power for the irrational and unjust distribution of those benefits. Those who seek a spiritual dimension in political activism are challenging not just the distribution of the benefits but our most basic conception of what a benefit is, and of the identity of the people who are to benefit. When satisfaction is keyed to individualism, consumption, success, and equality, too much is left out. The deep angst that permeates modern culture is a sign that—for all our wealth—something essential is missing. Spontaneous enjoyment, the satisfactions of compassionate connection, the cultivation of gratitude and joy, a simple sense that life has meaning, a feeling that one is more than a place holder for a global system of manufactured culture and financial transactions—all these need to be thought about by the same people who are talking about rights, equality, and oppression. Furthermore, the familiar progressive approach may well be missing a critical fact about recent social developments: that, as sociologist Manuel Castells claims, social life is increasingly structured around the opposition between impersonal global connections such as the Internet and financial networks and attempts at self-definition through a constructed sense of self-identity.[48] This opposition opens the door not only to fundamentalism's violent opposition to modernity but also to socially engaged spirituality in both denominational and nondenominational forms.

Detailed examples of the role of spiritual values in secular politics will be offered in later chapters, but to provide an initial clarification of the point, consider Lerner's treatment of American education. He begins with a devastating critique of the social and cognitive bankruptcy of the values that govern American educational institutions. This bankruptcy has led to violence and fear of violence throughout our schools, to falling intellectual performance and toxic school cultures, and to a "succeed at all cost" mentality (accompanied by widespread cheating), combined with an absence of respect for others, community involvement, or self-knowledge. In commenting on the particular horror of the shootings at Columbine High School in Littleton, Colorado, Lerner goes beyond the standard political accounts that stress either (by the right) repressive control of students and censorship of video games and movies or (on the left) the protection of individual rights, punishment of school bullies, and psychological "treatment" for unhappy students. Applying spiritual values to this social situation, Lerner suggests that if we want a world in which compassion and empathy are part of both private and public life, we should teach them in our schools. As one part of the alternative, Lerner suggests that parents demand course work in compassion and emotional intelligence throughout public school and that large amounts of public university scholarship funds be reserved for students who have excelled in these areas. If we can give scholarships to athletes and devote school funds to teaching driver's education, sex education, and the history of war, why not teach children how to handle their emotions and empathize with others? Although there might be serious disagreement over the nature of the curriculum and how to train those who will teach it, we know that work of this kind has already been done. Facing History and Ourselves, for instance, a yearlong course designed to teach morality, acceptance of difference, and citizenship by integrating lessons from the Holocaust and contemporary racial conflict, has been taught in over a thousand high schools.[49] Along with historical facts, the course includes material designed to defuse group hatred by developing empathy. Clearly, the best part of parenting, like the best part of traditional religions, also seeks to teach this.

The general point of this chapter is that historical and social changes have helped us realize that an adequate response to injustice and collective suffering will necessarily call on both political and spiritual values. To fashion such a response, however, each side has to be willing to receive the specific teachings of the other.

3

Politics Teaching Religion

If one wants change, any kind of change, support cannot be found within the traditional religious institutions . . . They represent and reflect the status quo, both past and present.

—*James I. Charlton,* **Nothing About Us Without Us**[1]

The church renews itself. We cannot preserve those structures in which sin has enthroned itself and from which come abuses, injustice, and disorders. We cannot call a society, a government, or a situation Christian when our brothers and sisters suffer so much in those inveterate and unjust structures.

—*Bishop Oscar Romero,* **The Violence of Love**[2]

One can find within the Bible excellent grounds for overcoming anthropocentrism and for care for the earth. But Christians did not do so until the insights of persons outside the church led to accusations against them.

—*John B. Cobb Jr.,* **Reclaiming the Church**[3]

Transformed by past history and present opportunities, religions are now able to offer profound gifts to political struggles without regressing to a repressive past. Avoiding such a regression, however, requires that religions learn some political lessons, lessons that will better enable them to assess, critique, and live out their own values. Clearly, secular political criticism of religion is

49

nothing new. What *is* different is that in recent decades, believers themselves have taken critical political insights seriously. Some of the faithful see that we cannot get to God *except* through a particular human community, via a particular set of beliefs, and by relying on our "local" ideas of what God could be. Even wordless mystical encounters with the Divine, once they are expressed in a human language to a human community, are subject to this condition.

To say that God is reachable only by humans in history is to say that religion always unfolds in the face of particular distributions of power and wealth, norms of justice, capacities for empathy and care, and ideas about morality. There can be no "final" religious truth until our communities have finally become perfected in all these dimensions. Since they are quite far from that point, so is our religion.[4] Further, religions not only live in political communities, they are political communities themselves, marked by their own successes or failures in the pursuit of justice and care.

If these reflections about the social limits and political nature of religion are commonplace, it is only because critical social theories have made them so. Just as the political power of kings and capitalism, abusive husbands, or racist communities have been challenged, so religious institutions themselves have come under political scrutiny—at times by the faith's own followers. These critical voices ask: To what extent does the internal organization or ethical teaching of our religion reflect the reigning injustices of the broader society? This question leads some to despair of ever reforming the "church" and therefore to abandon religion altogether. Others, however, maintain their religious commitment while struggling to transform the church politically. In doing so, they use insights from *secular* politics to make their own faith more authentic.

Let us take as an example one so obvious it might escape notice. It took the Catholic Church some time before it accepted the idea that the common people should decide on their own rulers. Now, however, the church's acceptance of democracy is taken for granted.[5] Yet the innovative idea of popular government did not emerge from the church but from secular political movements. As a *religion*, it had needed *politics* to make the change, and in this case, a particular type of progressive, world-making politics. Once developments such as this one occur, religions' self-understanding has to be seriously altered. Theologians must acknowledge that their own teachings have been made more holy and less historically limited by resources outside their boundaries.

These resources can prompt a reevaluation of some basic religious concepts. We have already seen, for example, how the emergence of nation-states and the global economy alters the meaning of "neighbor" in the

Golden Rule. Sin, prayer, forgiveness, repentance, peacefulness—to name but a few—may also be viewed afresh by seeing how our traditional understanding of them is determined by our social condition and how emerging political perspectives instruct us on why and how we should change them. When Rabbi Abraham Heschel said that in marching for racial justice with Martin Luther King Jr. "I felt like I was praying with my feet," he was telling us something new about *prayer*, which he could not have known if he had not learned something new from King's *politics*.[6] When Buddhist deep ecologist Joanna Macy recommends meditating on nuclear waste dumps in order to face the truth of our condition, she is teaching us something new about meditation, something she could not have learned without the global environmental movement.[7]

———

The moral purpose of the politics of social change is to comprehend, evaluate, and transform collective social relationships in accord with a vision of justice and true community. As opposed to traditional religious ethics, the focus is not on individual choices and virtues but on the social nature of human existence. This social nature conditions even our most private moral acts, and thus essential religious teachings about morality need instruction from political theory.

As a particular example of this phenomenon, consider how every religion teaches that the proper application of virtues depends on the setting in which we find ourselves. As Jewish philosopher Adin Steinzaltz puts it: "[T]here is no attribute that lacks its injurious aspect, its negation and failure, just as there is no attribute . . . that has not, under some circumstances, its holy aspect . . . All the attributes, all the emotions, and all the potentialities of the heart and personality are set on the same level and considered good or bad . . . according to the way they are used."[8]

But how are we to understand "the way they are used" without a political account of the social setting in which they exist? For instance, all religions teach us to be grateful for what we have. Traditional Jews begin each day thanking God for "returning their souls to their bodies." "Gratefulness," writes contemporary Catholic spiritual writer David Steindl-Rast, "is the heart of prayer."[9] And gratitude for the simple things of life—a child's smile, being able to get out of bed in the morning, a beautiful sunrise—surely warms the heart and makes us both morally better and more content.

Perhaps, however, we might ask whether what we are grateful for is properly ours—and whether it is the kind of thing for which we should be grateful. For instance, the traditional male Jew thanks God each morning for not being "made a woman." (There is no corresponding prayer for women!) Would gratitude for masculine identity have been possible without the rigid gender separation and hierarchy of traditional Judaism? Or without men's presumed theological and social superiority? Aren't the morning prayers themselves—which take at least forty-five minutes to an hour to complete—dependent on a sexual division of labor in which *she* cares for the children and the home while *he* talks to God? All of us face a broader version of this question: How many of the good things for which we thank God are held at others' expense? Or depend on privileges that we have and others lack? How much of our gratitude could we maintain if we lost the privileges that stem from our social position? Ultimately, given the global connections of the modern economy, and the way class, gender, and race shape our lives, how could we even begin to answer these questions without a political perspective?

In another example, consider how religions teach us the inevitability of suffering and the need to accept that our common fate, as limited creatures, is to endure pain. Buddhism claims that life itself is necessarily suffering and that the proper response is a heart and mind attuned to detachment and equanimity. Yet surely not all suffering is equivalent. My depression over my failed dot-com investments is different from the anguish of parents whose children starve while the world overflows with excess food. Refusing to recognize my mortality is not the same as refusing to tolerate getting cancer because a factory carelessly let toxins into the local water supply. Making peace with my particular mix of advantages and disabilities is not the same thing as accepting that local police can harass me because I'm not white.

At times, the spiritual virtues of gratitude or acceptance obscure humanly caused—and hence changeable—sources of injustice and suffering. At times the proper spiritual response is not to accept with gratitude but to question our own situation or resist larger social conditions. It is true that religions possess a great deal of wisdom about serenity, appreciation, joy in the moment, and substituting compassion for anger. Yet it is also the case that such virtues can be used as a kind of "spiritual bypass" (in Miriam Greenspan's apt phrase) in which pleasing emotions serve as an escape from threatening social realities. If religions can *teach* us a great deal about the limits of a mentality that sees the need to struggle and rage everywhere, religions also need to *learn* the political lesson of resistance to injustice. If peace and gratitude are important, so are anger and fighting back.

Because religious virtues cannot be adequately practiced without a political perspective, the Christian concept of a "confessing church," endorsed by Stanley Hauerwas and William Willimon as an alternative to a church unduly influenced by either conservative or progressive politics, is ultimately inadequate. The goal of the confessing church is to create a distinct religious community by withdrawing energy from the state and from a corrupt and violent culture, pouring that energy into an "alternative polis" in which people are "faithful to their promises, love their enemies, tell the truth, honor the poor, suffer for righteousness, and thereby testify to the amazing community-creating power of God."[10] My point, however, is that we cannot know who the poor are and why they are poor, what love is (or is not), or what righteousness consists in without using secular political resources to help us understand poverty, human relationships, and justice. We will not, for instance, understand love between men and women without the critical power of feminism to unmask domination posing as affection; nor will we see the injustice lurking in economic "free trade" without the political ideas of the antiglobalization movement. As in the cases of gratitude and acceptance, these virtues cannot be practiced by a purely religious consciousness, because neither consciousness nor community is ever purely religious.

Finally, religion has to learn from politics the concept of a *strategy* for social change, a way to make ethical values play a significant role in society. To explore this point, we can remember Marx and Engels's criticism of what they called "utopian" socialism.[11] Although Marx and Engels agreed with many of these earlier socialists' goals, their complaint was that, in a sense, goals were all that the utopians offered. A rational vision of how society might achieve them was missing. How would the powerful be made to share their power? How would the downtrodden learn to exercise legitimate authority? How would wealth and economic control be redistributed? Without a strategic *theory* of how such things come to be, of what social group(s) would initiate the desired change, utopian socialist demands were only escapist fantasies of what *would* be nice *if* it ever happened.

This criticism is relevant because religious writing about social issues often falls into a comparable error. We are instructed that a prophetic vision or the message of the gospel means that something "should" change. However, no strategic theory is put forward about how that change will come about, how current historic developments are making it likely that it might come about, or which actual social group would be doing the brunt of the work! We are told that poverty, war, injustice, and racism would be lessened if "we all meditated" (or prayed, or followed the Golden Rule, or thought about Jesus in a particular way). But what likelihood is there that this will happen? Who are the "we" that will bring it about? And on what basis does the speaker suppose that even if "we" want to, we'll actually have the power to do so?

Marx's strategic vision was rooted in the belief that the ever-larger working class would respond to ever-larger crises in the capitalist economy. Forming political organizations, workers would contest for state power and owner-ship of the forces of production. Obviously, his revolutionary predictions have failed to occur, and the industrial working class has not overthrown cap-italism as Marxism predicted it would. Yet the political activities of workers have greatly improved the condition of their class and for the most part have led to greater justice and fairness in society as a whole. And they have done so at least partly in conformity to the description Marx laid out. One lesson from this process is that a religious ethic without a strategic model is only half a vision. It is not enough to say what we want; we need also to have some idea how we might get it.

Let us consider some concrete cases in which religious values betray their de-pendence on existing, often unjust, social norms and in which they require a political corrective of their moral—and hence religious—failings.

We can begin with an obvious case. In *Blossoms in the Dust*, a study of prob-lems with Indian land reform written in 1961, anthropologist Kusum Nair reported on her experience in southern India.[12] She was asked to find out why land reform, a virtual economic necessity for the region's land-starved peasants, was faring so poorly. The recently elected leftist government had made land reform a priority and had hoped that the move would help the peasants alleviate their chronic poverty, debt, and illiteracy. Nair was asked to find out why the peasants weren't taking advantage of an offer that would al-low them to enlarge their holdings from as little as one-thirty-second of an acre to one-fourth or one-half acre. She did extensive interviews and came up with one general conclusion. The cause was the peasants' firm religious belief in the Hindu concept of karma: that their present social situation stemmed from their deeds in past lives and that a political alteration of their condition would violate what they in fact deserved. "In our next lives, if we are good in this one," they told Nair repeatedly, "perhaps we will be landowners. As for this life? It must be as God wills."

Can it be an accident that in this case religious dogma so clearly served the interest of one class over another? Or that the dogma was interpreted to al-low landowners to invest in machines or raise rents but not for poor peasants to get a little more land?

The happy end to the story is that a continued left-wing presence in Ker-ala has overturned religious bars to social change. Kerala has achieved a liter-acy rate and life expectancy comparable to developed countries. While poverty still remains, land is much more equitably distributed. Contempo-rary Hinduism, still the faith of the vast majority, has learned to coexist with political democracy and what can only be called economic decency. Beliefs around the idea of karma have been correspondingly changed.[13]

Other examples easily come to mind. Pacifists both secular and religious have long criticized religious support for wars, especially for those wars largely motivated by the pursuit of conquest and economic expansion. Despite the fact that religious pacifists have invoked spiritual values, in the vast majority of cases they have gone against the teachings of their own faith's current leadership. From Dorothy Day to Daniel and Philip Berrigan, the Catholic left has spoken up against militarism, nuclear arsenals, and the Vietnam War. Part of their point was that in publicly supporting the government's position, their own church had bedded down with the rich and powerful, ignoring its proper vocation as an embodiment of spiritual truth. The church hierarchy's typical response is summed up by a chapter title in a biography of the Berrigans: "Exile and Shunning."[14]

For another example, consider the harsh criticism leveled at religious authorities' tolerance of abuse within the family. In the words of a Lutheran theologian:

> The basic social structure of the patriarchal family, a structure that socialized women for domestic responsibility and men for dominance and aggression in public arenas, represents an important element in Christian theology. Christological doctrines use analogies to the patriarchal family to articulate the meaning of Christ. These doctrines assume the unquestioned norm of the patriarchal family. Hence, I believe such Christological doctrines reflect views of divine power that sanction child abuse on a cosmic scale and sustain benign paternalism.[15]

In other words, just as the war-endorsing church sides with the rich and powerful against the victims of aggression, so the patriarchy-supporting church sides with men against women and children.

———— • ————

Religious backing for unjust land distribution, denial of sexual abuse in the church, or lockstep support for nationalist wars are clear instances of religion's political failings. They also show how the moral teachings of religion, untutored by secular political and moral analysis, are inadequate in religion's own terms. But religions' limitations in this area cannot be redressed solely by the desire to be sensitive to issues of social justice. What is required is recognition of the ineluctably political nature of social reality. This is an especially telling point when it arises in thinkers already committed to bringing religion into the struggle for social justice, such as the five religious personalities from the last fifty years I discuss below. Diverse by religion, nationality, and ethnicity, they have in common remarkable accomplishments of intelligence, insight, and moral character. As we shall see, they also share an unintended blindness to the particular powers of political insight.

OSCAR ROMERO, JAMES CONE, AND THE PROBLEM OF SOCIAL STRUCTURE

Oscar Romero is perhaps the best-known victim of two decades of ruthless civil war in El Salvador, a largely one-sided struggle in which the country's landholding oligarchy directed its U.S.-trained and -equipped military against peasants, workers, and their supporters. Over 70,000 people were killed, as bombings, midnight "disappearances," torture, machine-gun fire on unarmed demonstrators, rape, and countless other forms of brutality became commonplace.

For the last three years of his life, Romero was archbishop of El Salvador. Appointed partly because of his conservative approach to theology and his personal connections to the upper class, he soon ended a lifelong avoidance of politics when a friend—a Jesuit working to support peasant land reform— was murdered. After saying mass for the victim and viewing his body, Romero was reborn as a passionate voice for the poor. Reversing his long-held conservative politics and his defense of the repressive government, he embraced the essential vision of liberation theology, which he had earlier dismissed as a "hate-filled christology." From his pulpit and in weekly radio broadcasts, through appearances in the slums and countryside, he embodied a religious voice of social concern.[16]

Romero's teachings were as simple as they were powerful: The poor and oppressed represent Christ on earth. Service to them—and sharing their plight— is the essential task of Christian witness. Nonviolent resistance to social evil is the responsibility of all those who espouse Christian morality; and, despite appearances to the contrary, the spirit of God ennobles and ultimately guarantees the victory of the poor. Just as Jesus was resurrected, so will be the humble and downtrodden of history. For repeating this message, for calling out to the government, "In the name of God, stop the repression," Romero was assassinated in 1980. When 150,000 people assembled for his funeral, dozens were killed by the military. It was five years before an open funeral procession for Romero was allowed, and another twelve before the shooting war ended.

As a religious thinker and activist, Romero embodied many of the central virtues that arise when religion enters social life to change the world. On the positive side, the religious call invokes symbols and narratives that maintain an immense hold on the imagination of most Latin Americans. To identify the poor with Jesus, to speak of El Salvador as "going through its own Exodus," to promise that "if they kill me, I will be resurrected in the spirit of the Salvadoran people" is to arouse vital emotional and moral responses. Similarly, Romero's insistence on the transcendent dimension of the human condition offered a kind of hope. In a social setting of almost Holocaust-like brutality, it may be possible to stave off despair and resignation only by believing this: "No one is conquered, no one; even though they put you under the boot of oppression and of repression, whoever believes in Christ knows that he is a victor and that the definitive victory will be that of truth and justice."[17] Where secular politics might have been stuck in despair, the Christian message—despite everything—offered joy.

Also, Romero personally modeled religious virtues of humility and self-sacrifice. He consistently refused "protection" from the government, asking rather that protection be extended to the poor.[18] He responded to criticism with principled openness. And he provided an example of someone who would not be stopped by the threat of violence, exemplifying the life-enhancing courage of those who do not believe *this* life is all there is. The spiritual imperative to *live* ones values—rather than only assessing their political consequences—provided a kind of integrity often lacking in purely secular political movements. Such integrity is one of the hallmarks of the great religious social activists, from Martin Luther King Jr. and Gandhi to Burma's Aung San Suu Kyi and our own Dorothy Day. (It is, sadly, *not* a hallmark of, say, the American Communist Party, the AFL-CIO, or your typical gathering of left-wing postmodern social theorists.)

As inspiring as Romero was, there were limitations in his perspective, both in its own setting and as a model for helping us understand the role of religion in political life. The key point is that Romero, who had been a devout Catholic all his life, after his friend's murder became more *fully religious* by becoming *political*. He came to understand the problems of El Salvador in terms of conflict between different social groups with vastly different interests and power. He learned that describing problems of poverty and violence in collective, social terms was a necessary development of religious ethics, not their betrayal.

Only then was he able to criticize "structural violence, social injustice, exclusion of citizens from the management of the country," to call for "a thorough change in the social, political, and economic system," and to identify the economic motives that helped prompt the repression. He was also happy to join in solidarity with nonreligious organizations, believing that the "true

Christian" is the one who serves the poor, not simply the one who espouses a particular religious doctrine. What we learn from Romero, then, is not only that "religion can do good in the world" but that in some circumstances "religion needs political insights in order to do that good."

Given his enormous courage and tragic martyrdom, it might seem positively boorish to subject some of Romero's statements to criticism. However, I believe that the more principled and passionate the figure, the greater weight these errors carry.

The basic problem is that Romero failed to push his structural analysis far enough. He tended to oversimplify his country's political situation by viewing it as a simple reflection of moral categories. For him—as for many religious thinkers and activists—moral categories enter the political world in a simple one-to-one correlation. Just as Christianity might talk of good and evil, or God and Satan, so there are also the poor and the rich, the downtrodden and the powerful. Now perhaps in the midst of a one-sided civil war, as in an ethnic cleansing or military repression, a simple appeal to the welfare of the poor is all that is needed. But even in El Salvador we might ask about the complexities of the political situation. The ruling class includes high-ranking military officers, top government officials, and large landowners. At the bottom we find the poorest peasants. But there are also all sorts of politically and morally intermediate groups: noncommissioned officers in the military, peasants conscripted to the army who kill other peasants, small businessman torn between justice and repression. Because of the many gradations that exist in situations of social struggle, a simple two-category model—good and evil, poor and rich—is inadequate. It is possible to accept democracy but still endorse a highly stratified capitalist system. It is possible to oppose the violence of the army without fully comprehending the violence of economic development that displaces the peasants in favor of export agriculture. The simple appeal of "no more repression" is direct and easily understood. But it leaves a great deal unsaid.

Further, Romero did not seem to recognize the tangled moral relations *within* "the poor." Are there not richer and poorer peasants? Was there no racism among different ethnic groups in El Salvador? Was there no sexism in poor families? Relying on an essentially religious vision, in which the differences between crucifixion and the resurrection, oppressor and oppressed, are comfortingly distinct, Romero's framework may not be equipped to comprehend a situation in which people have multiple social—and hence, moral—locations.

When liberation theology is adapted to other social settings, the situation is even more complicated. What does it mean, for instance, to identify with "the poor" in the contemporary United States? Are "the poor" those on welfare? The entire working class? Nonunionized workers? From the lower middle class on down? What about groups victimized in other ways: Upper-middle-class women who are abused by their husbands? Wealthy gay men threatened in the street by homophobic thugs? Rich teenagers assaulted by pesticide-laden food and arsenic-tainted drinking water?

That these issues are relevant to wider social contexts can be shown if we consider James Cone's extremely influential writings on a "Black theology of liberation." Cone was inspired by Latin American liberation theology and the more radical elements of the civil rights movement, and was deeply shaken by the murder of civil rights workers and deaths in ghetto riots. His response was a theology of oppression and liberation, of oppressors and victims. Explicitly modeled on Exodus, Cone made it clear that for him God was "on the side of the oppressed" and that the religious resources of Protestantism should support resistance against white America's violent racism. He asked: "Where is your identity? Where is your being? Does it lie with the oppressed blacks or with the white oppressors?"[19]

Cone presumes that God—like history, or righteousness—must be exclusively on one side or another. But perhaps God is on my side when I am, for instance, a black man shunted into a low-paying job because of my skin color but is *not* on my side when I'm abusive to my wife; God could support me when I'm a woman oppressed by my husband but not when I teach my children homophobia. And where is God when all of us who are employed pay taxes to a government that supports dictatorships? Or when we all participate in an economy that ravages the earth? If political activism is supposed to follow some moral simple model, it will be led in too many directions at once.

Further, a liberation theology that ignores the variety of moral positions generated by our multiple social locations will have difficulty coming to terms with an oppressed group's need for political alliances. Because of the complexity of any group's position in society, alliances must be made on the basis of more than the fact of virtuous victimhood. When the theological categories of good and evil, virtue and sin are read into society, the "good" (the victims, the downtrodden) are not likely to seek limited, compromise-based alliances. If white America, as in Cone's analysis, is homogeneously racist, you don't go trying to make alliances with, say, the white labor movement. If the "poor" are especially beloved of God, why should they make common cause with small shopkeepers or government employees? But, once again, except in the most extreme of situations, such *political* alliances are precisely what are needed in order to shift the political situation—and thus to lessen the suffering of the oppressed. In short, *political* complexity generates *moral* complexity. And to comprehend that moral complexity, it is necessary (though often not sufficient) to assimilate the lessons of political theory and the movements from which they spring.

Finally, we can raise a question that links Romero to political life rather than shows his need of it. This has to do with his unquestioned commitment to the church. With a sole exception, the other bishops of El Salvador resisted Romero's political commitment, denouncing him to Rome and at home. And despite some private encouragement, the rest of the church hierarchy was pretty much silent. Throughout the world, liberation theology in general was restricted by the Vatican. Even in the United States, where the stakes are considerably lower, Dominican priest Matthew Fox chose to leave after being silenced for his socially and theologically radical teachings. We might wonder whether Romero's combined passion for God and social justice (rather than simple charity) could have flourished better outside the Catholic Church than within it.

The question of whether to reform the dominant institutions or create new ones permeates the history of world-making political movements. In each case, the institutions we seek to transform both enable and restrict us. Romero's commitment to the church might be compared to antiwar activists remaining in the Democratic Party in 1968, to socialists working in the labor movement, or to socialist-feminists joining the National Organization of Women. In more recent times, we might consider the acrimony between liberals and leftists over whether to support Al Gore or Ralph Nader in the 2000 presidential election. Such dilemmas have given rise to countless strategic and moral debates about the conflicts between "reform and revolution" or about lesser evilism in electoral politics. Here, religion and politics can learn from each other's struggles over a dilemma faced by both.

REINHOLD NIEBUHR AND POLITICAL KNOWLEDGE

A world-famous theologian and political commentator, Reinhold Niebuhr was one of the last great public intellectuals of American life. Author of twenty or so books and close to a thousand articles, founder of a number of magazines linking religion to social life, impassioned public speaker and consultant to the State Department, his thought influenced people as diverse as Martin Luther King Jr., James Cone, and Thomas Merton.

In recent years, Niebuhr's theology has fallen into serious neglect. Indeed, as someone who has been writing on the relations between politics and religion for a decade, I find it extremely interesting that no one ever said to me: "You should read Niebuhr." Niebuhr was both deeply committed to a religious

(Protestant) worldview and also intimately knowledgeable of and in some ways sympathetic to liberal and Marxist perspectives. More particularly, Niebuhr strikingly anticipated many later political insights. He advocated nonviolent civil disobedience to achieve black civil rights twenty years before the Montgomery bus boycott and described patriarchal power in the family thirty years before feminism. He criticized cultural imperialism (even using the phrase) forty years before multiculturalism and recognized the need for a Jewish state before the Holocaust.[20]

Niebuhr's starting point—which is part of the reason the particular insights mentioned above were accessible to him—is the fallibility and selfishness of human beings, *especially* when they enter into social struggles for power, property, or privilege. His commitment to social justice, sympathy for the working class (his first professional job was as minister of a church attended by autoworkers), and ardent Christian faith coexisted with the belief that every movement, political party, or religious group was limited in understanding and liable to immoral self-aggrandizement. For the most part, he was immune to the kind of oversimplification that has plagued liberation theology. Unlike most religious visionaries, especially those in the Western tradition, he was highly critical of Christian claims to absolute knowledge, truth, and virtue. He was even able to assert that other religious groups—for instance, the Jews—often manifested certain virtues more completely than Christians.

Although he believed that religion was essential to a moral society and thus rejected the program of secularization, Niebuhr accepted many of the other central ideas of liberal modernity. He recognized that all concepts and beliefs were conditioned by history and social life, that political action should be used to improve the world, that the traditional view of the natural world offered by Christianity had been undermined by natural science, and that it was necessary to criticize religion for its parochialism and oppressiveness. Yet while he believed that the struggle for social justice was an unending necessity, Niebuhr also spent much of his life inveighing against the liberal naïveté that expected social betterment to be a natural product of historical development. In his most famous book, *Moral Man and Immoral Society*, he complained that liberals ignored the universality of human self-centeredness, especially in collective political action.[21]

For Niebuhr, this fact would not be changed by education, or reason, or technological developments. Uncritical reliance on any theory or group would always be a kind of idolatry: taking the part as the whole, confusing scientific facts with the full truth of the universe or human history, identifying our personal or limited group interests with those of "everyone." The task of religion was to provide a permanent position of transcendence by which to judge such errors and pretensions.

If Niebuhr's position sounds like a Marxist account of how ideology and political behavior express class interest, that is because Niebuhr constantly utilized (often without direct attribution) Marx's ideas. But unlike Marx, Niebuhr did not believe that there was a "universal class," the redress of whose wrongs would create a social utopia. Workers carried no more guarantee of virtue than the churches. Because everyone was morally fallible, political struggles were not to be aimed at finding the "right" group to run things but were to be about achieving a slightly better balance of power among contending groups. Niebuhr's skepticism about political movements had a conservative effect in some circles and caused his thought to lose favor with the rise of the New Left and liberation theology. However, by countering its naive romanticism about the inherent goodness of "the oppressed," Niebuhr's position would have done a great deal for the radical politics of the last thirty years. (His insights could be particularly important in ethnic or national struggles. One could only imagine what would happen to the Middle East conflict if Palestinians and Israelis began from Niebuhr's insight about the universality of human selfishness and arrogance.)

Despite Niebuhr's brilliance, he faces, like the other figures discussed in this chapter, some serious problems, problems based in a lack of understanding of the insights of specifically political perspective. His general "realism" about human sinfulness needed to be made more concrete through an understanding of specific political constraints and dynamics.

We can begin by noting his strange belief that Christianity was more fitting to our human condition than any other religion or philosophy. Only Christianity, he argued, could help us understand the universal tensions we face as human beings, those stemming from the fact that we are both part of nature and ensouled, good and evil, morally significant and insignificant, socially determined and free. Christian faith protects us from existential despair by connecting our historical existence to a transcendent God, from idolatry by reminding us that the divine infinitely transcends any particular human religious understanding or moral attitude, and from religious attempts to escape history (as in, for Niebuhr, Eastern religions or mysticism) by teaching that God entered—and continues to care about—history.

Besides being a theological error—Christianity does no more than other religions in this area—Niebuhr here commits a significant *political* mistake. Rooting the superiority of Christianity in its relation to a "universal" human experience presumes that we can describe that experience in some kind of neutral terms, unshaped by the particular perspective we began with. But of course we can't. Commentators on the human condition are always limited by their historical and social position, not to mention the contours of their individual lives. This is especially important in relation to Niebuhr's account of sin, which he tends to identify with pride and selfishness. But, as Valerie Saiving convincingly argued, the social situation of women, and therefore their psychological and moral habits, is culturally different from that of men. Women's experience of sin is less likely to involve pride and selfishness than it is a "sinful" lack of self-care, self-assertion, or taking of public responsibility.[22] In fact, there is no universal model of sin, because men and women are conditioned to experience life in very different ways. Niebuhr confused what he knew of highly individualistic, arrogant white men and the organizations they directed with "experience in general."

This serious flaw, one often committed by religious thinkers, is rooted in the notion that certain religious concepts or beliefs are "beyond politics," universally human, an antidote to the differences and conflicts that plague the rest of social life. In Niebuhr's case, as with other thinkers we will examine here, this belief leads to distorted generalizations. The point is not just that Niebuhr didn't see how fundamental political relationships caused essential differences between the men's and women's moral situation or that in taking men's particular experiences as a universal model, his account of sin was sexist. The problem, rather, is that because there was no women's movement during his lifetime, he could not *help* being sexist.

Those who write secular histories of religion and understand religion as a manifestation of social needs and a response to social changes would hardly be surprised by this observation. However, the point may well be at odds with the religious belief that spiritual truths exist outside of history. And it is this belief, I am suggesting, that is undermined when religions take needed instruction from secular politics. When the democratic movements of the eighteenth century redefined human freedom, they altered the European Christian idea of the proper relations between religion and the state. When Daniel and Philip Berrigan publicly challenged American racism, the Vietnam War, and imperialism, they offered American Catholics the opportunity to see the meaning of fundamental Christian beliefs—such as "Blessed are the peacemakers" and the Golden Rule—in a fundamentally new light. Religion shaped by politics teaches us that we cannot love Jesus without loving the poor, and that includes workers seeking a decent wage; that the full meaning of "Kashrut" (Jewish dietary laws) includes awareness of pesticides and the effects of meat eating on the environment; and that Buddhist "right livelihood" forbids making nuclear weapons. Such developments change the understanding of basic religious categories, refute some traditionally held beliefs, and reshape our conception of moral virtue. They teach us that any attempt to overcome the realities of social existence will always inevitably *reflect* that existence as well.

Of course, arguments will arise over whether these changes are the fulfillment of religion or its betrayal. Such arguments are just part of what religion is. Christians, for instance, share a common identification with the life, death, and resurrection of Jesus. Yet the meaning of those events is subject to wildly varying interpretations. To radical Christian pacifists like the Berrigans, faith in Jesus leads to civil disobedience against war and nuclear weapons. To more conventional Catholics, the message has nothing to say about resistance to the state whatsoever.

Returning to Niebuhr: Let us keep in mind that he wanted religion to be an antidote to human pride and selfishness in the public realm—to give our lives meaning, instruct us concerning our necessary humility before God, provide images of perfect love, show us that life is a mystery rather than a technical problem, and help guide us to make social life more just. But Niebuhr failed to see that although religious views can help heal the hurts of politics, political perspectives are equally necessary for the full sanctification of religion. Between religion and politics, the teaching and the learning need to go both ways. If religion is a permanent position of transcendence through which politics can be judged, *politics offers the same for religion.* Religion cannot be content with using politics in the way it uses auto mechanics or chemistry: as a purely technical knowledge that will help it fulfill unchanging values. Rather, political knowledge, gained from the experience of groups struggling for their collective interests and rights, will alter religious values themselves. The point is particularly important because similar presuppositions about the relations between politics and religion are held by contemporary spiritual writers who, like Niebuhr, see the sweetness of religion as something of an alternative to the brutalities of politics.

There is a final problem, which has to do with the practical implications of Niebuhr's insights about human fallibility—insights that place Niebuhr squarely in the center of contemporary views such as postmodernism, feminist theory, Marxism-after-Stalin, and postempiricist philosophy of science. Each of these stresses the inherently limited nature of any claims to truth, reason, or morality. Grand narratives about the direction of human history, attempts to construct a single standard of meaning for individual lives, or pretensions to objective standpoints in ethics or science—all have been rendered doubtful.

Yet a fundamental problem remains. Although it is valuable to teach humility and openness to recognizing errors, life—especially moral life—requires action. And every action or inaction is a commitment to one reality over another. "Humility" might make sense in setting the tax codes for different religious groups or setting the program for a "holiday" (not "Christmas," of course) school pageant. But what is "humility" when we encounter a rape, an environmental struggle, or a strike? We can act arrogantly or humbly, but any action makes the beliefs that inform it absolute—because any action points our energy in some particular direction and changes history accordingly.[23]

The consequences of missing this point come together in some of Niebuhr's later political views, when he asserted, contrary to some earlier writings, that the virtue of "tolerance" should inform relations between capitalists and workers.[24] Such a position is fundamentally mistaken, for "tolerance" is a virtue properly extended between equals, or at worst between those with more power to those with less. It is a virtue for situations in which justice already exists and where what is demanded is our ability to tolerate *difference*. Workers are not *supposed* to be tolerant of their employers, unless we want to pretend that those who toil in sweatshops are on an equal social footing with Bill Gates, or that monopoly capitalism embodies the most balanced and just social system we can imagine. And not unless "tolerance" simply means being pleasant while the power of the ruling group is dismantled. As Dorothy Day replied, when asked why her *Catholic Worker* newspaper concentrated on class strife as much as the love of God: "[C]omfortable people" need to "realize the unfairness of this existing order . . . If they cooperated with the worker instead of ranging themselves on the side of the employer, justice would prevail."[25] In other words, where injustice exists, it is our moral duty to take sides.

RELIGIOUS PEACEMAKING AND THE UNIVERSALLY HUMAN FROM THE DALAI LAMA TO THICH NHAT HANH

As with the other figures discussed here, the Dalai Lama and Thich Nhat Hanh are figures for whom I have the greatest respect. Their personal courage and ethical standing are of the highest order. Just because they are who they are, it means something to show that those who seek to embody religious faith in the social world are missing something when they fail to adequately take politics into account.

At a pubic lecture, the Dalai Lama said:

[T]here may be difference in cultural background or way of life, there may be differences in our faith, or we may be of a different color, but we are human beings, consisting of the human body and the human mind. Our physical structure is the same and our mind and our emotional nature are also the same. . . . If we emphasize specific characteristics, like I am Tibetan or I am Buddhist, then there are differences. But those things are secondary. If we can leave the differences aside, I think we can easily communicate, exchange ideas, and share experiences.[26]

The idea that human beings share essential aspects of their lives across differences is part of the wisdom of the religious perspective, a wisdom that political ideologies based in recognition of difference need to heed. How and why that should occur will be discussed in Chapter 4. Here, however, I want to point out the limitations of this view.

The Dalai Lama's desire to treat everyone "just as a person" expresses the Buddhist view that our psychology is both the core of human identity and the same everywhere. The prevalence of suffering in human life, Buddhism teaches, stems from the universal human tendency to grasp after that which cannot be controlled and to believe that "things" (money, social position, physical beauty, human relationships) can make us happy. When we truly understand the effects of this pattern, Buddhists believe, we will lessen our own self-created sorrows and have a complete and unforced compassion for those of others.

This perspective faces a basic limitation. When compassionate action aims at the underlying structural causes of suffering rather than simply responding to immediate distress, it is necessary to see how our social identities—rather than a universal psychology—are the sources of our suffering.

This point can be illustrated by considering the work of Tony Campalo, an acclaimed expert on urban ministry who writes about the church's role in responding to the dreadful urban decay of Camden, New Jersey. For Campalo, the church has often distorted its response to urban poverty by focusing only on the personal needs of the poor, on a one-by-one basis. More realistically, he argues, overcoming poverty requires an awareness that "it is not just individuals who have to be changed . . . this social system itself must be changed so that it doesn't turn out so many victims." While church officials support charity for the poor, "organizing for the kind of social action that is required to challenge those who maintain the oppressive social system raises all kind of questions for [the directors of churches]."

> There is no doubt in the minds of most church people that we are supposed to address the personal sins of those who live in urban ghettos, but when we begin to address the sinful ways in which institutions and corporate

structures can be demonic instruments for perpetrating injustice and oppression, we run into trouble. . . . we are often told that we are not "preaching the gospel."[27]

To explain the economic and social deterioration of Camden, Campalo
cites redlining by banks, taking taxable land out of the city to foster com-
muter roads to nearby Philadelphia, a town split in half by those roads, real
estate speculation taking advantage of racism, a GI bill that fostered segregated suburbs instead of urban development, slumlords paying off building
inspectors, and withdrawal of government programs for neighborhood support. To a great extent, these are large-scale institutional policies, not the
product of individual malevolence. And the poor who fall prey to them are
certainly not solely the victims of their own character flaws, but of social
pressures that might well undo any of us.

What happens when our compassion directs us to change the structures
and policies that have fostered Camden's urban blight? Then we will no
longer encounter the Dalai Lama's "people just like us" but will see people
acting as holders of particular social positions, powers, and roles. It is not as a
"human being" that the bank manager redlines or a developer destroys
a neighborhood. In other contexts, it is not as a "human being" that an executive withholds information about the toxic effects of his product, that hostile teenagers taunt a gay couple, or that Israelis and Palestinians kill each
other. In each, it is specific social identities that are at work. If we are to
lessen social suffering, we have to change the bank's priorities, alter patterns
of real estate development, limit the sovereignty of corporations, enlarge
what is acceptable in terms of sexual identity, and redefine the territorial demands and self-definitions of Palestinians and Israelis.

When we support or undermine social identities that provide power, privilege, or wealth, and that express deeply held beliefs and values, we are seeking political change. In each case, there are many people who are wedded to
the social roles in question and who will go to great lengths to preserve them.
Sometimes persuasion will work, but often it will be a question of whose
power is to prevail. Political changes based solely in convincing your opponent are rare indeed. More often, society improves when collective power—
an electoral victory, a strike, a revolt, a boycott, a series of public demonstrations—is brought to bear.

While the Dalai Lama talks of the centrality of "tolerance" as essential to
the Buddhist practice of happiness, he also is well aware of the difference between learning to accept interpersonal struggles with other people and responding to negative features of the social world. "Impatience isn't always

bad. For instance, it can help you take action to get things done . . . impatience to gain world peace—that certainly can be positive."[28] Yet achieving world peace means more than simply cultivating peacefulness within oneself and preaching it publicly. Rather, it means reducing the social power of those who benefit from war: from arms makers and generals to politicians who use the threat of war to justify repression at home. Such action commits us to one kind of social order over another and is likely to make certain people happy and others rather upset. To the arms merchant or the professional soldier, it does no good to appeal to the universally "human," for it is their livelihood that is being attacked in the pursuit of peace. This attack is likely to arouse profound resentment and resistance, even if it is done by smiling, patient, tolerant Buddhist monks.[29]

In a more analytical vein, we can find this tension between universal spiritual values and social identity arising in R. Scott Appleby's excellent account of religion's constructive and destructive contribution to contemporary politics. Because Appleby's account is both comprehensive and offered with a rigor that a religious leader like the Dalai Lama need not attempt, its dilemmas warrant some detailed attention.

Appleby makes a fundamental distinction between types of religious actors, some of whom he labels violent (he rejects these) and others, nonviolent (he endorses these). He identifies the violent side with a fundamental intolerance of other religions, a concentration on the well-being of the host religion as opposed to humanity in general, a willingness to use violence against others rather than accept redemptive suffering for oneself, a desperate sense that one's religious (and hence personal) identity is deeply threatened, and an attachment to a closed circle of leaders who possess absolute truth. His models for religious social engagement are those who "reject the use of deadly violence, identify enemies according to their deeds rather than their ethnicity or religion, and seek reconciliation with those enemies."[30]

These values are essential if religion is to act in the public world and respect democracy at the same time. However, the concept of violence can be quite problematic and cannot itself be made concrete without a particular political position. Clearly, car bombings and assassinations are more "violent" than peaceful demonstrations in favor of human rights. But what if a modern concept of rights—with its associated notions of individual autonomy, gender equality, and secular political authority—is felt to be an attack on one's own values and practices? What if, as Stanley Fish argues, enshrining the democratic "freedom to choose" is precisely what the "fundamentalist" believes is the biggest threat?[31] For some believers, it might in fact be that norms governing the Sabbath, gender roles, or sacred spaces are just as central to their conception of who they are as is their bodily integrity. For such people, threats to these things are as dangerous as bullets. In these cases, a seemingly neutral, "universal" distinction between violence and nonviolence will not do. Different beliefs about the sacred, the meaning of life, and moral responsibility are at stake, and we must simply be on one side or another.

For Appleby, the concept of tolerance is another essential dividing line between fundamentalists and religious peacemakers. He believes that peacemakers' willingness to listen to opponents, to communicate to each side the other's pain, to seek reconciliation rather than victory, and to hold to the basic value of every human being signals the presence of tolerance rather than intolerance. But the concept of tolerance faces problems similar to those plaguing that of violence. If we have any real point of view, it will exclude certain others. We cannot be committed and fully "tolerant" at the same time. It does not help to say that we should try to accept as many other points of view as possible, for we will have to judge a wide range of acceptance as a good thing, or not, depending on the situation. For instance, how many different views on rape or genocide do we wish to "tolerate"? In the same way, letting others make up their own minds will be reasonable or not depending on our attitudes toward the subject at hand. If we believe the subject is of great moral importance, such as child abuse or pollution, we are not likely to think it wise to let everyone decide for themselves.[32] Further, in certain matters—the status of the West Bank and Northern Ireland, women's rights in Afghanistan—it is not clear what "tolerance" could possibly be.

Religious peacemakers, it seems to me, are no more accepting than fundamentalists; they simply accept different things. Instead of the bland idea of "tolerance," religious peacemaking is better supported by providing as detailed an account as possible of what those things are. In Northern Ireland, peacemaking would mean the development of trust and the end of dead bystanders from bombings. Such a peace would be "intolerant" of extreme communal antagonism between Catholic and Protestant. A two-state solution of the Palestinian-Israeli conflict would be tolerant of two national identities but intolerant of the return of all the Palestinian refugees or the presence of 200,000 Israeli settlers in the West Bank and Gaza. Freedom for women in Afghanistan would mean religious authorities could no longer beat them for exposing an ankle. In each case, the peacemakers are opting for one political solution and rejecting others.

The range of actions open to religious peacemaking, Appleby tells us, includes making peace between warring groups, aiding communities suffering from poverty or disaster, and attacking the structural roots of social injustice. Yet without a detailed political account, how could we know which of these three is appropriate in a given setting? To seek forgiveness and reconciliation, for example, presupposes that the conflict in question is between roughly equal groups, both of whom deserve to be acknowledged and preserved. It should apply, for instance, to ethnic or national conflicts (e.g., Catholic-Protestant, Israeli-Palestinian). But what if the opposing groups are owners of enormous estates and landless peasants? Or capitalists and workers? Don't certain things have to change before the groups can be truly "peaceful"? Again, religious peacemakers speak out, as Appleby puts it, against the "abuses" of "business elites."[33] But from a socialist or Marxist perspective, *all* "business elites" (i.e., all capitalists) are abusive; and reconciliation with them is possible only after they give up their factories and mainframes. If people disagree with this goal, it is not because they are more tolerant or peaceful, but because they have a different political viewpoint.

These issues arise in the writings of Thich Nhat Hanh, the internationally respected Vietnamese Zen Buddhist teacher. A leader of the Buddhist peace movement during the Vietnam War, he was attacked by North and South alike for advocating a simple program of peace, democracy, and service to the poor. Since emigrating from Vietnam, Nhat Hanh has worked with refugees from Southeast Asia and has promoted an "Engaged Buddhism" that seeks to bring Buddhist compassion into social life.

Thich Nhat Hanh is a devoted, wise, and compassionate man. At the same time, he manifests the common religious mistake of believing he can enter politics and speak from a perspective that is somehow impartial, universal, and on "everyone's" side. If such a position were possible, doubtless people like he and the Dalai Lama would assume it. But, for the reasons just sketched, it is *not* possible.

Here is Nhat Hanh's 1992 programmatic statement issued to the Vietnam's Buddhist community and to the government. Vietnamese Buddhism, he tells us, should have "no political objective." Rather, it will "reject the path of seeking power, the manipulation of political power or *engagement in partisan politics.*" Buddhists should "wish to live in peace . . . with all other sectors of the Vietnamese people, without discrimination according to race, creed, and ideology *as long as they all share the willingness to protect the nature and the cultural heritage of our land.*"[34]

The contradiction is clear. What about people who do not want to protect nature or the cultural heritage? What about people who want Western-style economic development and cultural change? I do not believe for a moment that Thich Nhat Hanh would take such people as "the enemy" in any extreme sense. He would not revile them, put them in jail, or shoot them. But he would try to have their policies defeated, and in doing so perhaps remove their livelihood or social position. He tells us that his values are humanly neutral, universal. But others disagree and want society to move in another direction. No matter how generous, openhearted, and nonviolent he may be, the result is a political struggle.

—————

One of the great gifts of religion is its capacity for a joyous celebration of the whole of existence. Much (though not all) of religious thought stresses the underlying unity of the universe: all of it created by a God who saw that it was good, or a form of Divinity itself (as in Hinduism, Wicca, or some indigenous traditions). Rabbi Marcia Prager expresses this thought in her interpretation of Judaism's most important prayer, the Sh'Ma ("Hear, O Israel, the Lord our God, the Lord is One"). Reminding us that the Hebrew term usually translated as "idols" (as in "Do not serve false idols") is better understood as "something that is less than the whole," Prager interprets the Sh'Ma as instructing: "Wake up! Understand! The smallest patterns you can see are reflected on a cosmic scale in the patterns of the universe. Don't focus on a mere part imagining that it is the entirety."[35] We can find a similar revelation toward the end of the Bhagavad Gita, perhaps the most important text of Hinduism. Prince Arjuna, after having been instructed to fulfill his "duty" as a warrior even though that means having to fight his own kin, sees his human charioteer—really the god Krishna in disguise—metamorphose into dozens of different forms. Arjuna is left with a vision of the whole of the universe as embodying divine energy, as each incarnated soul turns into another in an endless chain of godly existence.

Such images are not merely a matter of theology. The emotional technologies of prayers, music, ritual, and meditation exercises are designed to induce feelings of awe and appreciation for the universe. Spiritual critics of the secular left tell us that political organizations must learn to recognize the hunger for these feelings and the negative consequences of their absence.

Yet it is at this point that a political sensibility must sound a cautionary note, to make sure that the bliss of celebrating the divine does not come at the expense of forgetting something. It is, after all, extremely difficult to emotionally experience "the whole." Often, what is called "the whole" is really a small part. We hear a newborn baby coo and forget the ones starving to death; we walk on a beautiful beach and forget the millions of gallons of oil dumped at sea each year. Dorothy Day, whose own religious fervor was always tempered by a hardheaded awareness of political reality, lamented that when we remember the "horrors" of our time, we cannot help but ask: "How can we be happy today? How can we transcend this misery of ours? How can

we believe in a Transcendent God when the Immanent God seems so powerless . . . ?"[36]

Political perspectives, although at times trapped by their own habits of
constant criticism, offer a corrective to spiritual escapism. "If you would celebrate existence authentically," they caution, "do it from the middle of
Auschwitz. Or tell us how joyful life is while you are watching people starve
to death." I am not suggesting that it is impossible to do both at the same
time. I am emphasizing, however, that religious perspectives need the input
of politics so we may remember not to concentrate on the former while ignoring the latter.

4

Religion Teaching Politics

Central to any new politics will be a new spirituality—indeed, a renewal of some of our oldest spirituality—creating a moral sensitivity that refuses to separate political ideas from their consequences for human beings and for the rest of the creation.
     —Jim Wallis, The Soul of Politics[1]

If we divide reality into two camps—the violent and the nonviolent—and stand in one camp while attacking the other, the world will never have peace. We will always blame and condemn those we feel are responsible for war and social injustice, without recognizing the degree of violence in ourselves.
     —Thich Nhat Hanh, Love in Action[2]

Justice, reason, and community—these are the rallying cries of the great progressive social movements. Activists for political and economic democracy, worker's rights, women's equality, love of the earth, protection for animals, and liberation for oppressed groups have demanded that society recognize the wrongs it was doing to its victims and the waste and unhappiness it was creating for everyone—and then change its ways.

The enormous accomplishments of these movements can be read from the details of our daily existence. In the United States, women vote, workers can form unions, the poor and elderly are supported by something of a social safety net, legal discrimination against racial minorities has ended, attempts to redress the effects of the history of racism are in place, and in many (although not enough) cases, economic activity is restricted by concerns for our collective environment and the inherent value of the natural world. Throughout the developed world, comparable accomplishments have been achieved or are being struggled for. Even in highly traditional or repressive settings, we find that the most patriarchal of religions is aware of feminism's challenge, and the most brutal of dictators may be embarrassed by revelations of human rights abuses. Virtually every nation has groups resisting ecological destruction and the excesses of the new global economy.[3]

Despite its accomplishments, the moral weakness and psychological immaturity of both the rank and file and the institutional leaders have often rendered these attempts to remake the world much less successful than they might have been. To redress this dysfunction, they can turn to religious traditions for help. If political theory can *teach* religion lessons about strategies for social change and the political dimensions of spiritual concepts, politics can *learn* from religions something about how to be human and moral in the midst of political turmoil. Alongside the political understanding of people as bearers of social roles resisting or inflicting injustice, religious values (at their best) offer a sense of the moral worth of people as individuals and as victims of collective emotional trauma. In addition, any progressive political movement that wants more than individualistic democracy, a free market, and group entitlement can use religious resources to construct a substantive vision of a just social order.

———— • ————

One of the great insights of world-making politics concerns the collective nature of human existence: that what we learn and where we live, what we can expect out of life and how social authorities treat us are all shaped by our society and our place in it. It teaches, rightly, that almost everything about our lives has a political dimension. One of the great mistakes of progressive politics is to sometimes forget the universally human aspects of our lives, as well as the experiences and demands we face as individuals.

In various ways, the resources of religion can help political movements overcome these limitations. These resources include beliefs about the divine, the meaning of life, or the path to human fulfillment, and practices such as prayer, meditation, and communal worship. There is also what might be called the "culture" of religion. By this I mean an emphasis on certain virtues that are not necessarily religious but typically do enter social life associated with a spiritual impulse. These virtues include compassion, forgiveness, self-examination, and reconciliation.

PASSION AND DETACHMENT

Every person possesses some gauge of self-worth, evaluates himself or herself according to some standard, and has a sense of what makes life meaningful. These forms of self-understanding and appraisal organize our day-to-day existence. They connect a pattern of effort and experience into a more or less unified life. In the context of world-making politics, people tend to do this by focusing on quantity and consequences, by comprehending their personal worth on the basis of measurable achievements. To know how well they are doing and whether their lives make sense, they ask: How much have we raised worker's living standards? Lowered defense expenditures? Increased support to the poor? Limited the power of corporations? Increased rights? Changed laws?

But if we only measure our lives in terms of what we have done, then our sense of ourselves as persons is morally and emotionally (one wants to say "spiritually" as well, but we might have to wait for that) dependent on factors outside our control. What happens if the campaign or the movement is not a success? Having given everything we have to a strike, a campaign for the Equal Rights Amendment, the overcoming of anti-Semitism, or the establishment of a homeland for Palestinians, and *then* to be faced with failure—where does that leave us?

In reality, activism rarely yields a final success. As environmentalists, we might protect one wetland and lose two others or ban a cancer-causing pesticide only to see a new and just as lethal one appear on store shelves. As feminists, we get more women into Congress and see a simultaneous rise of misogyny in movies. In our campaign for human rights, we save one indigenous group from extinction even as another totters on the brink. Further, in the modern world of politics many activists are well aware of the connections among different causes: women's liberation and environmental protection, poverty and ethnic violence, gay rights and disability rights. A victory in any one of these is often accompanied by a sense of the still-to-be-accomplished tasks in others. Like the rest of life, and probably even more so, political struggle is finite and imperfect.

The consequence of all this is that many activists share a personal psychology of agitation, fervor, and—eventually—despair and burnout. A sense of the desperate importance of the task combines with a lurking sense that one has never accomplished what one should. In the contemporary world, the stakes are so vast and those who hold the actual reins of domination so distant and powerful that any victory tends to seem temporary and local at best. In the face of global environmental devastation, countless repressive governments depriving people of food to feed their military machines, and the spread of a seemingly unstoppable popular culture of violence, impersonal sex, and joyless consumption, we cannot help but feel that we have not done enough.

Anyone who has done political work will recognize the dangers and effects of this dynamic. In concrete terms, we might remember the example of Helen Caldecott, devoted leader of the nuclear disarmament movement, who burned out after a few years of overly intense work, having in the end begun to alienate coworkers and the public by her shrill desperation. As critically important as her political work of trying to teach sanity in a decade of nuclear madness was, she had no sense of personal identity left when she seemed not to be succeeding. For a more recent example, consider the antagonism, desperation, and hostility that sometimes marred the 2001 U.N.-sponsored international forum on racism in Durban, South Africa. There were constant struggles over which group was the most oppressed and victimized, widespread incapacity to consider differing views, and conversations that degenerated first into arguments and then into shouting matches. And all this among people who shared, at least initially, a concern with making the world more just! Despite the valuable connections that emerged, much was unnecessarily lost.[4]

An antidote to this self-defeating pattern can be found in religious accounts of personal worth. In contrast to the standard political emphasis on measurable success (and hence also on measurable failure), religious traditions teach that purity of motive is the gauge of devotion, and devotion the test of merit. It is our task to be responsible for trying, being dedicated, and aiming in the right direction. The trick—easily stated, but requiring a lifetime (at least) to master—is to commit all the passion, skill, and intelligence you can, and then relinquish attachment to "results."

Religion also teaches that my intention is itself of cosmic spiritual importance. There is a kind of hidden calculus in which any good act carries weight. In the words of a nineteenth-century rabbi:

> Let no one in Israel . . . say to himself: "What am I and what can I accomplish through my humble deeds in the world?" Let him understand, rather, let him know and let him fix in his thought that not one detail, from any moment at all, is lost of his deeds, words and thoughts. Each one goes right back to its root in order to carry on in the height of height, in the worlds and among the pure superior lights.[5]

As the French Jewish philosopher Emmanuel Levinas comments: "In spite of his humility as a creature, man is either in the process of damaging or protecting the world."[6] The ultimate personal meaning of this mystical claim is that my personal passion, not my public performance, is the ultimate measure of my worth. Because the purpose of human existence is to manifest morality, it makes a difference if I've done the right thing—even if I can't see the immediate effects. No good deed is ever lost.

This way of understanding our lives has the added benefit of helping overcome not only the kind of despair that affected Caldecott but the twin temptations of arrogance and self-hatred. It is a moral perspective that can help sustain us as persons in a life of political struggle, a good deal of which necessarily will not bear the fruits we seek. As Kierkegaard observed, if it is only effects that matter, then the world historical figures who Do Great Things are the only people who are Truly Great. The rest of us are, well, Nothing Very Special. However, if ethics (as Kierkegaard believes) is "subjective"—if what matters is intent and devotion rather than measurable consequences—then the kind of self-contempt that often attends those who measure their lives by public accomplishments is misplaced. Each individual has infinite worth, because each individual has the chance to construct a moral stance before God.[7] Being "great" is something that is available to each one of us, a matter that is totally under our own control.

Do we have to have a straightforward belief in God to experience this shift in perspective? I do not think so. For many in the modern world, including many who might be described as religious believers, talk of "saving worlds" or "leaving it up to God to determine the outcome" is understood metaphorically. (And we can even find in tradition a nonliteral, subjective approach to Divinity. Medieval Christian mystic Meister Eckhart said that "the eye of God is the eye with which I look at God." A Hasidic rabbi suggested that people are mistaken when they think they pray *to* God. Actually, "prayer itself *is* of the essence of God.")[8] What is important is that the moral emphasis on our own passion replaces a calculating—and often depressing—concentration on results. And this replacement seems, ironically, more rational than the frantic secular drive to "succeed," even to succeed at progressive social change. Anyone who has ever raised a child, helped a friend through emotional turmoil, taught in a classroom, or sustained a marriage knows that despite our best efforts, the outcome of our actions on other human beings is a chancy affair at best. The indeterminacy of the effects of our actions is magnified a thousandfold when we attempt to remake the political world. The *spiritual* perspective of passion for the goal but detachment from the outcome—whether or not it is surrounded by *metaphysical* claims about God or the sustaining of worlds—embodies our understanding of this simple, but extraordinarily important, truth.

VIOLENCE AND DESPERATION

The ethical flip side of a personal desperation to achieve political goals is the willingness to engage in violence to do so. Arrogance that asserts that "we alone know the way to a society of justice, freedom and human fulfillment" paves the way for intimidation, deceit, humiliation of opponents, ostracism of those who disagree with the movement, needless splitting of political movements over small differences, and a painful inability to listen to anyone other than ourselves.

Psychically, these self-destructive behaviors originate partly in an overweening ambition: to remake the world. And here there arises a paradox that haunts religion and political life alike. Both of these have at their heart the desire to bring about wide-ranging change, and both can be a source of hope, progress, and human happiness. But precisely because the goals are so sweeping and the stakes so high, both religion and politics give rise to a sense of personal desperation and fanatical self-importance.

In the case of politics this has contributed, countless times, to failure. Consider perhaps the greatest political disaster of the twentieth century: the degeneration of communism from a genuine movement of dedicated and courageous revolutionaries into an assortment of corrupt, repressive, economically inefficient statist regimes. Obviously, I cannot provide even the approximation of an account here,[9] but one particularly important moment carries the weight of the point I'm trying to make. The year is 1924, in the Soviet Union. Following a brief and intense internal struggle for leadership of the Communist Party and the Soviet government after Lenin's death in 1921, Stalin is consolidating his power as national leader. Standing against him is Leon Trotsky: one of the earliest Russian socialist revolutionaries, leader of the Red Army during the civil war, internationally respected Marxist theorist. But Stalin holds the reins of the party, and Trotsky—as a Jew and as a late joiner of Lenin's faction of Russian socialism—is held to be something of an outsider. Stalin defeats Trotsky on several important policy issues and demands that Trotsky prove his continuing allegiance. Trotsky makes a remarkable declaration: "In the last analysis the party is always right, because the party is the single historical instrument given to the proletariat for the solution of the fundamental problems . . . I know that one must not be right against the party, for history has created no other road for the realization of what is right."[10]

The Party can never be wrong! And therefore it not only commands the personal allegiance of Trotsky but by implication is entitled to any violation of human rights, any breach of moral principles, in order to achieve its ends.

Arthur Koestler's haunting novel *Darkness at Noon* described how this perspective flowered in a regime of absolute repression of dissidents and the public humiliation of any leaders who supported different policies.[11] Koestler revealed in fictional form a basic truth: that fundamentalist arrogance in political life slips easily and naturally into self-aggrandizement, the pursuit of power for its own sake, and a self-deception about revolutionary virtue masking an ever-increasing use of violence.[12]

This is an extreme example. But the same dynamic can be found in the history of virtually every activist political movement. The seeds of fanaticism have, sadly, flowered in countless places. If not the massive violence of Communist regimes, we find self-justification for unprincipled compromise, competition with other groups for success or publicity, and the sense that worthwhile political goals justify corrupt means.

How might religious values or insights counter this disastrous pattern? For one thing, the psychic desperation that says "Only I" (or, "Only my party, group, movement," and so on) can save "the world" ("history, the environmental crisis, the condition of women," and so forth) would be mitigated by an acceptance of the necessarily limited and partial nature of any person or group. The image of effort combined with emotional detachment from results could encourage a more balanced and judicious understanding of political life. A trust in the ultimate goodness of the universe—or at least an understanding that we are but a small part of the whole—might help us remember that no single party or movement or group has the task of saving the world. Holding one's political passion with a corresponding sense of spiritual calm, peace, detachment, and acceptance, with a longer and broader view, can diminish the violence that inevitably flows from desperation and can soften the arrogance that is so often a mask for fear. This spiritual perspective will help create a more effective politics and a more humane form of life for political activists themselves.

Desperation, arrogance, and political violence are also likely to be lessened by a religious or spiritual perspective that human beings—whatever their political beliefs or social position—possess a common spiritual identity across political differences. We all experience grief and joy, love our children, and seek happiness. In such facts there are no barriers between us. These commonalties are sometimes expressed by the claim that we are all children of God, or that we all have souls that are sparks of the original divine fire, or that we all suffer and are in need of enlightenment. Writing in the context of struggles for pacifism in the face of the emerging Cold War, Catholic poverty and peace activist Dorothy Day reflected: "Whenever I groan within myself and think how hard it is to keep writing about love in these times of tension and strife which may, at any movement, become for us all a time of terror, I think to myself: What else is the world interested in? What else do we all want, each one of us, except to love and be loved, in our families, in our work in all our relationships?"[13]

These insights eliminate neither political differences nor the need for political struggle. That the slave owners were human beings and children of God does not mean we allow slavery to continue—even if the slave owners are emotionally devastated when their slaves are freed. It does mean that our desperate need to accomplish our political goals by altering social life is combined with a more compassionate and gentle sense of the humanity of even the worst of our opponents.

John Paul Lederach, a Mennonite peacemaker engaged in brokering agreements during the civil war between the Sandinista government and Nicaragua's Miskito Indians, tells a marvelous story about his own experience of "creating an enemy." Waiting at an airport on the Honduran border with Nicaragua, he saw a Honduran helicopter pilot—dressed in fatigues and wraparound sunglasses, clothed in military authority, engaged in contact with an obvious CIA operative. The "colonel," as Lederach imagined him, was a symbol of the corrupt and violent American and Honduran regimes, collaborating to devastate the peaceful Nicaraguans. In Lederach's imagination, the colonel was totally alien, having nothing in common with Lederach's own chosen vocation of devoted Christian peacemaker. As the colonel rose to meet an arriving plane, Lederach visualized the kind of corrupt, evil contact he was about to make. To his shock, Lederach saw that the arriving passenger was a handicapped ten-year-old girl, limping along on crutches, assisted by the awkward but clearly loving colonel. In amazement and moral chagrin, Lederach thought: "The colonel is a father, just like me!"

The lesson, Lederach writes, is that the creation of an enemy is in part a mental process. We identify differences between us as people and we forget similarities; we make the whole being of ourselves and the Other synonymous with the differences; and we value our own characteristics over those of the Other. In the end, *we* are wholly good, and *they* are wholly evil: inhuman, dehumanized, deserving of any fate we might visit upon them.

At the beginning of a new millennium, we can too easily bring to mind a few of the countless contexts in which such thinking operates: the Middle East, Northern Ireland, the Punjab, Chiapas, Serbia, the treatment of gays and lesbians, the destruction of the World Trade Center and much of American rhetoric in response.

Unfortunately, Lederach doesn't discuss the sad fact that in some instances, the essential humanity of an adversary is comparatively unimportant.

The Nazi officers who directed the mass shootings of Jews in Poland and Western Russia before the existence of concentration camps used to come back to the barracks after a hard day's work to read Shakespeare and listen to Beethoven on their portable phonographs. On their leaves home, they would bring flowers to their wives and play with their children. Just like the Jews they killed, they were fathers. So what?

Lederach's reply here, and I think it would be a good one, might be that not all adversaries are the SS. Most of the time, there are sparks of humanity in our foes; and if we are to have peace as well as justice, forgiveness as well as truth, we had better remember that fact. That *some* people are completely incapable of making peace does not mean that *all* people are. Wherever it is possible to reconcile, we need to find some common ground. We should at least start with the presumption that all of us are children of God, or essentially human, or suffer and love and fear and rejoice in pretty much the same way. And we should try to hold onto that presumption as long as we possibly can.

In the aftermath of the truly soul-destroying violence in Nicaragua, Lederach tells us, unlikely groups learned to work on common projects for a common end. These groups included former enemies, survivors of violent assaults, and people who had lost friends and family to the other side or had been guilty of murders themselves. Cambodians who had made peace after similar cruelty and suffering told Lederach that they could work with each other for the sake of the children because they did not want civil war and violent repression to ruin the lives of the next generation. The desire of victims to prevent a recurrence of what happened to them, Lederach says, is perhaps the strongest desire to come out of people who have undergone traumatic violence. At times, it will even take precedence over the desire to tell their stories and have their suffering publicly acknowledged.

But if we are to make peace to end the suffering, how must we think of our adversaries? I wonder if there is any way to do it except in religious or spiritual terms. After the pain and suffering we have felt, only a devotion to something like the Golden Rule, or the belief in a common humanity, or a spiritual commitment to reconciliation can bridge the gap of grief and loss.[14] We will need, as feminist ethicists and psychologists have maintained, to pursue neither power over others nor undue self-sacrifice but a realization that true selfhood lies in healthy human connections. And we will want to see that although a certain amount of competition and conflict may be inevitable, we badly need to balance such "adversarialism" with a mutuality that "assumes deep fulfillment in social connections and a more or less peaceful relationship with oneself."[15]

This perspective can be adapted to the activist's mentality. As Thich Nhat Hanh put it during the Vietnam War:

> In the peace movement there is a lot of anger, frustration, and misunder-
> standing. The peace movement can write very good protest letters, but
> they are not yet able to write a love letter. We need to learn to write a letter
> to the Congress or to the President of the United Sates that they will want
> to read, and not just throw away. The way you speak, the kind of under-
> standing, the kind of language you use should not turn people off. The
> President is a person like any of us.[16]

Avoiding the mental creation of enemies is especially critical because in political life *anyone* can become an enemy: not only the social "oppressor" but those on your own side with whom you disagree. The history of radical politics overflows with internal struggles that have at times assumed truly frightening dimensions. The treatment of differences within the Party in all Communist countries is one example of this phenomenon. Stalin murdered not just the rich peasants and aristocrats but perhaps half a million Communists as well.[17] Closer to home, we find extreme antagonism between more reformist and more revolutionary members of the German Green Party, between supporters of Gore and supporters of Nader, between environmentalists who stress animal rights and environmentalists who stress the integrity of ecosystems, between black "womanists" and white "feminists." In its early days, Students for a Democratic Society (SDS) was castigated by the older generation of American leftists. And when feminism emerged eight years later, the male leaders of SDS (and SNCC) responded with contempt and scorn. The more radical members of the antiwar movement called the less radical forces "peace creeps," while SNCC activists mockingly referred to Martin Luther King Jr. as "de Lawd."[18]

These attitudes have long been the norm in many arenas of left politics—including both small left "sects" and widely respected icons such as *The Nation* magazine. Consider, for instance, the hyperbolic exchange over America's response to the terrorist acts of September 11, 2001, between well-known left spokesmen Christopher Hitchens (a *Nation* columnist) and Noam Chomsky. Along with erudition and intelligence, there was a conspicuous inability to see the exchange as anything but an opportunity to "win" a debate by confirming a long-held view. It brought to mind Jean-Paul Sartre's forty-five-year-old description the French left's responses to the Soviet invasion of Hungary: "Later there was news, a great deal of news: but I have not heard it said that even one Marxist changed his opinion."[19]

I am not suggesting that we stop arguing for what we believe or dissolve all political differences in a warm bath of spiritual mush. I am simply saying that the hard-hearted pursuit of differences and rejection of adversaries makes for bad politics, extremely ineffective political movements, and a political culture that wears out its activists. Spiritual values of universal love, respect, and care might help us to combine personal peacefulness with the pursuit of justice. If they did so, political movements would see greater internal cooperation, a much easier job of making alliances, less splitting of groups over not-so-great differences, and the creation of a culture of political life that is much more humanly nourishing.

We might compare on this score, for instance, Gandhi and Lenin. Lenin was the dominant figure in the Bolshevik Party in the years leading up to the Russian Revolution, and he was surrounded by highly intelligent, disciplined, and strong-willed men. Disagreements over the proper strategy frequently arose. This was especially true when Lenin, having been exiled to Switzerland during World War I, returned to Russia after the monarchy had fallen. When strategic differences arose in this setting, Lenin had one characteristic response: Excoriate his opponent and claim absolute rightness for his own views. If those methods failed, he would frequently seek to expel his opponent or threaten to resign if his beliefs were not accepted.[20] Lenin's basic mode of operation, even within the Party, was coercive. His views, he believed, had to succeed at all costs. Whatever the political differences between Lenin and Stalin, and they were many and important, Stalin's totalitarian repressiveness reproduced on a grand scale the same attitudes that Lenin had exhibited within the Party.

Like Lenin, Gandhi was also engaged in a long and difficult struggle, and again like Lenin, he had a very definite political objective. But unlike Lenin, Gandhi proceeded on certain religious or spiritual assumptions: that all people were united by their essentially divine nature, that anyone—himself included—could act immorally or ineffectively, that therefore the correct method of personal interaction and collective change was persistent, active nonviolence.

Gandhi was also the leader among an inner circle of strong-minded men, many of whom held him in a kind of special reverence. When disagreements over policy arose among his comrades, Gandhi, believing that nonviolence was the correct method for personal spiritual life and for politics alike, took the exact opposite tack of Lenin. When his close associates disagreed, they often said that they would defer to Gandhi because of their respect for him. No, he counseled, that would be a larger mistake. The most important thing is for you to proceed with integrity on your own beliefs, even if that means you follow a course *I* think is wrong.[21]

Gandhi's approach, I believe, makes not only for a better spiritual life but for better politics. It is more likely to bring out the best work in each person in an organization, to cultivate younger and less-experienced activists, and to avoid the political errors of sectarianism and violence. Over the long haul, mutual respect is likely to get us further than conflict and intimidation.

Thich Nhat Hanh offers a method for handling disagreements within Buddhist communities, including and especially those engaged in social action. His suggestions include warnings not to be too attached to one's opinions, not to force one's views on others, and not to "maintain anger or hatred."[22] The rules presume that emotional violence is a dangerous thing and that active feelings of hatred, contempt, or rage do not further *anyone's* cause. Christian prayers stressing humility and the need for God's forgiveness carry the same message, as does the Jewish bedtime prayer that reads, "I hereby forgive anyone who angered or antagonized me or who sinned against me." Once again, these values are not *necessarily* religious. They can and do emerge in secular settings. But it is also a simple fact about our culture that they have most often been articulated by spiritual activists, not secular ones.[23]

I saw a dynamic of destructive antagonism play itself out many times during my own years of political activism, especially in one instance that I remember vividly. In the late 1970s, I helped form a small group of Jews to do political work around the Middle East conflict. We were all veterans of leftist politics from the 1960s on; all strongly identified as Jews. We believed that both Israel and a Palestinian state had a right to exist and were all emotionally affected by the region's continuing violence. Holding this "two-state" position in 1978 made us anathema to American Jews who saw the Palestinians as nothing but terrorists to be suppressed and to leftists who thought Israel was a "colonial-settler state" (like the white regime of South Africa) that ought to be eradicated.

Passions ran high in our tiny group, and we lacked the personal maturity and spiritual resources to handle them. We argued violently about the exact way to express our position: the right amount of emphasis to place on Zionism's colonial roots, or the anti-Semitism of the Arab nations, or the Holocaust, or the plight of Palestinian refugees. Deeply committed to "the cause," all our desperation, emotional violence, frantic desires to "do something," fear of failure, and corresponding hatred of "the enemy" began to be reproduced within the group. We fought increasingly, eventually splitting into two rival groups: one with seven members and one with eight. Fifteen of us, in actuality extremely close in our political perspectives and passions, were going to solve the Middle East conflict. And we couldn't even get along with each other! This trivial example would mean little if it were not a microcosm of the antagonisms, splits, and wasted energy that have plagued virtually every arena of the secular left for over a century.

JUSTICE AND TRAUMA

Part of the reason for the failure of our little group, a failure writ large in a great number of movements, was our collective inability to realize that political struggles frequently (though not always) include two dimensions. In the first dimension, that of justice, we work to defeat the accumulated power of the oppressor and use concepts like comrade and enemy, our side against their side, winning and losing. In this context, we are not particularly concerned with the fate of the oppressor. If making society more just bothers men used to abusing their wives, corporations accustomed to polluting without penalty, or Third World dictators who shoot union leaders, so much the worse for them.

In the second dimension of social struggles, we find collective trauma: histories of collective antagonism and victimization without a neat division between oppressor and oppressed. In this dimension, a too simple view of either side's moral standing often engenders new injustice, and the traumas of violence are reproduced from one generation to the next. The attitudes of antagonists bound up in such struggles are well described by peace activist Colman MCarthy's account of the psychodynamics of war:

> Most . . . nations go into battle convinced, I'm right, you're wrong; I'm good, you're evil . . . I'm going to win, you're gong to lose. Even if one side does win, the first reaction of the loser is, I want a rematch; I'll come back with meaner words, harder fists and bigger bombs. Then you'll learn, then you'll be good and then we'll have peace forever. *This is an illusion, but few can give it up.*[24]

Perhaps—to choose a particularly tragic example—one reason the Israeli-Palestinian conflict is so intractable is that it contains both of the dimensions of justice and trauma, and to an extreme degree. On the level of justice, we have the Israeli occupation of Palestinian land, with vast inequalities of power, wealth, and support from world powers between the two. Historically, however, we may also see the existence of Israel as a response to 2,000 years of Christian anti-Semitism that culminated in the Holocaust, and the fact that nearly a million Jewish refugees from Arab countries fled to Israel. On the level of intergenerational grief, fear, and rage, we have two peoples violated by history. Each at times sees in the other the image of the historical

oppressor. Arab anti-Semitism all too easily calls to the Jewish mind the image of Nazism, while to Palestinians, Jews are another variant of European
colonialists. Both sides have their dead, their grief, and their understandable
distrust of the other. Whatever resolution of the Middle East conflict
emerges (if one ever does), some unjustified loss and bitterness will result:
Someone's home will be lost forever; someone will be made unsafe; some injustice will be suffered.

In the dimension of justice we ask: Who is right and who is wrong? What
must be done to overthrow the powerful in favor of the weak? In the dimension of trauma we implore: Tell me about your pain, and please listen to mine.
We try to remember that parents on both sides love their children, want to
live in peace, and carry painful memories that prompt collective violence; and
we dare to hope that our common suffering might bring us together.

Here we can dream against despair with Leah Green, the founder of Mid-
East Citizen Diplomacy, who leads citizen delegations to the Middle East to
practice what she terms Compassionate Listening. She describes the effects
of a meeting with a Sufi sheikh, a Palestinian spiritual teacher who preaches
peaceful reconciliation with Israelis.

> As we walked outside, about forty children and assorted adults were
> mulling around—undoubtedly attracted by the chanting and singing com-
> ing from the mosque. Tonight we are staying at Nevve Shalom/Wahat as-
> Salamm/Oasis of peace, an intentional community of Israeli Jews and
> Palestinians living together and raising their children together in peace. A
> vision fulfilled! . . . We are filled with joy! We spent our time together
> tonight mostly laughing. What a blessing after the incredible darkness and
> confusion we have witnessed on this trip . . . Enemies can find paths to one
> another . . . *if you believe it's possible.*[25]

Or we can marvel at a joint Palestinian-Israeli organization of parents
whose children were killed by the other side. The founder of the group,
Yitzhak Frankenthal, lost a son to Hamas terrorism, but still helps frame the
collective call for reconciliation. "We, who paid the dearest and most painful
price of all, sit together discussing peace. We lost a child yet we do not seek
revenge, only peace. If *we* can sit and talk, so can anyone."[26]

Few political struggles are only about justice, few are only about trauma.
Even the Nazi terror had some roots in Germany's terrible losses in World
War I, the harsh terms imposed by the Allies, and the economic tribulations
and social unrest that followed. Even the most violent misogynist probably
carries within himself the emotional pain of a typical male upbringing: the
repression of feeling, the haunting fear of failure, the hatred of all parts of

himself that might be perceived as "weak" by others. These experiences do not *excuse* Nazism or misogyny. They do help make the perpetrators human, less completely alien to those of us who oppose them.

The great religious social activists, typically much more than the secular left, have spoken to both the justice and the trauma sides of social conflict. This understanding is not just a theoretical matter but something that helps them to be more effective in their response to violence and oppression. As Thomas Merton put it: "Without compassion, the protester tends to become more and more centered in anger and may easily become an obstacle to changing the attitudes of others."[27] Moreover, religious love can be a source of knowledge, for part of love is empathy, which can give us knowledge of another's emotional state, and part imagination, which drives us to put ourselves in the place of someone whose life experience—and socially based suffering—may be very different from our own.[28]

In practice, this has meant groups of peaceworkers actively engaged in some of the great social and political struggles of the last fifty years.[29] There has been a religious presence in national, religious, and ethnic conflicts worldwide—including South Africa, Ireland, Israel, Southeast Asia, and Central America. For instance, there is Sant'Egidio, a lay Catholic body that was inspired by Vatican II and Pope John XXIII's stress on outreach to the non-Catholic world. It has been instrumental in peace and reconciliation efforts in Mozambique, Uganda, Burundi, Algeria, Kosovo, and Guatemala. The Mennonites, despite their long tradition of withdrawal from the perils of modernity, have successfully found a third way between quietism and civil disobedience. They have created a "professional class of peacemakers" (such as John Paul Lederach) who reach out not just to Christians but to all "those who reject coercion and violence." Their practice is a "benign engagement with others that emphasizes listening, care, and gentle patterns of interaction."[30] These values have been practiced "militantly," by well over a thousand members of "Christian Peacemaker Teams" working in Haiti, Hebron, and other dangerous hot spots. In Burma, devotedly nonviolent Buddhist Aung San Suu Kyi has struggled for democracy, justice, and freedom against brutal repression in Burma.

For such efforts, the goal of reconciliation among human beings is central. Concerns for justice and truth are not eliminated but are joined to those for peace and forgiveness.[31]

MADNESS

Ethnic or national strife has always contained a kind of irrationality: all those resources wasted, all those precious lives lost. Yet beyond the traumas of ethnic

or national conflict, there are even more extreme social events that seem animated by a kind of collective madness. For example, the threat of nuclear war
or the use of other weapons of mass destruction and the continuing environmental crisis cannot be conceptualized solely under the familiar concepts of
justice and oppression.

These issues do require some political analysis. The nuclear threat is
partly a product of the social interests of munitions manufacturers and the
military; toxic pollution is not just a problem for "everyone" but falls disproportionately on the poor and people of color, while others make a great deal
of money selling products that cause illnesses. However, nuclear weapons
and environmental destruction are simultaneously a universal human threat.
They put everyone in danger and create a common human need to respond.
Here the religious perspective, which concentrates on what we share, despite
differences in social position, nationality, race, or gender, is fitting. A spiritual
approach can enable both political resistance and a kind of emotional wisdom
in the face of overwhelming danger. As James W. Douglass, who organized
protests against nuclear-armed submarines and the transport of nuclear war-
heads on railroad tracks, wrote:

> Evil's power to destroy life comes from our denial of its presence and our
> refusal to accept responsibility for it. The essence of our life-destroying
> evil lies in our unseen, unacknowledged cooperation . . . As we began to
> claim personal responsibility for the missile propellant shipments and
> sought to express our love for the train employees, we experienced the faith
> to overcome the evil which was in us and on the trains; faith in the redeem-
> ing power of nonviolent love, faith in the cross. Our growing community
> of faith and nonviolent action made the tracks linking us a double sym-
> bol—of not only holocaust, but hope.[32]

In this eloquent statement, we find the essential themes of religious social
activism. There is a refusal to see those who produce or transport the
weapons as "enemies." One acts out of love, no matter how great the stakes.
There is the ability to mobilize energies despite the overwhelming odds.
Douglass was part of a few hundred people facing the American military-
industrial complex. Because of his faith, because "nonviolent love" has a "re-
deeming power," he can join the vastly unequal battle. Yet love is not simply
an emotional overflow but a commitment to truth. It requires acts of witness
against real threats. Ethical victories emerge only from a resolute commitment to act morally no matter how strategically weak one is. Last, Douglass
can act without desperation, bitterness, or hate—*despite* the magnitude of the
issue—because he trusts that each loving act has infinite value.

In a society that creates the madness of the arms race, isn't this attitude—which is so much more likely to emerge from religious or spiritual values than from purely secular politics—exactly what is needed? Would an emotional state of frenzy and fear convince the millions of small cogs in the nuclear machine—from low-level engineers to factory workers, from engine repairmen to truck drivers—of the danger of the weapons and their corresponding insanity? The goal, as Merton says, is at least in part a change in attitude among those whose lives and incomes are not completely bound up in the nuclear threat. But these people will rarely have their attitudes or values affected by shrillness and desperation. Such approaches are more likely to call forth stiffness, defensiveness, and hostility.

This issue is especially important given the class structure of advanced industrial societies. In the traditional Marxist model, the process of capitalist accumulation is supposed to create a richer and increasingly smaller and more powerful ruling class. The working class, by contrast, was expected to get continuously larger and more homogeneous. As more and more people became wageworkers for large, impersonal corporations, their differences in nationality, gender, religion, and ethnicity were supposed to become increasingly less important. So far, this account has proved inaccurate in many ways. Most important, there remains an extremely complicated stratification of the "working class." If we define "workers" as those who do not control corporations and do not set the terms of their own work (as many professionals still do), the category still includes industrial workers, service workers, union and nonunionized labor, engineers, teachers, janitors, day care providers, migrant farm labor, pharmacists, technicians, computer repair personnel, and on and on.

In any confrontation with the enormous social power of those who control global corporations, governments, and transnational organizations like the World Bank and the IMF, this heterogeneity creates some difficult questions. Can these groups find enough common ground to act together? And can they get along enough even to find out what interests they share? To do so, there will have to be a general atmosphere of respect for differences, an ability to listen carefully to other people, and a genuine attempt to see commonalities as well as divisions. The overall approach must aim at preserving humane connections even in the face of real differences in income and social position. Such an atmosphere is much more likely to produce the kind of wide coalition required for significant social change—whether that change is initiated by electoral campaigns, activism in the street, or nongovernmental organizations.

The same situation obtains in the case of the kinds of politics emphasized by what have been called "new social movements," that is, movements based around race, gender, ethnicity, religion, or sexual preference rather than

class. At the very start, we find issues arising in these movements that concern diversity within the group itself. Blacks are in different classes and gen-
ders; women have varying racial status; gay men and lesbians have significant
income differences. If the movements are to have some effective political
unity—or at least cooperation—spiritual activist skills and values of self-
examination, listening to others, and compassion are needed. The history of
the left over the last thirty years has seen countless painful examples of overinflated rhetoric about who is the "real" victim, about who has the right to
speak for the movement, and about how suffering guarantees political purity.
These ways of acting have only served to provoke counterproductive personal and organizational hostility and to alienate potential allies by an abu-
sively hostile style. In terms of effectiveness, spiritual values of seeing the divine in each person or of recognizing our common humanity are much more
likely to get men to be supportive of women's rights or whites to deal with
their inherited cultural racism than is overinflated bombast about "male
chauvinist pigs" or "redneck honkies."

This does not mean that some people are not male chauvinist pigs or redneck honkies or that political groups should be unprincipled in naming sexism or racism where they exist. It means that if we are to build large and successful movements, we need to find the most effective way to get allies.
Openness, calmness, a lack of unnecessary hostility, and principled actions
without self-indulgent nastiness would seem to stand the best chance. That is
why bringing spiritual attitudes into social and political struggles can be
tremendously worthwhile. Of course, the use of spiritual nonviolence is no
guarantee of success. Sadly, such guarantees are impossible to get in any case.

IMAGINING THE REVOLUTION

How are we to know that life can be better than it is now? What enables us to
hope for a world in which injustice and irrational pain have been dramatically
lessened? One standard political response—and not a very good one—is simply to offer verbal criticisms of what we don't like and expect people to be
convinced by the brilliance of our insights. Unfortunately, however, just because most people are fully entangled in the society at hand, they are unim-
pressed. Utopian notions of alternative social orders typically do not move
the masses.

A much more realistic picture comes from the Marxist notion that any
given society contains contradictions—essential characteristics that both make
the society what it is and lead it to change. Marx believed that in the case of
capitalism, there was a fundamental contradiction between technological ac-

complishments and social failures. Technological abundance combined with recurrent economic collapse would, Marx predicted, lead to the eventual transition from private to social control of the economy. Yet while class-based conflict was the source of political progress for a good deal of the late nineteenth and early twentieth centuries, capitalism's ability to deliver (a lot of) the goods, combined with the mind- and soul-numbing effects of mass culture, seem to have sapped working-class revolutionary potential.

Because of the inability of socialism to take root in the developed world—and its poor track record elsewhere—radical political thinkers have sought for the source of social change in other places. Herbert Marcuse speculated that those marginalized by the "triumphs" of modern capitalism—racial minorities, women, students—could be the source of a new "great refusal" to accept society as it is.[33] Other political visionaries have hoped that the reality of environmental degradation or the loss of community might provoke a sweeping desire for social change.[34]

The bleak truth is that people are usually not motivated to change society simply because they believe it is unjust or irrational. Short of feeling that our very lives are threatened, most of us are politically passive. Political activism is at best hard, tedious, and time consuming; at worst, it involves real dangers to oneself and one's family. In order to act, people need to believe—and to feel deeply—that they are both entitled to and capable of changing social life, of taking more power, responsibility, and happiness. If these feelings don't exist, distrust of the social order gives rise mainly to cynicism, inertia, and despair, or to vicious scapegoating of a minority. No matter how bad things are, without a certain sense of our own value we do not feel that *we* are competent to change them or that we deserve to have something that's better. Despite the political freedom characteristic of most advanced industrial societies, we experience ourselves as powerless. Our very selves are dominated.[35] We do not exercise the power we could.[36]

How then do people get a sense of what a fundamentally different society would be like? And how can they learn that they themselves are able to create it?

Because the experience of religious practice can provide a sense of hope, community, and personal value to counter their absence in secular society, spiritual life can be a source for overcoming this surplus powerlessness and political passivity. To develop this point, let us examine an analogy from a decidedly nonreligious source. The Hungarian Marxist Georg Lukacs, one of the originators of the anti-Communist tradition of Western Marxism, argued that revolutionary political consciousness would emerge from the contradiction between workers' knowledge of themselves as real people and the fact

that they were treated like commodities by their employers. Knowing that
I'm a person and yet being treated like a thing (seen simply as a source of labor time and profit) by the factory owners, said Lukacs, can cause me to resist
the owner's economic and social power.[37] One can think of corresponding experiences for other groups: women struck by the contradiction between their
felt personhood and their sexual objectification; African-Americans provoked
by the tension between serving in the army in World War II to defend a freedom abroad that they were denied at home.

In this context, paradoxically, religion offers hope in a way that secular
politics does not. If in social life we feel we don't matter, in a religious setting
we are told that each soul is precious. If in society at large I have no power,
here my devotions and prayers connect me to the universe's ultimate reality.
If I generally feel depressed, anxious, or numb, an ecstatic religious service—
or just a spirited hymn—can provide a little authentic joy in living and an appreciation of the universe. By providing us with vital occasions of community
and celebration, the experience of religious life can belie the escapist nature
of its theology.

Christian hymns talk of the saving grace of Jesus. The Aleinu prayer,
which ends all Jewish services, speaks of the time when "all people will call
upon the name of God and all the earth's wicked will turn towards God."
Buddhist mediation imagines a perfection of mind of spirit in which all suffering is held with compassion.

Because all these look like fantasized alternatives to what is *really* going on,
many leftist critics of religion have missed the fact that the otherworldly content of theology is not its sole meaning. It is the experience that counts as
much as the words. It is not the conceptual content—what the religious beliefs assert or claim—that is at issue here but rather the *emotional experience of
that content*. In experiencing awe at the mystery and holiness of creation, we
can personally feel that environmental pollution is at odds with what is most
important to us. In having an emotional experience that we interpret as being
of divine love and grace, we no longer see ourselves as unworthy to speak up
in the secular realm. In feeling the emotional bonds of the religious community, we no longer take the soulless impersonality of the modern city as inevitable. In the experience of religious joy, we relearn the childhood knowledge of the difference between shopping at the mall and our heart's delight.

Doubtless, the joys and insights that flow from religious experience can
become trivialized by being identified with what happens after we die or left
as a purely private form of enjoyment. A slightly hard-edged, watchful political eye is needed to keep the exaltations of religious experience from turning
into an apolitical dead end.[38] But since *every* form of religion or politics has

its dangers, describing those dangers does not refute the positive possibilities they also contain. It is hardly news to say that religion can be escapist! My point is that it can *also* be inspiring. And inspiring not just for the overflowing heart in a sacred moment, but for activist political change.

As an example, consider the practice of keeping the Sabbath. In Judaism, this is meant to be a fixed time period during which no labor is performed, with "labor" being traditionally defined as activities needed to build the ark of the covenant.[39] More broadly, the Sabbath is, in Abraham Heschel's poetic description, a "palace in time."[40] In this palace, we are told, we will find a little foretaste of heaven. In Michael Lerner's words:

> The basic principles of this practice are . . . : Rejoice! Dedicate this day to joy, celebration, humor and pleasure. Let Go of Worry. It is forbidden to worry about work, money, power, control or anything else. . . . Gratitude! All week long we focus on what is not yet happening and what needs to be changed in the world and in our lives. . . . On Shabbat the energy goes in a different direction . . . The goal is to celebrate . . . For one day out of the week, don't try to change, shape or transform the world. Respond to it with joy, celebration, awe and wonder. Open yourself to the miracle and mystery of the universe.[41]

On the Sabbath, we are called to experience happiness without buying, self-love without unending competitive performance, delight in tradition that can comfort us in our own mortality, and a sense that the universe—which is, after all, where we reside and which breathed us into being—deserves awe and joy as well as work and disappointment. In this way, religious life can prefigure the kind of celebration and delight that we hope could mark life in a liberated society.

Although the modern world—beset with wars, unnecessary poverty, repression, and ecological misery—is very far away from such a society, it will do us good to have a taste of what it is we are fighting for: to know that we can have more than a system composed, in Jurgen Habermas's trenchant phrase, of "social engineers and the inmates of closed institutions."[42]

LIBERATING VALUES

There are certain culturally spiritual values that are particularly useful as countervailing forces to the dominant culture. Their political importance resides in the fact that they offer alternatives to the values that bind people to the dominant order. As Herbert Marcuse argued, if our sense of identity is

tied to ideals and images that make us dependent on the system, no alternative to the system is possible.[43] As an example, consider the contemporary
American addiction to consumption. Selfhood is, for many, measured by
their ability to consume. Buying becomes equal to happiness, as more and
more of the virtues or personal characteristics that were traditionally held as
the source of human fulfillment become commodified. To paraphrase Marx,
who intuited this dismal prospect in its earliest stages: In a society shaped by
money and consumption, I do not have to be beautiful, smart, talented, or
good, for beauty, intelligence, talent, and goodness are—like everything
else—things I can buy.[44] We are then wedded to environmentally damaging
high consumption, to the capitalist system as a way of delivering the "goods,"
to our (possibly polluting) jobs.

As an alternative, consider how a spiritual emphasis on gratitude, self-
awareness, and a deep enjoyment of nature could counter our attachment to
buying things. This emphasis is a potential corrective both to conventional
social attitudes that see human happiness as residing in commodities and to *political perspectives*—those of liberal Democrats, for example—that accept the
primacy of consumption and simply desire it to be more equitably shared.
When the *American Prospect*—a glossy bimonthly magazine seeking to revi-
talize the left wing of the Democratic Party—defines liberalism as democracy
plus government support for living conditions and social benefits, it manifests this constricted vision of what politics can be. When the American
union movement adopts the shortsighted position that every job must be
protected despite all possible environmental consequences, it does the
same.[45] For years, the right took advantage of this lack of vision and captured
the soft, cultural issues of family life and community concern. However, as
commentators from Cornell West and Michael Lerner to Sharon Welch and
Jim Wallis have observed, it is a crippling limitation of progressive politics to
confine itself to matters of income and social services. A qualitative—not just
quantitative—change in social life is required. Our images of collective life
need to include different sets of values, not just greater distributive justice regarding the "goods" that are produced already.

It is a noteworthy weakness of liberalism to be shortsighted in this area.
From Marx's dream of a society without alienation to the radical feminist
idea of gender freedom, the radical political traditions offer more substantial
images of human freedom and collective fulfillment. But even the most ambitious of *political* programs, I believe, could be enhanced by resources from
spiritual traditions.

We might consider how spiritual practices are designed to cultivate mental
self-awareness and moral virtues that can be vitally important in social life. The

goal of these practices is a kind of profound personal change. Of course, political movements have also called for personal change. The Old (Communist) Left talked about the "new Socialist man"; radical feminists called on women to "remember a time when you were not slaves . . . or failing that, invent."[46] But with the exception of the groundbreaking contributions of consciousness-raising developed by the women's movement in the late 1960s and early 1970s, few actual *techniques* have been offered to make these changes real.

Religious traditions approach the question of personal change seriously and systematically, far more so than political ones do. Buddhism, for example, has an enormous repertoire of meditative techniques designed to help people develop their self-awareness and lessen their egotism, aggression, and self-important posturing. These techniques can help us discover how our mind constructs an interpretation of daily life and to recognize that this interpretation is often an overlay that obscures reality rather than revealing it. Engaging in disciplined meditation practice could help activists realize when they are manifesting a tendency to dominate, seeing adversaries when there are merely different opinions or pursuing power rather than principle.[47]

Imagine, if you will, social activists who meditated on their intentions as a prelude to meeting about a controversial policy decision, who were well aware of their own internal tendencies to violence as well as the "external" manifestations of violence by the "enemy," who took as their model political militants motivated by commitment to service rather than the personal accomplishment of—and recognition for—"great deeds." Imagine a political leader who had no fear of her repressive jailers because "she did not hate them."[48] Imagine members of a group that could believe, in the words of a Mennonite peacemaker, that to transform global conflicts, they first had to "identify our own violent patterns" and "do so humbly, contritely, and honestly."[49] Imagine a group of people that felt a seamless connection between self-transformation and social transformation, who felt that their ability to continue to do the good work of political action depended in part on sustaining their own self-awareness and capacity for compassion and who also believed that spiritual development required participation in world-making politics.

In fact, we need not tax our imaginations overmuch, because such groups have existed. Rooted in different religious or spiritual beliefs, they have contributed to political struggles over issues of racial justice, peace, poverty, democracy, and the environment.[50] Although no systematic study has ever been done comparing their track records with those of the conventional left, it is hard not to suspect that they leave much less of a trail of burnt-out activists, alienated publics, and groups crippled by infighting.

IMAGINING LIFE

By their very nature, political responses to life are oriented to the ways in which society shapes human experience and causes unnecessary human suffering. Spiritual traditions, by contrast, offer resources to help people comprehend and respond to the universal features of human existence: to such experiences as giving birth, raising children, celebrating love, aging, and death.[51]

I came to understand this distinction personally when, after a decade of intense activist politics, my wife and I had a son who was born brain-damaged and who lived—never leaving the hospital—for only sixty-five days. Obvious as it should have been, I realized with a shock that certain kinds of pain cannot be explained by an unjust social relation, an oppressive person in power, a violent heart that should be reclaimed for peacefulness. I understood that vulnerability and loss cannot be eliminated through politics. My blindness here may have also been part of the late-twentieth-century American middle-class culture, where so much of life seems amenable to control. Clearly, it was endemic to a leftist culture that concentrated only on socially caused pain.

In any case, as I found, spiritual traditions and those who practice them are often quite at home with death, loss, and pain. There are rituals for burial, services and prayers designed to comfort us in affliction, a simple habit of asking God for help with our grief and loss. Religion offers a constant reminder of the universality of loss—as in the famous Buddhist parable in which a woman whose only child had died was comforted when she saw how death had visited every home in the village, not just her own. Further, spiritual teachings suggest that we can feel God's presence in our pain. The Twenty-third Psalm tells us, "The Lord is my shepherd . . . though I walk through the valley of death." Even without a literal belief in a literal God, these words can suggest a way out of the loneliness and emotional isolation that facing death often provokes. One will look in vain for any of these resources in the secular left.

Similarly, there are certain forms of joy—over the birth of a child, the celebration of a marriage, the turn of the seasons, the delight of harvest—that generations of religious practices have learned how to sanctify.

At this point, it might be argued that politics should deal with justice and collective irrationality and leave rituals of celebration and mourning to private life. While important, such things are not really "political," any more than is one's taste in food, clothes, or sex. I believe, to the contrary, that as citizens, political activists, and progressive thinkers, we need a political culture that nourishes us, as well as a set of political goals for which to work. At the very least, we need to be aware of the fundamental incompleteness of a purely political viewpoint and to end the long tradition of antagonism with spiritual traditions—the better to enable the most ardent political activists to receive the help that spiritual life can offer.[52]

The pains of politics have also to do with activists' everyday experiences. By this I mean that extended periods of time contemplating and resisting oppression, war, ethnic hatred, poverty, or environmental damage are extremely draining. It is not just a matter of the psychic desperation I spoke about earlier in this chapter, but of the emotional toll taken by endless images of present human suffering and threats to our collective future. My own experiences of activism—in the antiwar movement, in dealing with the Middle East and chronicling the Holocaust as part of the Jewish left, and in environmental politics—led me at times to be able to think of nothing but burning bodies, mangled lives, and a poisoned earth. And I certainly do not think I am any more sensitive or emotionally vulnerable than anyone else. For me, as for many others, such near-continuous grief and anger take a heavy toll.

Emotional responses to political life are often sources of information and insight, not neurotic feelings that need to be "cured."[53] But we do need direct, intuitive, meditative practices as sources of calm and reassurance to enable us to hold them. For want of a better word, I call such practices "spiritual," in part because they typically derive from a culture of religion. Quieting the mind in meditation, using intuitive resources in visualizations; invoking ritualized forms of compassion, repentance, and joy as ways to connect to other people and to other forms of life—all these can soothe the troubled heart and allow anguish to coexist with celebration. We can remember that eighteenth-century Hasidic Rebbe Nachman proclaimed that it was a great "mitzvah" (religious obligation) "always to be joyful"; or that, as Dorothy Day reminds us, Christians should learn to "rejoice in tribulation."[54] Along with changing the world, the activist needs to live within it, and to do that, he or she needs to be sustained. Religious traditions, at their best, can help in that essential task.

———

Up to this point, my claims about the necessary interdependence of religion and politics have been supported by comparatively brief examples. Many of these examples have been negative: how various religious thinkers or political movements *would have been better* if only they had utilized the resources or insights of the other side. Now we need to see how the interchange between world-making religion and politics has played out in practice.

Part TWO

5

Redemptive Suffering and the Civil Rights Movement

> *I tell you today that there are some things in our social system to which I am proud to be maladjusted. I shall never be adjusted to lynch mobs, segregation, economic inequalities, the madness of militarism, and self-defeating physical violence. The salvation of the world lies in the maladjusted.*
>
> **—Martin Luther King Jr., as quoted in Let the Trumpets Sound[1]**

> *We've got to make people see that love is a strong, positive force for the happiness of oneself, not just for others.*
>
> **—Aung San Suu Kyi, The Voice of Hope[2]**

Martin Luther King is justifiably celebrated as a model of integrity, personal courage, and charisma. He and the spiritually oriented civil rights movement have a great deal to teach secular political groups seeking social change. Their most important lesson is that religious passion, directed toward the ethical transformation of manifest social injustice, can create a powerful mass movement—even among those who possess little social standing or clout.

But is the popular story of the positive role of religious values in the civil rights movement adequate to the historical record? I think, rather, that it is somewhat one-sided. The conventional view accurately attributes some of the successes of the movement to its distinctly religious character, yet it fails to reflect how that character also contributed to the movement's limitations. Although religion provided a surprisingly effective motivation and self-understanding, the movement's long-term effects were determined by the degree to which inspired religious action could lead to sober political effects.

———————

By the end of 1959, some two and a half years after Martin Luther King Jr. and the black community of Montgomery had won the unprecedented victory of compelling the city's bus lines to treat black passengers fairly, the public presence of the movement in general and King in particular had dramatically dwindled. There had been no significant victories after Montgomery, and the struggle to achieve legal equality seemed stalled in the tenuously held and rather dim hope that the federal government might intervene in Southern racism. Meanwhile, African-Americans in the South continued to be virtually disenfranchised, with only between 2 percent and 20 percent allowed to vote. Blacks were subject to white violence, mired in crushing poverty and illiteracy, and denied access to restaurants, bus waiting rooms, theaters, rest rooms, hotels, public beaches, and virtually every other public facility whose use helped mark white citizens as full members of the surrounding society.

King and the organization that had grown out of Montgomery, the Southern Christian Leadership Council (SCLC), were mired in organizational difficulties, strategic confusion, internal struggles for a political presence in the enormous national organization of black Baptists, and King's personal difficulties with fabricated charges of tax fraud. The great success in Montgomery—in which ordinary blacks had sustained a boycott for nearly a year—had nevertheless left other common public amenities untouched. And even the bus victory was limited. No one had ever denied blacks the right to ride the buses. They had simply won the right sit in them anywhere they liked—and only in one particular city.

King was the acknowledged leader of the direct action dimension of the movement of black rights. While the older, more established, more institutionally connected side of black politics, especially the National Association for the Advancement of Colored People (NAACP), leaned toward a strategy of victory through long and technical court cases, King's religiously inspired vision called for direct confrontation with the white world over issues of immediate personal concern. Such confrontation necessarily required the participation and support of a large number of ordinary African-Americans, not the legal expertise of upper-middle-class black lawyers.

But where and how to move next? With its large black population, numerous black churches, and active NAACP leadership, Montgomery had been fertile ground for a beginning. The bus issue had galvanized the black community of Montgomery, which had been provoked for years by rude and even vicious treatment by drivers. Rosa Parks, made forever famous by her refusal to "sit in the back of the bus," was not the first black woman in that period to be arrested for refusing to follow the rules, but the third.[3] After the city surrendered, however, another effective focus was not found. King's eventual victory, including his steadfastness in the face of Montgomery's stubborn resistance, bombings, and police harassment, had made him an international celebrity. In less than a year, he and his ideas had more national visibility than leaders who had worked for decades. But after Montgomery, it was clear that King and the SCLC did not know where to go or what to do.

It is against this background that the next stage of the national civil rights movement erupted—not as a planned campaign orchestrated by well-known black leaders and their established organizations, but as an upheaval of black youth, mainly college students in their late teens and twenties, who took King's religious orientation toward social change and lived it with their bodies. Their passion pushed King and the "adult" movement far beyond the goals and methods of Montgomery. King had not sought to "end segregation" but only to make it fairer; and he had directed a legal boycott, not purposefully illegal sit-ins. The young people's willingness to expose themselves to jail, physical violence, and the threat of death constituted an example of religiously inspired courage that fed back into King and the more established organizations. From the sit-ins and freedom rides of 1960 and 1961 emerged the systematically planned King-led campaigns in Birmingham, St. Augustine, and Selma, which attracted the attention of the nation (and the world) and ended black disenfranchisement and legal segregation.[4]

Religion was crucial to this process. Many of the movement's leaders were ordained ministers or divinity students. Key meetings were almost always held in churches. The rhetoric of the movement invoked God's promises of liberation from slavery as often as a secular language of rights.

Yet the religious heritage of African-Americans was decidedly ambiguous on the subject of political action. On the one hand, writers like James Cone claim that black theology was essentially a theology of liberation. "Unlike white churches, which separated religion and politics when the racial question was involved, black churches have always viewed them as belonging together, *especially* in regard to race. When their dignity was being disregarded, blacks used religion and anything else in their possession in order to fight for their right to be treated as human beings."[5] Frederick C. Harris sums up a good deal of research in suggesting that religion promoted "mainstream and protest activity" (though not "political violence and separatist black nationalism").[6]

Still, many of the religiously inspired figures of the movement have re-ported personal dissatisfaction with the political quietism of the religion they learned in their youth. A few pages after the above assertion, Cone quotes King's own criticism of the Negro church for (in Cone's words) "its one-sided, anti-intellectual focus on the heaven theme to the exclusion of prob-lems on earth," or as King himself said: "[A] minister cannot preach the glo-ries of heaven while ignoring social conditions in his own community that cause men an earthly hell."[7] John Lewis remembers that following the 1955 Mississippi murder of Emmett Till (whose "crime" was asking a white woman for a date), he decided he could no longer live like his religiously minded parents, "taking the world as it was presented to them and doing the best they could with it."[8] James Bevel, who later became an enthusiastic and creative leader of nonviolent struggle, first reacted to movement ideas by flatly asserting that they were contrary to the gospel.

If, as Stephen Carter observes, the black church could not be separated from politics because it was the central institution of the black community,[9] nevertheless the dominant "political" message of the black church before this time was not that of political activism. If Sunday morning gave African-Americans "a rare though passionate affirmation of their humanity," it typi-cally provided little carryover to the rest of the week.[10] In fact, some black political organizations, such as the NAACP, were founded to compensate for the otherworldly orientation of the churches.[11]

If it was religion that helped inspire the movement, it was religion trans-formed by politics. The peculiar way in which these two combined gave the movement some of its strengths and its weaknesses—and was responsible both for its spectacular victories and some of its most telling defeats.

In some ways, the catalyst for the civil rights movement's next stage was a di-vinity student named James Lawson, who had embraced religious nonvio-lence in his youth. At age ten, he slapped a boy who had called him "nigger." His mother did not congratulate him but said "What good did that do? . . . It's just ignorant words from an ignorant child." You are, she reminded him, deeply loved by your family and by God. Violence is simply unnecessary.[12]

From that time on, Lawson committed himself to not hitting back against racism but to finding a better way to overcome it. In college he was deeply influenced by liberal Christian pacifist A. J. Muste, who showed him that re-ligious faith and political dissidence could be combined. He then spent over a year in federal prison for refusing the draft during the Korean War and stud-ied the nonviolent heritage of Gandhi in India. While in India, Lawson read about the Montgomery bus boycott, experiencing a special thrill to think that a southern black Baptist was carrying on Gandhi's ideas in the United States. A few years later, while a graduate student at Oberlin College in Ohio, Lawson spent an evening with King. Come south, King told Lawson. Don't wait until you finish your schooling. We need people like you now. And so Lawson took a job as a Southern staff member for the Fellowship of Reconciliation, a Quaker-inspired organization dedicated to the religiously oriented use of nonviolence to solve problems of daily life and world politics. He enrolled in Vanderbilt University Divinity School and started offering seminars and workshops in nonviolent social change to Nashville's African-American college students.[13]

These students were varied: middle and lower class, Northern and Southern, religiously oriented and secular. Some were made hopeful by the Brown decision of 1954 promising the end of segregated education, others angered by the contrast between Northern and Southern racial practices. Together, they shared an attraction to the force of religiously guided nonviolence as the way to overcome segregation. Knit together by Lawson's teaching, they responded to a spontaneous sit-in at Greensboro, North Carolina, by launching a sustained and comprehensive effort to desegregate Nashville. Months of sit-ins, demonstrations, and an emerging national presence followed. Out of their actions would come the Student Nonviolent Coordinating Committee, the freedom rides, and voter registration drives in the dangerous, fanatically racist Deep South. They reignited the fire of the Montgomery movement and sparked King into the famous campaigns in Birmingham and Selma.

After the Nashville group inspired a national movement and had organized themselves into the SNCC, Lawson wrote the following definition of nonviolence for the SNCC handbook:

> We affirm the philosophical or religious ideal of nonviolence as the foundation of our purpose, the presupposition of our faith, and the manner of our action. Nonviolence as it grows from the Judaic-Christian tradition seeks a social order of justice permeated by love . . .
>
> Through nonviolence, courage displaces fear; love transforms hate. Acceptance dissipates prejudice; hope ends despair. Peace eliminates war; faith reconciles doubt. Mutual regard cancels enmity. Justice for all overthrows injustice. The redemptive community supersedes systems of gross immorality.
>
> Love is the central motif of nonviolence. Love is the force by which God binds man to Himself and man to man. Such love goes to the extreme; it remains *loving and forgiving even in the midst of hostility*. It matches the capacity

of evil to inflict suffering with an even more *enduring capacity to absorb evil*, all the while persisting in love. By appealing to the conscience and standing on the *moral nature of human existence*, nonviolence nurtures the atmosphere in which reconciliation and justice become actual possibilities.[14]

These words capture the religious spirit animating the most successful entry of spiritual ideas into political life in American history. Three years after they were written, however, Lawson was not even invited to the SNCC's annual meeting. His message of religious nonviolence had ceased to be the organization's guiding ethos.

More broadly, during this time the civil rights movement as a whole had shaken the nation, transformed the public status of black people in the South, and provoked a fundamental realignment of American politics that was to last for decades. Its singular role in American history seemed largely rooted in its inspiring religious message and inspirational spiritual leaders. Yet little more than a decade after it began, its victories sharply dwindled; and a short time after its greatest triumphs, it began to fracture and falter.

Why?

——— — ———

Let us recall the criticisms of religion by Karl Marx and Friedrich Nietzsche. In a sense, the power and effectiveness of religious ideas in the civil rights movement both confirm and reverse these criticisms. And such criticisms, it should be realized, are not just historical oddities but are still widespread in progressive political circles.

When Marx called religion "the opium of the masses," he was referring to its painkilling properties, the way it can alleviate the sorrows caused by poverty and class subordination. In the religious imagination, poverty, humiliation, and drudgery become less real, and an anticipation of heavenly glory transforms a present seen as merely temporary. Expectation replaces, or at least softens, a painful present.

Yet even though it lessens pain, Marx believed, religion is a form of alienation. Religious belief involves the projection of our own, quite human powers and capacities onto some *other* Being, an imaginary one at that. The consequence is political passivity and a lack of class solidarity. Quasi-addicted to the false happiness promised by the church, peasants and workers lacked the willingness to overturn the system and bring happiness down to earth. In essence, religion's offer of false happiness made real happiness less accessible.

What happens if we agree with much of what Marx says, *except*, however, his assertion that attachment to the pleasures of religion make actual satisfaction harder to come by? What if the "false" happiness of religion could, under certain circumstances, make real happiness—and passionate political action in pursuit of that happiness—*more* rather than less accessible? What if people need some sense of joy, some modicum of human satisfaction to be psychologically able to act on their own behalf? And if the black church described by John Lewis as a place to find "joy and meaning in the midst of hardship and pain,"[15] could it increase commitment to political change rather than subvert it? What if imagining that a future of God's love awaits us makes it possible not just to endure the daily humiliations of white-dominated society but also to undertake the actions that would transform it? What if the nightly mass meetings, so essential to the crucial civil rights struggles in Birmingham, St. Augustine, Selma, and other cities, imbued demonstrators with a religious fervor that gave them respite from the beatings, arrests, and threats and *also* inspired them to go back to the streets and jails the next day?

Nineteenth-century philosopher Friedrich Nietzsche argued that Judaism and Christianity begin in a reversal of existing moral values by people too physically and socially weak to express their aggression directly. Religion was a "workshop where ideals were lied into existence," where powerlessness was equated with holiness, and an allied force of infinite power was imagined to compensate for actual impotence.[16] Nietzsche's approach in some way parallels that of Marx, but Nietzsche's stress on power complements rather than repeats Marx's stress on happiness. The imaginary power of God promises that our present condition will be avenged, says Nietzsche. When God rules the earth, and when God's judgment is visited on the unrighteous, then "we" religious folk will have the power, position, and prestige that are so far beyond us now. "The last shall be first" is an attractive slogan precisely for those who are last now, those who have in this life neither the ability nor the opportunity to become anything else.

The result of this religious transvaluation, says Nietzsche, is that a personal philosophy of powerlessness and meekness became enshrined as the dominant model of ethics, and a class of exploitative priests who deny their own and their followers' lust for power became socially dominant.

What if Nietzsche, like Marx, is half right? What if religion does lead us to see dominant social forces as weak and the socially weak as strong? But what if, contra Nietzsche, this imaginary strength can give rise not to continued alienation but to the actualization of potential personal power that had been lost? What if imagined strength and virtue can give rise to real action? What if the religious sanctification of powerlessness becomes in itself a real power? And this not in the form that Nietzsche loathed—a sanctimonious and bureaucratic organization of parasitic priests—but in the form of a mass movement that engages, empowers, and liberates those that join in?

Of both Marx and Nietzsche we may ask: What if the *religious imagination* can be part of the process of developing collective, democratic *political power*?

———————

Well into the Montgomery boycott, the young, highly educated, but in many ways inexperienced King ran directly into the full force of Southern racism. His life and his family's were in serious danger. Hateful phone calls permeated the atmosphere of his home. Dozens of threatening letters came each day. Even as the African-American community of Montgomery was holding fast to the boycott, the white community seemed to be getting harder and more hateful. One January night, awakened by a call in which a harsh voice threatened to "blow your brains out and blow up your house," King went into his kitchen, made himself some coffee, and decided to quit. It was too hard on him, and more important, he had no right to put his wife and daughter at risk. Bowing his head, he prayed for guidance, confessing that he was ready to give up. As historian Stephen Oates describes it:

> Then he felt something—a presence stirring in himself. And it seemed that an inner voice was speaking to him with quiet assurance. "Martin Luther, stand up for righteousness. Stand up for justice. Stand up for truth. And, lo, I will be with you, even unto the end of the world." He saw lightening flash. He heard thunder roar. It was the voice of Jesus telling him *still* to fight on. . . . He raised his head. He felt stronger now. He could face the morrow. Whatever happened, God in His wisdom meant it to be . . . And for the first time God was profoundly real and personal to him.[17]

Experiences like this do not fit into the Marxist or Nietzschean criticisms of religion. Nor are they easily integrated into the standard liberal account of religion, in which spiritual passion is, at its best, a private affair.

From that day on, King was able to pursue basic civil rights with a religiously guided fervor, a fervor that increased, rather than limited, his commitment to world-making political change. In this process King was not perfect. He made strategic errors, had a taste for the high life, and was sexually promiscuous. Yet his use of religion in public life was clearly a development of democracy, not a subversion of it. His sense of God's immediate presence—a sense lacking during all the years of theological study and ministerial training—enabled him to make that contribution in the face of enormous and frightening opposition. And what that sense did for him personally, it also did for much of the movement as a whole.

———————

For the religious protester, the goal of nonviolent civil disobedience was not simply to overthrow a particular law or the system of segregation. It was, rather, to create something distinct and positive in itself. In the passage from the SNCC handbook quoted above, Lawson uses the phrase "redemptive community" to describe this goal. For Martin Luther King Jr. and John Lewis, the term was "beloved community." This was, in Lewis's words, a "commitment to seeing the spark of the sacred in every human being, no matter how vile or how violent."[18] After Montgomery, King said that the real aim was not to defeat the white man but "to awaken a sense of shame within the oppressor and challenge his false sense of superiority . . . *the end is reconciliation; the end is redemption; the end is the creation of the beloved community* where all men would treat each other as brothers and equals . . . There are great resources of goodwill in the southern white man that we must somehow tap."[19] Like Anne Frank, the religiously motivated members of the black civil rights movement seemed, despite everything, to believe that that people were "really good at heart." This goal, and the moral tone of the early civil rights movement as a whole, clearly moves beyond the secular, liberal aim of legal equality. What activists like King and Lewis were talking about was a new form of collective relationship, not simply a more equitably distributed autonomy.

It is important to stress, however, that the religious activists' vision of a truly moral community is not based in some unsophisticated naïveté. In fact, a spiritual understanding of political life as turning on personal moral choices does not necessarily make one incapable of simultaneously utilizing political theories about impersonal social structures. King understood that basic social institutions—patterns of ownership, education, law, and political power—were essential causes of racism against African-Americans, and indeed of other systematically oppressed groups throughout the world. Doing his first round of graduate work at Crozer Theological Seminary, he was sympathetic to a Marxist-style analysis of the effects of capitalism and said that he was tending toward the necessity of an "armed revolt" to improve the social position of blacks. According to Michael Harrington, long a leader of American Socialist politics, by the early 1960s King was a "closet socialist."[20] In a press interview during the Montgomery bus boycott, King said: "The oppressed people of the world are rising up. They are revolting against colonialism, imperialism, and other systems of oppression, including American segregation."[21]

Yet King added something to these standard leftist critiques of systematic injustice: a deep-seated concern with the methods by which injustice was to be overcome. Most of the secular left (and the secular right, as well) seemed unaware that the struggle for one's legitimate rights could too easily lead to the creation of yet another set of powerful, unresponsive, oppressive institutions.

King, partly influenced by Niebuhr's warnings about the tendency of any social group to pursue narrow self-interest, sought a political method that would
truly end oppression, not just shift it around. He rejected the idea that one
should be, in the manner of political groups from the Communist Party to the
Republican Party, so enamored of one's own interests and goals as to be willing to sacrifice other people to further them.

Religious nonviolence is a response to this problem, a way of getting
power to resist an unjust *system*, without sacrificing either love or justice. Systematic nonviolence is active and decisive, the very opposite of passivity, yet
it promises, as much as anything can, that success will not require or cause a
betrayal of the goals that led one to act in the first place. It is not merely
a moral way to act. It is a way to get power without turning that power into
something destructive. It can thus fulfill religious values and also serve as a
highly effective *political* strategy, that is, if "politics" means justice as well as
self-interest, if it is the pursuit of a better life for everyone, not just about
getting this or that interest group (or its leaders) a better deal. It was part of
King's gift that he saw the necessity of striving toward both of these goals. In
a 1967 speech, he declared: "There is nothing wrong with power if power is
used correctly. . . . [P]ower without love is reckless and abusive, and love
without power is sentimental and anemic. Power at its best is love imple-
menting the demands of justice, and justice at its best is power correcting
everything that stands against love."[22]

Part of King's response to injustice was an appeal to the better nature of
the oppressor. His rejection of violence is particularly important here. On the
one hand, as King repeatedly pointed out to those members of the movement
who wanted to take up arms, blacks were only 10 percent of American society. Despite his own youthful flirtation with the idea of armed insurrection,
he knew that in any violent struggle, blacks would be hopelessly outgunned.
In largely white America, where the vast majority of people supported the
government, appeal to armed revolution was "blatantly illogical." "In a violent racial situation, the power structure has the local police, the state troopers, the National Guard and, finally, the army to call on—all of which are
predominantly white."[23]

On the other hand, and more important, King believed that violence always obstructs the development of the beloved community. It was not just
that he couldn't win the battle but that as soon as he engaged in battle he
would already have lost the war! That is so because the war is not about "winning," but about creating a society no longer made up of winners and losers.
Only a strategy aimed at awakening the conscience of the oppressor could accomplish this objective. Only the use of one's own spiritual power would

both *compensate* for the existing inequality of power and *prevent* a repetition of that inequality in a new form. For this struggle, a new kind of fighting force was needed. As he explained in describing the mass meetings in Birmingham: "We did not hesitate to call our movements an army. But it was a special army, with no supplies but its sincerity, no uniform but its determination, no arsenal except its faith, no currency but its conscience."[24]

What was the source of that special army's strength? Its ability to endure redemptive suffering—to take onto itself suffering that was undeserved. This willingness to suffer was not simply an exercise in masochism but part of an overall rethinking of the way in which Southern blacks understood their social situation. As such, it was a highly effective way to mobilize an economically and emotionally depressed population. In this dramatically new perspective, the unjust social superiority of the oppressors could now be seen as a weakness; and the lack of money, numbers, or institutional power of the oppressed took a back seat to their moral fervor and capacity for self-sacrifice.

Imagine yourself as part of a group subject to long-term humiliation and social subordination. How do you get to the point where you feel powerful enough to act? You see your power as coming from within, from the strength of your determination to undergo suffering to pursue justice. How do you see powerful oppressors as vulnerable? You see them as fundamentally at odds with their own spiritual nature, contradicting their own truest identity. How do you have the courage to resist the established (white) authorities? By seeing yourselves, in essentially spiritual terms, as ultimately *more* powerful! How can *you* be more powerful than they? Because you have God—and the oppressor's own essential nature—on your side!

This new sense of selfhood could sustain the movement even in the worst moments. After four black children were killed in a church bombing in Birmingham, King spoke to the community's grief and rage:

> We must say to our white brothers all over the South who try to keep us down: we will match your capacity to inflict suffering with our capacity to endure suffering. We will meet your physical force with soul force. We will not hate you. And yet we cannot in all good conscience obey your evil laws. Do to us what you will, Threaten our children and we will still love you . . . bomb our homes and . . . our churches . . . and we will still love you. We will wear you down by our capacity to suffer. . . . We will so appeal to your heart and your conscience that we will win you in the process.[25]

One reason redemptive suffering is so powerful is that it emphasizes the unique personal power held by the oppressed, a power they are *always* capable of manifesting. Whatever else is true about oppressed people, they can always, if they will, choose to suffer more. But a suffering that is chosen instead of merely "endured," that is invited rather than inflicted by another, is a suffering transformed. People who *choose* their suffering are no longer victims. They have become active agents. Further, when hardship is chosen and accepted, the person undergoing it has, quite clearly, won a highly significant victory over fear. The habitual avoidance of pain expresses a kind of subservience: Fear guides us away from what is forbidden by those who can inflict pain on us. Thus, the white community's persecution of African-Americans—personal humiliation, loss of jobs or bank loans, physical violence—was a strategy of control. Once the persecuted willingly chose to suffer, that control was broken.

Finally, the idea of redemptive suffering redefines the social situation. By allowing "success" to be achieved regardless of oppressors' actions, those actions became increasingly irrelevant. Success and failure were now in the oppressed's own hands. Regardless of the social outcome, previously powerless movement members could know that they had oriented their lives according to a moral reality of greater value and power than anything the white power structure had at its disposal.

Consider this description of John Lewis, who had grown up terrified of ever being in jail, reflecting on how he felt after his first arrest in Nashville: "Jail was not crushing; it was . . . he thought to his amazement, liberating. 'I had never had that much dignity before . . . It was exhilarating—it was something I had earned, the sense of the independence that comes to a free person.'"[26] Consider the charisma of James Lawson. His appeal was not based on his social position or any rational guarantee of future success for the movement. "He just had a way about him. An aura of inner peace and wisdom that you could sense immediately upon simply seeing him."[27]

Such comments should remind us of two of the key themes discussed earlier. The first theme is that at its best, a religious sensibility can combine the passion to act with a confident, peaceful detachment from results. This is a familiar theme in spiritual writings. In Søren Kierkegaard's *Fear and Trembling*, biblical Abraham is described as a supreme model of faith because he can carry out God's command to sacrifice Isaac, risk everything he holds dear, and still proceed with confidence and equanimity. In a Zen Buddhist teaching story, a monk, pursued by a tiger and about to fall over a cliff, manages to grasp some wild strawberries and exclaim, "How delicious!"[28]

In the movement, activists had to shape this kind of combination of faith and detachment, action and trust, into a political force. They had to fully engage in a dangerous and difficult course of action, while knowing that the end result was really out of their hands. In the early years, they certainly could not trust in a rational calculation of victory, for measured in terms of secular power, they had little hope of success. Lawson, for instance, could not promise a "revolution" because of some assessment of potential African-American political power. Paradoxically, however, by his willingness to act despite the dangers and inequality of physical power, Lawson had *already* triumphed in the battle against Southern segregation, which was a battle for a kind of elementary self-respect. Whatever would happen in regard to lunch counters, interstate bus travel, or voting rights, once self-respect was achieved, the most important victory was won. The spiritual redefinition of existence that helped make that achievement possible.

The second theme is the way the actual experience of religion helps us imagine "the revolution"—or at least significant social change. In the civil rights movement, we see that these two themes are related, for the experience of religious inspiration helps people to act with a combination of passion and detachment.

Everything in the segregated South (and a good deal in the North!) said that blacks were without value. Yet a religiously transformed experience of their situation contradicted the racist view. Out of that contradiction, action could be born. If whites said that blacks were frightened, incompetent, ignorant, and passive, a nonviolent religious movement told them that their suffering made them beloved of God, privy to the secrets of the universe in a way their oppressors had forgotten or never known. Believing in their own value, they lived with a courage that destroyed any image of inferiority. Their very prayers were actions, their high spirits in the face of danger a spiritual triumph foreshadowing a political one.

Besides changing the condition of the oppressed by giving them a new sense of their autonomy and value, redemptive suffering also transvalues our sense of the oppressor. The social power held by the white sector of society no longer had to be seen as a badge of racial superiority, for social power itself, when at odds with spiritual truth, was devalued. Unjust power, power held in opposition to God's will, began to look a lot less like real power. At least, that is, when viewed through the lens of the beloved community.

As in Nietzsche's perspective, the existing social valuations of groups are reversed.[29] It is not the police chiefs, mayors, or white businessmen who are the bearers of power and value, but the black folks willing to undergo pain not only to prove their own essential value under God but also to *help white folks come to their senses*. Nonviolent civil disobedience is not only a form of struggle; it is also a gift of conscience to the *entire* community—to black and white alike. As Lewis said: "All I knew then was that I believed that most people, regardless of race or any other distinction, were kind and had a conscience—or were *capable* of being kind and having a conscience . . . I pity those filled with anger and hate because they are victims just as much as the people they attack."[30]

But who can give a gift except the wealthy? Who can sacrifice to awaken the conscience of the oppressor except those strong enough to endure pain without resentment? And if one is *that* strong, how could one ever again be considered an inferior? Adopting this view of their own actions enables the socially weak to feel the power of their own virtue, giving them hope of success not based in money, numbers, or arms. The reversal is possible because from a religious point of view, politics is not simply a tale of the power of groups, but an arena of moral testing for the individual. If I can stand up to the forces of evil without surrendering my sense of love, then I have won a great victory—over myself if not over the social system that oppresses me. Freely entering into redemptive suffering, the oppressed shake off their ingrained sense of inescapable inferiority.[31]

In short, the spiritual tone of the civil rights movement changed the African-American's basic everyday experience and provided a distinctive advantage over purely secular accounts of political struggle. In a secular vision, it may very well be impossible to imagine how to alter the situation of an economically marginalized minority group like African-Americans. Traditional Marxism, or any class-based political framework, sees the working class as possessing potential power because of its size and central role in the economy. This class needs only political organization to manifest that power. For feminism, the sheer number of women and their essential role in the household economy and in personal life gives them a comparable potential power if they, too, organize.

For a racial minority, the situation is quite different. It may in fact be that a religiously understood entry into redemptive suffering was the *only* way to begin to overturn the experience and the social reality of black inferiority. In December 1959, as Lawson's workshops entered into the critical preparatory phase for the first round of sit-ins, there was great emphasis on creating a sense of inner strength and overcoming "the shame of being black in a white nation." The goal was to create not just pride in themselves but the ability to rise above the existing structures of anger and hate. Religiously speaking, the essential message was that we are all "children of God" and that violent racists were simply blind to this essential fact. In being violent, they simply revealed that they did not really feel powerful, confident, or well loved. Once blacks understood that neither their own feelings of inferiority nor their social situation were their own fault, they could be more tolerant of their oppressors' delusions. "They were to be teachers as well as demonstrators." But to do so, "they had to value themselves . . . they had to end that longstanding self-hatred."[32]

But what a difference in perspective! No longer to see one's acts as the desperate striving of an underclass or as an attempt to prove one's worth to the socially powerful. But, rather, to see oneself as a gentle but learned teacher of ultimate truths, facing enormous physical danger to educate the basically good, but deeply misguided, white oppressor.

Part of what led to this victory was the sheer exuberance of throwing off fear, of breaking artificial and unjust bounds that had been set by others. No longer constrained by the threat of jail, beatings, death, or hated racial epithets, the men and women who regenerated the movement were for that time the freest people on the planet. As Robert Moses, initial architect of the movement in Mississippi, wrote in response to the original lunch counter sit-ins: "[B]efore, the Negro in the south had always looked on the defensive, cringing. This time they were taking the initiative." After his initial demonstration, he observed, "From the first time a Negro gets involved in white society, he goes through the business of repressing, repressing, repressing . . . When you do something personally to fight prejudice, there is a feeling of great release."[33]

Theirs was not merely a willingness to suffer, but in some respects a *pursuit* of suffering, for in their eyes the suffering itself had real power in the social realm. As King said, explaining why Freedom Riders refused bail and stayed in oppressive jails, it is "a matter of conscience and morality. They must use their lives and their bodies to right a wrong. Our conscience tells us that the law is wrong and we must resist, but we have moral obligation to accept the penalty." Only in this way can we "save the soul of America."[34] Similarly, during one of the freedom rides, Lawson attempted to turn away police protection from the marauding white mobs that had already torched a bus on which an integrated group had ridden. His nonviolent philosophy, he said, directed him to endure whatever suffering was coming. "We will accept the violence and the hate, absorb it without returning it."[35]

If a religious self-understanding is not the only way to generate this viewpoint, it certainly was essential to the way it was accomplished in the civil rights movement. No secular politics can embrace suffering for its own sake or accept that suffering is ever "redemptive." Such perspectives might celebrate the strength of solidarity, but they cannot revalue the social dominance of the ruling group, for they have no conceptual basis to understand that rulers are violating their own essential nature or that "real" power lies elsewhere. For a secular politics, social power is the only power there is. Nor can a secular political movement[36] believe that there are metaphysical guarantees of success—that God, or Spirit, or the spiritual soul that every individual (even the most racist) possesses is on the side of the oppressed. Suffering can be redemptive only to the extent that there is a spiritual (or at least psychological) mechanism by which it has an effect. In the religious perspective, that mechanism is God—or at least the essentially spiritual nature of humanity and the universe. Thus, only in a *religious* view do the actions that led to the civil right's movements *political* victories make sense.

———————

Despite its spiritual genius, the civil rights movement was not the simple embodiment of religious principles. For one thing, as I have mentioned already, a good deal of black religion in the United States had clearly been otherworldly, passive, and deeply accommodating of the status quo. This was so not only for theological reasons but also because black pastors had reached positions of comparative wealth and social standing. Political activity put that at risk.

Connected to a community and a larger historical situation, the African-American church shaped and was shaped by larger forces. As historian Charles Payne put it: "If the pre-1950 history of the rural black church conforms to this [socially conservative, politically passive] model its history since then suggests that there is nothing inherently conservative about the church, that its message can as easily be packaged in order-threatening as in order-preserving ways."[37]

The transformation of Southern black Christianity involved the adaptation of religious ideals and self-understanding to the dynamics of the mobilization of social power. The accounts it gave of itself, and what it actually was, were not always the same. Thus, if in the civil rights movement we find the church transforming the world, it is also the case that the religious viewpoint was not the only force at work.

Consider the following statement by King, delivered at a 1961 rally in Richmond, Virginia, addressed to white racists who wanted to close public schools to prevent integration: "We will wear you down by our capacity to suffer, and in the process we will win your hearts . . . Nothing is more sublime than suffering and sacrifice for a great cause."[38] Although this statement expressed the movement's standard public self-representation, a bird's-eye view of the struggle reveals that success was typically dependent on mobilizing political power in conventional, secular ways, and not by initiating a moral change among white Southerners.

The complex reality of the movement can be understood if we again ask: What is violence? Plainly lynchings, bombings, and beatings are more "violent" than peaceful demonstrations in favor of basic civil rights. But what if the sight of a black person in a white setting is experienced as a direct assault? But what if an end to racial inequality is felt to be an attack on one's own way of life? Thinking that "violence" is an easily understood concept depends on the assumption that the body is central in a way nothing else is and that assaults on the body therefore have a distinct and particularly important role in social life. But for some whites, preserving racial superiority was as important as their own physical well-being, and threats to that superiority were as dangerous as bullets. Or if not quite as dangerous, clearly dangerous enough to provoke a rage felt to be completely justified.

That such a reaction was inevitable becomes clear once we realize that a serious *nonviolent* campaign, even one in which the participants agree to legal penalties and refuse to strike back when attacked, is nevertheless to some significant degree *coercive*. A wide range of desegregation activities—boycotts, blocking movie theaters, refusing to conform to accepted social norms (for example, by not sitting in the back of the bus)—were experienced as a violation by the people against whom they were directed. Although such actions were not violent in the narrow sense, to someone who expected subservience from "Negroes," they were highly threatening. They interrupted the normal course of life, caused significant loss of business revenue, and created a climate of fear in citizen bystanders. Such actions are perhaps among the least aggressive possible courses of action open to victims of repression. However, they are not nearly as benign as their practitioners sometimes claim. That is why when these campaigns succeeded, they usually did so like campaigns in secular politics: by using social pressure to secure their objectives, not by awakening the hearts of those still clinging to racial privilege.

According to John Lewis, the initial desegregation of Nashville lunch counters was less the result of changed hearts than of economic pressure and the threat of widespread violence after a prominent black citizen had his house bombed. Similar dynamics unfolded in Atlanta; Columbia, South Carolina; New Orleans; Little Rock; and even Jackson, Mississippi.[39] A religious understanding might have been essential to *motivating* the actors, and it might have been hoped that spiritual nonviolence and universal love (even for the oppressor) would win the day. But the *power* the movement produced was not unlike that of nonreligious groups like the AFL-CIO and the antiwar movement. In the end, collective pressure organized by ministers singing gospel songs about Jesus was often indistinguishable (except for the music) from secular struggles.

From the beginning, leaders of the movement lived a creative tension between the pristine values of nonviolent spiritual awakening and the nuts and bolts of national and even international power politics. These politics were not a prelude to the beloved community but involved the oppressed acting against the oppressor in socially tolerable ways in order to enlist the aid of third parties whose power would overwhelm the oppressor. Whatever the demonstrators' rhetoric, success came when the oppressors were defeated, not converted.

For example, in order to be successful, the movement had to attract and retain press coverage. Wonderfully aware of the political possibilities of the media age, the movement soon recognized the newly created ability of television to enable a national audience to witness local conflicts. Television was instrumental in mobilizing national sentiment against the regional practices of exclusion, humiliation, and violence. Nightly news footage of black children assaulted by dogs and fire hoses in Birmingham helped shaped public opinion and set the stage for key legislative victories.

To achieve those victories, the movement had to galvanize support from the federal government. While the ostensible appeal of marches and sit-ins was to the surrounding white communities in the South, in many contexts the actual focus was an attempt to motivate the federal government to provide police protection and then pass new laws. In this attempt, activists took advantage of Cold War competition for Third World allies by alerting the world to democracy's failures in the home of its self-proclaimed champion. Violent racism was not the image President Kennedy wanted to project to emerging nations whose allegiances he sought.

In the end, it was laws or federal rulings that made the difference for the movement. For example, the well-known bus boycott in Montgomery, which proved to be the activist beginning of the civil rights movement and catapulted King to international prominence, was won not because white folks changed their mind but because racially restricted bus seating was ruled illegal by the Supreme Court.[40] The long and difficult campaign in Birmingham, where peacefully demonstrating school children were assaulted by police dogs and fire hoses, achieved only a minimal local settlement and was followed by the devastating murder of four black girls in a church bombing. There was, to say the least, little noticeable change in white sentiment. Yet nationally, the campaign stimulated wide support for the federal Civil Rights Act of 1964, which made segregation in public facilities illegal. Freedom rides by black and white activists were greeted by burnt-out buses, mob violence allowed by local police, and murder threats. Only behind-the-scenes action by then Attorney General Robert Kennedy led the Interstate Commerce Commission to forbid segregation in transportation facilities.[41]

Perhaps most important, the Selma campaign of 1965, culminating in the filmed assault by state troopers and local "deputies" on an attempted black march to Montgomery, was essential to the passage of the Voting Rights Act later that year. This act guaranteed federal protection for black registrants and paved the way for massive black entry into the political process in Southern states. (A few years afterward, stalwart segregationists would be courting African-American votes and proclaiming themselves "friends of the Negro.")

Whose interests were awakened and whose were threatened in these campaigns? Northern states had their own less obvious or legally identifiable but equally pernicious forms of racism, but they had no investment in keeping blacks from lunch counters and voting booths. It was part of John F. Kennedy's foreign policy of competition with the Communist bloc over emerging nations to have the United States appear as the bastion of democracy. For these reasons, the struggle for civil rights was supported by the federal government and the Northern states when it was compatible with their perceived interests or when it seemed to support values that were essential to the reigning ideology and not particularly threatening to dominant institutions. It should be remembered that as early as 1950, the number of electoral votes in non-Southern states where blacks could be influential in elections outweighed the electoral votes of the *entire* South by a margin of almost two to one.[42] Hence, in the national elections of 1964, not a single congressperson who voted for the 1963 Civil Rights Bill was defeated, whereas twenty-two who voted against it were. Thus, national political responses to the civil rights movement, themselves often couched in the language of rights, were also motivated by familiar considerations of electoral politics.

Other factors at work included a fundamental restructuring of the Southern economy, a restructuring that seriously diminished the economic role of traditional forms of racism. Ultimately, some writers argue, the victory for civil rights in the South reflected the displacement of cotton production by new urban businesses and industries. The social fabric of segregation fit with rural blacks as captive labor for old-style cotton plantations, but not with the new South of mechanized farms and factories.[43] Of course, many whites were attached to a "tradition" of racial superiority, and so a few years of violence and turmoil were inevitable. But the more up-to-date capitalism of the "new South" could do without segregation, and therefore the real powers of Southern society were willing to let it go. In short, the hope of a religious awakening on the part of the oppressed might have inspired the actions of protesters; but in reality, the protests translated into changed public policy only when someone else was moved to act and when the goals fit in with the broader social and political structures.

In just this way, the civil rights movement was a political movement; and, I believe, some of its crucial failures arose because it was *not political enough*.

———— • ————

The spiritual brilliance of the civil rights movement unfolded in a context of competing political and economic interests that cannot be comprehended without recourse to the theoretical tools of secular progressive politics. These tools stress opposing forces rather than moral values and are oriented toward finding ways to mobilize oppressed or disenfranchised groups to create a more just society. The universality of Christian love, accessible to each particular individual, has little role here. In practice, when progressive alliances and federal interests were not at work, the movement stalled. Beyond the tightly knit African-American communities of the South, the goal of a public "dignity" disconnected from concrete changes in economic conditions had little relevance; and goals more suited to the concerns of African-Americans in urban, industrial settings could not be achieved simply by the willingness to suffer.

Thus, Northern cities applauded King's efforts to desegregate the South but were less than enthusiastic when he challenged their own racist housing or employment patterns. Chicago, for instance, responded to the SCLC's fair-housing campaign with widespread resentment and violence. Similarly, California voted overwhelmingly in favor of a referendum to allow for segregated neighborhoods and to reverse a fair-housing statute.[44] The political fact of the matter is that the social alienation, minority status, and economic impoverishment of African-Americans gave them little leverage for social change.

In speeches in Chicago, during King's ill-fated campaign for fair housing, the exchanges went like this:

> "*What* is our problem?" King would ask.
> "Tell us?" the people would cry.
> "It is that we are powerless—how do we get power?"
> "Tell us, Martin!"
> "By organizing ourselves. By getting together."
> "That's right!"
> "We are *somebody* because we are *God's* children."
> "That's right!"[45]

But what were they to do once they "got together"? They lacked, for instance, the power to strike and halt key industries that made the AFL-CIO a social force. Racism, which had been nourished by slavery, legal segregation after the Civil War, the use of blacks as poorly paid strikebreakers, and the confinement of them to the worst jobs, kept them in isolation from other actual or potential sources of resistance to the social status quo.[46] In many cases, white workers identified more with their employers than with black workers. And the federal government had little interest in dismantling the complicated threads of Northern urban racism, unlike the internationally embarrassing dramatic forms it had taken in the South.

An oppressed, economically marginalized minority, whatever its absolute spiritual worth, simply cannot get economic power without creating powerful alliances. By definition, they lack economic clout and an irreplaceable economic role. Where then will their power come from even if they do "organize"? Eliminating the last vestiges of slavery by defeating segregation was a great victory, but it posed little to no threat to more modern social structures. Eating in restaurants of their choosing and sitting anywhere on the bus they liked, African-Americans could still suffer poverty and political powerlessness. Pervasive forms of structural racism remained after Jim Crow was defeated. Old-boy networks, ethnic ties, and cultural differences maintained informal, but quite real, barriers to advancement.

Further, as economic analyses of racism have shown, there is good deal of economic rationality in creating a "dual labor market" in which the poorest paid, least secure jobs go to a racial minority. Labor solidarity is weakened, and there is a permanent group of workers who will have to accept low wages and bad working conditions. A general climate of racism allows for blacks to be scapegoated for problems stemming from a highly stratified economy. White workers receive a free sense of superiority via their racial privileges, and their allegiance to the existing social order is increased. Thus, modern capitalism may not need segregation, but it still has a role for racism.[47] And, as historian Bruce Nelson observes, race is "encoded" in working-class identity, and white workers were often active agents in promoting and maintaining their racial privileges. The spiritual tone of the civil rights movement was unable to challenge this arrangement.[48]

The inability to form enduring alliances with the white labor movement spelled the end of the civil rights movement as a national presence. The collapse of whatever black–labor union alliance existed led to the resurgence of the Republican Party and a significant desertion of the Democrats by white working-class men. Fundamentalist religious visions grew to compete with liberating ones, and alternative interpretations of the new social movements led to opposing sides in a new culture war. Clearly this is not all the "fault" of African-American political strategies, but it does point to some of the political limitations of a religious vision. A movement animated by a purely religious sense of political life cannot forge the kinds of alliances that will join fundamentally different communities. Alliances require a sober recognition of each other's secular interests, not just a shared spiritual vocation. The vicious racism manifested in the struggle over forced busing in Boston is an example of how little the spiritual virtues of redemptive suffering could transcend communal differences. Without recognition of common material interests, the communities remained at war. Ironically, the poor and working-class

African-Americans and whites had common interests in better schools and in broader policies to improve their respective social positions. However, the encounter became defined as one centered on racial antagonism. As a result, neither community won very much of anything.[49]

To overcome these obstacles it would have been necessary for the civil rights movement to join the spiritual passion of its early years with a heterogeneous political coalition that could have addressed the complexities of at least class and race, and perhaps gender as well. A politics of spiritually redemptive suffering could not do this. Far from being "universal," the distinct blend of moral fervor and Christian ideas put forward by King was that of a very particular group. It was unlikely to mobilize *other* groups. The kind of rainbow coalition that was needed, however, could not be centered in any one community. Images of the exodus from Egypt, or of the crucifixion and resurrection, so fitting to the African-American experience and Baptist culture, simply would not do for a political movement in which black *and* white interests were to be joined. Broad alliances can be animated by a widely held ideological fervor, but this fervor cannot be rooted in the cultural experience of only one group.

What was needed, though (sadly) perhaps not possible, was the development of formal and informal political ties between blacks and the white working class. Around what issues could such an alliance have unfolded? Possibilities include job training and security, reducing military budgets in favor of social expenditures, across-the-board improvements in education and health care, environmental legislation protecting cities and suburbs from pollution, rewritten tax codes to favor workers and the poor rather than the wealthy, controls over runaway shops, and increased attention to occupational safety and health. Such concerns might have brought a lasting racial unity that would have seriously strengthened the left wing of the Democratic Party by providing a basis for solidarity between unionized workers and the more impoverished. Instead, resentments over affirmative action devastated the party that seemed guaranteed national hegemony after the Republican disgrace of Watergate.

Perhaps such a black-white alliance was simply not possible at the time. In post–World War II America, white workers had been accommodated by a compromise that guaranteed them higher wages and better working conditions at the cost of any kind of radical social presence.[50] With the exception of some maverick labor leaders with radical pasts (for example, United Auto Workers head Walter Reuther), the predominant feeling among union leaders and rank and file alike was that voting rights and access to public facilities were enough for "the Negro." Seduced by "Americanism," increased material comfort, and the privileges of color, the white working class for the most part saw its best chance as lying with the powers of capital while generally opposing all but the most rudimentary black demands. Limited to extending basic democratic rights to blacks, the union movement could not see beyond what it took to be its own immediate self-interest. This seemed fine in the short run. In the longer term, we can see that the racial fracturing of the working class is one reason all parts of the class are close to powerless in the global economy.

Without a broader alliance, the urban black communities were left to take power in the only ways they could. First, they elected sympathetic local governments. Yet while it helped to have black mayors in Cleveland, Atlanta, and Los Angeles, local politicians were highly restricted in how much structural change they could effect. Economic power still rested in large corporations and the federal government. Despite a dramatic increase in the number of elected black officials between 1970 and 1999 (from 1,469 to 8,936), African-American influence remains limited. "Even with a 36-member bloc in the House of Representatives, the congressional Black Caucus finds itself marginalized and must fight to get the attention of party leaders on issues such as election reform and the criminal justice system."[51] As William Julius Wilson has powerfully argued, while the life experience of African-Americans is shaped as much by class as by race, the experience of class is also always "colored" by race.[52] A good deal of the African-American middle class feels itself only tenuously accepted by white society. And a good deal of black political power is held only because it can deliver social services to, and votes from, the nearly 40 percent of African-Americans who remain in poverty—as well as the nearly one-third who often teeter near the brink. The stark differences of the poor and the near poor versus the one-third who have risen leave African-Americans with a steadily diminishing sense of communal solidarity. Ironically, as Manuel Castells argues, blacks still bear a collective stigma of racism but nevertheless lack a coherent collective identity.[53]

Outside of conventional politics, African-Americans were left with the "power" (or powerlessness) of violence. In the 1960s, and a few times since then, urban riots in large and medium-sized cities caused property damage, loss of life, and a government response in the "War on Poverty." Yet federal and state entitlement and affirmative-action programs often hardened racial divisions. They were represented as an instance of big government empowering blacks at the expense of whites. The depressing result was a fundamental realignment of American politics, the "Reagan Revolution," in which much of the white (preponderantly male) working class deserted the Democratic Party. Reagan—who had opposed virtually all federal support of civil rights legislation in the 1960s—coded his political message with explicit appeals to white racism. Also, the racialized understanding of contemporary social life has, if anything, in some ways increased in the last two decades. There have been racist aspects to the public discussion—to name but a few—of immigration, the energy crisis of the 1970s, economic downturns, and America's conflicts with the Arab world.

———— • ————

African-American willingness to be beaten for trying to vote or to refuse police protection out of willingness to suffer during a freedom ride was powerful but inherently limited. The movement's moral authenticity needed to be inserted into a secular political strategy of shared interests of highly different communities, and an understanding of how economic interests are essential to basic social change. A willingness to suffer might integrate a bus terminal, but it could not create an alternative economy, promote control over multinational corporations, or reorient technological development away from environmental destruction. In the absence of such victories, the effects of the movement were quite partial. An increased level of social integration (though not in housing) and a new black middle class coexists with continued social powerlessness for the majority of African-Americans. Jobs move to other countries; blacks suffer disproportionately from pollution.[54] In an ironic example, the Montgomery city bus service, scene of the movement's first real triumph, has fallen into a state of semicollapse that is disastrous for the city's poor blacks.[55]

The period from 1963 to 1965, with the passage of the two major civil rights bills, was both the high-water point of the movement and the beginning of the end. This decline was signaled most clearly in the response of SNCC workers to the failure of the Mississippi Freedom Democratic Party (MFDP). Refused entry to the political process in Mississippi, SNCC and its local allies had decided to create an alternative. Involving more than 70,000 Mississippi blacks in substitute elections, they chose delegates for the Democratic convention. But except for two "at-large" delegates, their slate was rebuffed, and all of the lily-white delegates of the "regular" Mississippi Democratic Party were seated instead, even though most of them rejected party nominee Lyndon Johnson because of his support of civil rights. Lacking white allies within the party, allies it would have taken years to create, the MFDP had no leverage at the convention. Reeling from the strain of organizing in violent Mississippi, shocked into angry despair by the Democratic Party's rejection, SNCC turned away from religious nonviolence and toward black power.[56] That is why Lawson, who had been the most respected SNCC leader, could be rejected only a few years after the group's creation.

This turning point led many in the civil rights movement away from its founding values of the beloved community, nonviolence, and the spiritual understanding of social change. Key figures such as pioneer Mississippi activist Bob Moses dropped out. John Lewis, whose steadfast support of a religious nonviolence made him a SNCC bedrock, was deposed as its chairman in favor of Stokely Carmichael, who had little confidence in nonviolence and wanted SNCC to be an all-black organization. During the June 1966 "Meredith March" (in which several civil rights leaders continued a march started by quickly wounded James Meredith), the slogan "black power" made its first appearance.[57]

This slogan was a rejection of the fundamental values of religious social action. Instead of the premise of the essentially spiritual commonality or bond between all human beings, it offered the notion of competing power groups. Instead of the desire to *awaken* the oppressor, the express goal was to generate more power and thus defeat him. But black power was premised on a fundamental mistake: that African-Americans could generate real power without a multiracial alliance. It was one thing for Black Panthers to parade around Sacramento or Cornell University carrying rifles or to train a few hundred ghetto youths in self-defense. But the overwhelming power of the government and the white majority made these gestures a kind of fantasy. It was politics, all right, but of the wrong kind, a kind of "alternative utopianism for embittered idealists."[58]

It was, in fact, a desperate inversion of the most simplistic form of religious thinking about social issues. Instead of God and righteousness to guarantee their purity and triumph, however, they now had the all-powerful forces of worldwide revolution, the non-white groups challenging European imperialism from Cuba and Ghana to Vietnam and Algeria. But what, in the end, did this have to do with African-Americans? In fact, virtually nothing. Outside of a few conferences and some catchy slogans, there was neither a structural nor a political basis for real solidarity. Like it or not, the future of the American black community resided in alliances with sympathetic, similarly placed whites. Without such alliances, a fundamental transformation of the group's social position would not be possible. And thus with the exception of the small black middle class, the fate of the majority of blacks in the United States, at least in economic terms, has not improved. Neither has, with some few exceptions, that of the working class as a whole. The real hope for African-Americans and for the country as a whole, as Cornell West argues, is "a multi-racial alliance of progressive middlers, liberal slices of the corporate elite, and subversive energy from below," which might create some "radical democratic accountability" and "restructure the economy and government so that all benefit."[59]

In response to the most concrete manifestation of black power, urban riots, government pacification programs of transfer payments were instituted. However, as Frances Fox Piven and Richard Cloward have argued, the structural effect of such programs was a moderate increase in welfare, the siphoning off of black leadership in jobs with government programs, continued black-white alienation as whites saw programs for blacks exclude them, and—most important—a dependence of the black community on the largesse of the federal government.[60] In some ways, the federal government replaced the white plantation owner.

In Mississippi, for example, public programs initially staffed by movement veterans and the rural poor were co-opted and taken over by professionals, the black middle class, and white moderates. With the help of federal policymakers, government programs and funds were channeled toward "acceptable" forms of action and familiar, "safe" leaders. Without a class base of poor and working-class whites to supplement the black community, the drive for black freedom and social development degenerated into antipoverty programs that treated blacks as clients to be handled rather than as the source of their own social power.[61] The meaning of the racial "community" became defined by acceptability to the white establishment. Its "leaders" were determined by their access to what the white power structure could dispense. The struggle for justice became the struggle for government funds, as a political movement was transformed into a dependent group of welfare recipients and their administrators. Political action was redefined as qualifying for benefits.

Religion without adequate politics had become bad politics. And politics that had lost its spiritual spark became business as usual, with much of the African-American community locked in despair. Lacking a cross-racial alliance, white workers also failed to utilize the power they could have had. Seduced by the promise of keeping its privileges, its standard of living experienced minimal growth for twenty-five years, while wealth and income continue to concentrate in the upper 1 percent of the population.[62]

In the end, of course, it might be that a strategy of fundamental class alliances was beyond King and his comrades. Perhaps the relevant communities (white industrial workers, the white urban and rural poor) could not have responded in any case. Perhaps just because the religious civil rights movement could spark courage in and provide comfort to one very *particular* marginalized community, it could not at the same time serve as the basis for a secular politics of shared interests among *differing* groups. But if this is true, then my point is supported: Religious motivation and self-understanding by themselves are not enough. Until the motivation is combined with political alliances, with calculated (though not unprincipled) strategies for different constituencies, the religious community will remain virtuous, but ultimately in many ways ineffective.

A similar problem faced that other icon of nonviolent social change, Gandhi. Like King, Gandhi was a moral exemplar who helped inspire collective action in a deeply demoralized and subordinate population; also like King, he turned to a religious framework to overcome the racist oppressiveness of a ruling group that prided itself on being liberal and democratic. Yet while Gandhi's methods were effective in achieving the basic elements of modernity—political independence and democracy—they were powerless against the highly stratified class structure of twentieth-century capitalism, and the religious and communal violence that continue to this day. Gandhi sought a decentralized India of spiritual values and a modest but decent standard of living. He also wanted to avoid the class-based rhetoric of communism. Yet at times he invoked a kind of moral nationalism that could fuel feelings of Indian superiority and special Hindu virtue. In the end, modern India came to be dominated by a concentrated ruling class no more committed to the collective good of the ordinary Indian than England had been. Even with the recent growth of a consumerist middle class, the vast majority of India's people are politically powerless and desperately impoverished. Shortly after Gandhi's death, India's government embraced militarism and a nuclear weapons program—draining resources from its 100,000 villages that lacked clean drinking water while celebrating the resolutely nonviolent Gandhi as its greatest cultural figure.[63] Once again, a religious vision that prided itself on its lack of political calculation and organization led to a social situation in which bad politics remained in power.

It is part of King's genius that he recognized the need for a basic transformation in American society and that in his last years he returned to a political vocabulary that included concepts like "capitalism" and "structural change." He frequently talked about the need to join ideological, economic, and political power together. "In the future we will be called upon to organize the unemployed, to unionize the business within the ghetto, to bring tenants together into collective bargaining units, and establish cooperatives for the purpose of building viable financial institutions."[64] As early as 1964, he hoped that a Voting Rights Act would make cooperation possible between blacks and white labor, and by 1967, he looked forward to the potential power of black unity with "millions of white workers" that would lessen racial antagonism through the "cohesion in union organizations."[65]

Despite his own personal growth toward a more inclusive politics, the historical meaning of King and his movement has become identified with religious virtue. Its purity and power are associated with the manner in which it was "spiritual and moral" *rather* than political. As such, it is often presented, at least in popular culture and on one Monday in January each year, as a victorious *alternative* to politics. Understood this way, the nation seems happy with King's hard-won, but limited, victories. My point is that if the movement had been more political, and in the right ways, its victories might not have been so limited.

6

After Patriarchy:
Feminist Politics and the
Transformation of Religion

*Whatever diminishes or denies the full humanity of women must be
presumed not to reflect the divine or an authentic relation to the
divine, or to reflect the authentic nature of things, or to be the message
or work of an authentic community.*

—*Rosemary Radford Ruether, Sexism and God-Talk*[1]

*The relation of Torah to women calls Torah itself into question. Where
is the missing Commandment that sits in judgment on the world?
Where is the Commandment that will say, from the beginning of
history until now: Thou shalt not lessen the humanity of women?*

—*Cynthia Ozick, "Notes Towards Finding the Right Question"*[2]

The story of Exodus has supported world-making criticisms of injustice by
Jews and Christians alike. This critical stance was echoed by the Prophets,
who stressed compassionate social relationships as much as ritual purity. Despite the powerful social resonance of these moral imperatives, it is also true
that original Judaism—like its Christian heirs—had a partial and selective vision of ethical relationships. Those who lived in the Promised Land before
the Jews arrived could not have been too thrilled to learn that their homes
were promised to another people. Rare is the Christian church that consistently loved *all* its neighbors or even attempted to forgive its enemies.

129

This partiality is nowhere more clear than in the Torah's treatment of women—and in the way that treatment is repeated throughout all of traditional Judaism, in other biblical religions, and is in fact echoed throughout world religions in general. This patriarchal character remained almost completely unchallenged until recently, when it has been contested by women (and some men) who have been decisively affected by a secular political movement. Feminist politics have entered religion, seeking to overthrow a patriarchal order always represented as timeless, divine, and non-negotiable.

In this chapter, I will sketch some of the essential aspects of the feminist challenge, emphasizing broad lessons about the relation between religion and politics as two ways of world making. These lessons turn on the essentially historical and human dimension of all spiritual systems and the need such systems have for insights and correctives stemming from secular emancipatory politics. My discussion of Martin Luther King Jr. and the civil rights movement in the United States was, so to say, a picture of religion going forth to alter and improve the political world. Here I will describe a dramatic and instructive instance of how politics enters—and changes forever—the world of religion.

During the last forty years or so, we have witnessed an unprecedented rise of women's social power throughout all of social life. Although women are still not equal to men in wealth or social power, virtually the entire developed world has fundamentally lessened its legal and cultural constraints on their lives. Women have access to more jobs, political positions, scientific and scholarly pursuits, sexual freedoms, and personal choices than at any previous time in history. Almost every nation has organizations dedicated to pursuing a better and more just social position for women. Even in despotic Afghanistan, where the position of women has approximated a kind of social slavery, underground organizations have risked severe punishments to educate girls.

I believe that three basic historical developments lie at the root of these changes. First, there is the full flowering of a commodity or market economy, in which a separate sphere for a home-bound "wife" is much less necessary, possible, or desirable. As almost everything costs money in today's society, most households need two wage earners to have enough money to buy what is needed or desired. For households to get that much money, women must perform paid labor, in addition to caring for children and doing housework. As women enter the labor force, men's power over them is reduced and the image of femininity as bound to a powerless private realm is harder to sustain. Second, there is the continuing extension of the principle of equal rights. This principle has moved, although too slowly and only with a great deal of prod-ding, from its limited application to white male property holders across the original boundaries of both race and sex. Extended to women, it first erodes women's unequal status in the political realm. Voting, property rights, and edu-cation are acquired. Then, however, equality begins to enter the realm of pri-vate life as well. Marriage, sexuality, and child raising are critically analyzed. Fi-nally, all of patriarchal culture from art to theology is seen through a feminist lens. The third factor accounting for the rise of feminism is the global cultural hegemony of the West. For better or worse, many of the West's ideas and val-ues have spread to parts of the world where neither democracy nor a fully de-veloped commodity economy are the norm. The ideals of political equality, in-cluding the equality of women, have become available everywhere—if in certain places only to a certain segment of the population.

The feminist challenge begins with the simple but profound observation that all the world's widely held religions have been deeply patriarchal. Their founding texts were male authored and interpreted; men have held virtually all positions of institutional authority; and in numerous ways their theologies have bolstered the idea of male spiritual superiority. Many of us now see these points as obvious, but before feminism it was—except for rare and mar-ginalized voices[3]—close to impossible to see traditional religions *as* patriar-chal. Male power was the standard, believed to be a necessary consequence of unalterable realities of gender, divinity, and religious knowledge. It could not be seen, as feminists have taught us to see it, as one possible form of religion among others.

In a breathtakingly short time, feminist theology, woman-oriented rituals, and female power in religion's institutional life have led to the most dramatic change of religious structures in history. Consider, as a small example, the "Declaration of the Parliament of the World's Religions," accepted by a meeting of more than 6,000 representatives of all the "major" religions, as well as indigenous peoples and followers of Wicca. The 1993 document pledges "a commitment to a culture of equal rights and partnership between men and women" and names patriarchy as a sin.[4] Similarly, the National Council of Churches, with its thirty-three Protestant and Orthodox denomi-nations and its combined membership of about 51 million, asserts in its "In-clusive Language Lectionary" that although it was true that Jesus was a man, his gender is spiritually irrelevant to Christian faith.[5]

Of course, many in religious life have not been won over by feminist argu-ments. Islam, the Catholic Church, and Orthodox Judaism retain a male-only clergy and support their gender hierarchy with appeals to a timeless tra-dition. In societies where women lack social power generally, they cannot be expected to achieve it in religion. What is decisively new is not the accomplishment of women's equality, but the struggle for it. Patriarchal religious authorities, no matter how much they may claim to be unreachable by feminist criticisms, are well aware that such criticisms exist. They know, that is, that they are in a fight for the soul of religion, a fight between competing visions of the tradition's fundamental meanings.

In some ways the feminist enterprise within religion—as opposed to efforts of those women who simply abandon tradition altogether—can be illuminated by an image used by physicist Otto Neurath to describe the process of scientific innovation. Science, suggested Neurath, is like a boat that must be repaired while we are sailing on it. We can't question all our scientific beliefs at once, for that would give us nothing to sail on, so we repair some while relying on others.[6] Similarly, women throughout the world are attempting to rebuild—in a way that reflects their collective experiences and interests—what they believe are their own traditions. They will change the faith while they remain within it.

Those feminists who choose to "stay and fight," rather than abandoning religion altogether or opting for the women-centered goddess or Wicca traditions, emerge as piercing *religious* critics of the male establishment. They do not seek to abandon the faiths of their fathers—and mothers—but to make them more holy. Judith Plaskow, perhaps the most widely respected Jewish feminist theologian, tells us she went through "a gradual process of refusing to split between a Jewish and a feminist self. I am not a Jew in the synagogue and a feminist in the world. I am a Jewish feminist and a feminist Jew in every moment of my life."[7]

Plaskow's process and comparable ones undergone by women throughout the world have a great deal to teach us about the relations between religion and politics when considered as two ways of world making. To uncover these lessons, let us examine some of the major themes in feminist theology.[8]

———— • ————

The first female rabbis in Judaism's 3,000-year history were ordained in the early 1970s, and by now the United States has several hundred. Writing in the magazine *Reconstructionist Judaism*, Rabbi Rebecca Alpert tells us that in the Jewish community, "[w]omen's viewpoints are now taken seriously, and women's voices have been included at the centers of power. Although the situation is far from perfect it certainly can no longer be said that women hold the same marginal place in Jewish life that they did two decades ago when I entered the rabbinate." By 2001, Rabbi Elaine Zecher of Boston could say she never felt she had to struggle with being a feminist in the pulpit of the large and high-profile Reform Jewish Temple, where she has served for more than a decade. "The way was paved for me by the first generation of women rabbis."[9]

Of course these changes are not universal within Judaism. For almost all of Jewish orthodoxy, female rabbis in particular and women's equality in general remain an anathema. Yet even within orthodoxy, voices are raised to ask how it is possible to learn "from the women's movement" to "enhance the quality of our lives as Jews"[10] while leaving as much of the tradition intact as possible. What this learning involves, says Blu Greenberg, perhaps the leading feminist spokesperson who identifies herself as part of Jewish orthodoxy, is "[t]o measure the halachik [legal] and religious status of Jewish women *against the feminist notion of equality of women*."[11]

It is interesting that the liberals Zecher and Alpert and the orthodox (albeit an unorthodox orthodox) Greenberg agree on the spiritual importance and moral validity of feminist insights. Before feminism, it could not have occurred to a self-identified Orthodox Jew to challenge the "halachik" status of women in terms of a standard not explicitly Jewish! And progressive Jews, less wedded to Halachah (law), would nevertheless not have had feminism to call on. These are profound *religious* shifts based in part on *secular* political insights.

Religious feminists do not reject the holiness of their traditions, but they do challenge their traditions' claims to self-sufficiency. For them, religion-as-it-has-existed reveals by the very fact of its patriarchy that it has fundamental flaws in need of repair. Whatever essential holiness is there, the feminist critics maintain, coexists with historical limitations, partiality, and "sin." Awareness of such sin permits—some might say, demands—women to question virtually every aspect of their faith. They ask: Does any given rule, value, claim, or role presume the second-class status and inferior value of women—of their souls or intellects, their bodily functions or moral character? Armed with the answers to these questions, feminists separate the spiritual wheat from the sexist chaff: Whatever is holy cannot entail the degradation of women.

To put the point another way: With the advent of a feminist critique, women can sense that what has been defined as their *religious* identity, ordained as necessary by God or their nature, is actually in some ways a reflection of their *social* situation. As such, that definition is deeply colored by contingent arrangements of power, privilege, and status—a reflection of the long history of the wars between the sexes. But this insight is exactly what a purely *religious* interpretation of religion must deny. From a traditional viewpoint, religious claims, including those about gender, escape the partial and limited character of social life.

As a key example of how feminist criticisms change our sense of religious life, let us return to the Prophets, whose urgent calls for social justice and compassion are a hallmark of the relation between monotheistic thought and social criticism. What the Prophets say, in no uncertain terms, is that God lives in history and places certain demands on people to act morally *within* history. If we are to serve God, we must not fast while ignoring the poor, or perform sacrifices today and accept bribes tomorrow. When Jesus laments the treatment of the poor and cautions, "Whatever you have done to the least of these, you have done to Me,"[12] he repeats the message. The prophetic God, as it were, keeps popping up where you least expect it. For Moses, God is the thunderous voice in the clouds, for Elijah a "still, small voice," and then (surprise!) God is "in" or "is" the beggar on the street corner, the starving orphan, the servant without enough blankets to keep off the nighttime chill.

Yet along with clarion calls for justice, there is another theme in prophetic literature—one that is deeply patriarchal and misogynistic. This theme is the repeated description of the people of Israel as womanly and of God as male and the identification of Israel's moral and spiritual weaknesses with those of "women."

> In graphic depictions of adulterous sex, the prophets equate woman's desire with the appetite for idolatry, women's eroticism with betrayal of the covenant. The prophet pulls the reader into a shared voyeurism, recounting these forbidden sexual pleasures and the stripping and punishment that follow them. "Abandoning me, you have gone up/On the couch you made so wide. You have made a covenant with them./You loved bedding with them." (Isaiah 57:8–9)[13]

In this metaphoric marriage between God and His unfaithful Israel, it is often presumed that "a husband has exclusive ownership over his wife's sexuality, her desire, her very body. He can threaten to strip the unfaithful woman and leave her to die of thirst (Hosea 2:5) to cast out her children (2:6) to block her flight to her lovers by holding her prisoner (2:8), to humiliate her publicly by exposing her genitals (2:12)."[14]

The feminization of Israel and Israel's sins against God has many pernicious consequences. It identifies women with lack of self-control, hypersexuality, and the need for men's instruction and chastisement. It projects an entire nation's failings onto one part of the nation, obscuring the fact that it was almost always men, rather than women, who *led* the nation. Because of the violence of the imagery, as one commentator puts it, the God of the Prophets, for all His attention to social justice, is also an abuser of His "wife." God is thus represented in a way that legitimates violence against women in purely human marriages.[15] This theology of male domination appears throughout traditional religion—from the original Buddhist teaching that nuns must be subservient to monks to the Book of Revelation's feminizing of a community of sin—and has been used to legitimize physical and emotional abuse of women for centuries.[16]

The misogyny of the Prophets is but one example of traditional religions' sexism. For example, some key passages in the Torah are essential to defining the Jewish people, yet are formulated so as to seem only to be addressed to men ("Moses warned the people to stay pure . . . And he said . . . 'Be ready for the third day: do not go near a woman.'").[17] A strict gender division of labor allotted religious authority and advanced education exclusively to men. Under Talmudic law, women cannot testify in religious courts and are dependent on men for divorce.

Besides the legal differences between men and women in Jewish law and the frequent historical absence of women in narratives shaping Jewish identity, key expressions of Jewish spirituality ignore the differences in men and women's typical life situation. Two examples of this last issue deserve mention, for they apply to areas that are not bound to orthodoxy but are potentially relevant to virtually every form of Jewish life. Further, as broadly spiritual concerns, they can easily be extended to any religious path whatsoever.

Consider, for example, how the Baal Shem Tov (the mystically oriented eighteenth-century founder of Hasidic Judaism) suggested it would be a good thing to meditate for an hour to clear one's mind and focus one's attention *before* reciting morning prayers. Now most people who take religious life seriously can appreciate the importance of prayer and of using meditation as a way to deepen both the immediate experience of prayer and the morally beneficial changes in personal behavior that prayer can bring about. Yet what mother in a traditional household would have that quantity of time at her disposal? And what traditional rabbi would have recommended an equitable division of household labor so that women as well as men could engage in meditation to purify their prayers? The original suggestion is offered as a way to develop the spiritual life of "Jews," without acknowledging that it develops that life for Jewish *men* while depending on (and possibly increasing) the domestic labor of Jewish *women*. The unstated fact is that the spiritual activities of any family member are made possible by the domestic labor that supports it. Traditional Judaism's answer to this problem was to excuse women from almost all regular prayers. No need for them to meditate beforehand, since they had little obligation to pray in any case. But what then happens to their need for the emotional and spiritual sustenance that prayer can provide? How will women get some regular, scheduled spiritual isolation from daily tasks, the kind men get when they pray? If we are then told that women are naturally more spiritual than men and don't need regular observance, we might wonder why this "natural" gift is not reflected in women being trained as rabbis and teachers.

Even more central to the entire practice of Judaism is the commandment to honor the Sabbath. As discussed earlier in Chapter 4, the Sabbath is traditionally understood as a time when no work is done, with work defined as the forty-two kinds of labor needed to construct the tabernacles of the covenant. Those who perform that kind of labor get to rest, pray, celebrate the miracle of existence, remember the exodus from Egypt, and study the tradition. Yet certain kinds of labor—the care of children, the old, or the sick—cannot be suspended on the Sabbath. Infants need to be fed, bathed, and supervised; the disabled need help with the basics of life. Given the traditional gender division of labor, therefore, women must "work" on the Sabbath. What is rest for carpenters, wagon drivers, electricians, cobblers, jewelers, farmers, computer programmers, or any other "male" worker is another day of caring labor for their wives, daughters, or mothers. Today, even if both husband and wife have paid jobs, women are much more likely to be responsible for domestic labor.[18]

There are ways around this dilemma—such as having men do half the housework and child care; but these ways will not be found until domestic labor is recognized *as* labor and some ethical energy is put into sharing it equally. Unfortunately, what is most striking is not that the division of labor limited the restfulness of the Sabbath for women but that even liberal twentieth-century theologians and spiritual writers who celebrate the Sabbath missed this obvious problem until feminism arrived (and many of them missed it even after feminism arrived). The great contribution of the Sabbath to world civilization and to maintaining the Jewish people was celebrated, but its unequal meaning for women and men was invisible. Before this inequality can be seen, we must have a feminist movement that creates an awareness of the gendered division of labor, the invisibility of "housework," and the devaluation of the culturally "female" labor of nurturing and care.

The point is not just that the traditions are sexist. It is, again, that their sexism could not be recognized, challenged, or overcome without the analytical tools and human community of a secular political movement. Religions cannot know their own limitations by themselves. Holiness requires politics.

——— · ———

Of course, it is hardly news to say that secular forces alter religion. Ever since Max Weber and R. H. Tawney argued over whether the rise of Protestantism was a result or a cause of capitalist individualism, we have been familiar with the idea that changes in theology may be the result of changed social conditions.[19]

But when sociologists argue about changes in religious life, they are clearly not assessing those changes in terms of religious aspirations. They are *explaining*, as outsiders, what they do not *accept* as insiders. Within Christianity, people disputed (and died!) over whether Protestantism was an improvement of Christianity or a distortion of it. Whichever position believers took, they could not see their beliefs as a product of history. They argued in religious terms, and they did not (and could not) appeal to forces external to religion.

Yet when self-consciously Jewish, Christian, or Buddhist feminists invoke standards of fairness, equality, and justice, they are importing *into* religion secular ideas aimed at making religions more . . . religious! And when they invoke a feminist understanding of what fairness, equality, and justice mean, they are reinterpreting some of their religion's basic moral ideals in political terms.

How is this done?

The basic principle is that aspects of religion that demean the spiritual validity or limit the religious participation of women are thereby, as Ruether puts it, "presumed not to reflect the divine." Yet how can women know this? That is, by what insight or revelation do they revoke centuries-old traditions of patriarchy while claiming that they themselves remain within the traditions they are altering?

Here we return to a theme developed in Chapter 2: how modern religions have learned to combine acceptance of theological differences with a greater concentration on human relationships. Feminism's critique of religion continues this trend. Certain ethical principles, or ways of understanding ethical principles, become primary. The ethical, as it were, becomes the limiting condition of the metaphysical. What we are willing to believe about God is now bounded by what we can believe about justice. Whatever else God is, God can no longer be a support for social inequality. In other contexts we have seen changes from support of slavery to support of abolition, from acceptance of segregation to its rejection, from participation in anti-Semitism to realizing that anti-Semitism is evil. Now the issue is the treatment of women.[20]

If by "tradition" we mean what people actually did, then sexism is traditional—however much reformist theologians may argue at a later time that earlier views were distortions of the "real" meaning of the faith. Challenging sexist norms in favor of new ones requires a profoundly *new* interpretation of the original revelations, a new interpretation built on a specific political movement and ideology. John Cobb captures the essential point: "One can justify [gender] equality by using certain scriptures, but one is unlikely to do so if one is motivated only by conformation to the canon. Only when one accepts insights coming out of contemporary feminism is one likely to find that these are supported in scripture."[21]

Feminism uses two basic tools of progressive political theory to accomplish its revision. The first tool is the value of democratic equality. Human beings are born, says liberal political theory, in a condition of political equality, and any political inequalities that exist must be rationally justified as a deviation from that original condition. Inequality cannot be inherited or presumed.[22] Although the original liberal target was the privileges of the aristocracy, feminism has extended the principle. It has denied that physiological differences between men and women justify political inequality, any more than differences in wealth (or height, for that matter) justify them among men. Once this principle is accepted, religious teachings are placed in a defensive position. On what initial basis, it is asked, *can* you distinguish between a man and a woman? If the traditionalist's response is: "On the basis of our original Revelation or Teaching," the feminist reply is: "You have misunderstood or misinterpreted that teaching." The traditionalist's rejoinder is likely to be: "But the tradition has always been what *we* say it is!"

At this point feminists employ their second tool, which is another principle of secular political life—the critique of ideology derived from Marxism.[23] (Typically, such usage occurs without attribution or even knowledge of the tool employed. Like the principle of democracy, Marx's critique of ideology has simply become common knowledge.) This critique asserts that what people believe is always to some extent shaped by their personal interests, historical experience, and social position. The dominant ideas of an age, Marx claimed, tend to favor the group in power, and usually do so while purporting to be divinely inspired or objectively rational. Because the social elite has a special power over education, religious institutions, the media, and cultural life in general, belief systems tailored to the interests of some particular group are presented as being in the interests of everyone. In this theory of ideology, democracy is extended from the realm of political rights to that of knowledge and values. Since an elite group will always tend to support beliefs that reinforce their power, a community where power is not subject to collective control cannot generate trustworthy beliefs.

The application of this point to women and religion was phrased nicely by Rabbi Zecher: "What we understand as the Word of God will depend on who gets to report on their religious experiences. Women, for millennia, were simply not allowed to report."[24] Women's experience, and the beliefs and values to which such experience would give rise, are absent. Religious traditionalists reply by saying that equality is a secular value, not a religious one and that in any case there are good *religious* reasons for the inequality (as, for instance, there are good secular reasons for us to delegate authority to cops or senators). The feminist response is: "How can you know what good religious reasons are, since you have systematically prevented women from contributing to our sense of what religion is or should be?" In other words, what we know of God, our rules for religious living, our sense of moral rules and ethical virtues, will be deeply flawed unless the full community can participate in framing them. Without inclusion, the interests of the particular can masquerade as the universal: the desire of men to perpetuate their social power at the expense of women and maintain their positive religious valuation at the expense of the religious devaluation of women will all too easily cloud men's judgment.[25]

Christian writers such as Letty Russell, Rosemary Ruether, Mary Hunt, and Beverly Harrison express this point by asserting that since God is understood only by a community, how much holiness we can perceive depends on how just our community is. Therefore, realizations about ways in which the community is unjust necessarily lead to changes in religious understanding. In this view, the originally egalitarian texts or insights are not misunderstood by a sexist culture (as, for instance, Rita Gross claims happened in Buddhism). Rather, the religious systems created then had the inevitable limitations of the communities that produced them. Therefore, the task is not to find the "real" meaning of the old texts "but to forge a just community that will allow a liberating message to emerge today."[26]

———

Feminists criticize traditional religions' basic teachings about women, especially religion's assertion of women's second-class status in religious institutions, the family, and the public realm. Two other issues, perhaps less obvious but surely of critical importance, are also of concern.

The first has to do with access to the particular, vital resources for human living that spiritual practices can offer. When feminists challenge the religious meaning of the tradition and the place of women within it, they are engaging in a political struggle over some of the fundamental benefits of social life. Communal worship, myths to help us understand the structure of life, comfort in our afflictions, inspiration to carry through in hard times—all these are part of what religion can offer. When women are denied full participation and devalued within religions, their access to these "goods" is lessened.

In traditional Judaism, women can only participate in important communal rituals in segregated, screened-off areas, so their access to the benefits of prayer and the tradition are minimized. When the countless prayers of blessing for life's little miracles (for food and drink, for seeing sights of nature, for success, and so on) that give Judaism part of its particular richness fail to include a single formula for experiences like first menstruation, menopause, and pregnancy, it is clear that resources for a spiritual life are distributed unjustly. Comparable problems arise in other religions when women cannot see female role models as priests or meditation teachers. In such cases, women's spiritual identity is limited because they cannot identify with socially affirmed spiritual models. The demand that these resources be equally accessible to women is a political struggle just as much as women's pursuit of equal pay, professional advancement, and freedom from violence.

Yet it is not only equality that is sought, but also a fundamental change in some of the basic concepts and practices of religion itself. Consider, for instance, women rabbis (and the point, I'm sure, can be extended to women ministers, priests, and spiritual "masters" as well). As Laura Geller points out, female rabbis have often shown a significantly different set of priorities than men. Rather than pursuing an ever-larger congregation, public presence, or prestige, women rabbis place more priority on empowering their members, balancing work life and home life, and maintaining intimate connections with others. As one of the first Reconstructionist women rabbis says: "Women's version of reality is not a hierarchical model where the goal is to move up, to be alone at the top, but rather a network model where the goal is to connect with others, to be together at the center."[27] We might add that the typical male rabbi always needed a wife if he was to have a family life. When the rabbi *is* a wife, we are likely to get some new models of both what it is to be a rabbi and what it is to be a wife.

In another example, Judith Plaskow questions the very status of law (Halachah) as essential to Judaism. Perhaps, she muses, a rigid, controlling theology issuing from those at the top of a religious hierarchy is not the model that Judaism—and by implication any religion—should take.[28] Here Plaskow, like other feminists, is consciously or inadvertently using Carol Gilligan's widely cited distinction between female and male styles of moral reasoning. Gilligan claimed that in ethical dilemmas, women tended to reason in terms of empathy, connection, and compassion rather than by seeking a single set of hierarchically ordered abstract principles. It was relationship rather than judgment, empathy rather than universal reason to which they appealed. With Gilligan and other writers like her, the very structure of moral reasoning was put in question.[29] Feminists do the same with familiar religious concepts.

That is why feminists who discuss the nature of God do not stop at questioning traditional claims about how God wants women to be subservient to their husbands or desires only male priests. Rather, feminists question the names by which God is known and the concepts used to describe God. Instead of solely masculine pronouns, women introduced female ones, and thus invited worshipers to imagine God as a mother as well as a father, as a birth giver as well as a bodiless creator, a source of compassion as much as a law-giver. Nel Noddings suggests that serious ethical failings may result when God's omnipotence and omniscience are stressed and other, more relational attributes, are ignored:

> [T]he religious tradition has blinded us ethically. Since God, who clearly has the knowledge and the power to do otherwise, inflicts or allows the greatest of suffering, the inflicting of pain cannot be a *primary* ethical abuse. Since God hides himself from us, the neglect of a loving personal relation cannot be a primary evil, and the responsibility for remaining in contact falls to the weak and dependent. Since God presents the world to us in impenetrable mystery, there is precedent for mystification and the dependent and powerless must learn to trust authority.[30]

Similarly, Plaskow offers a clear rule for what may, and may not, be used: "Traditional images like lord and king, for example evoke by definition relations of domination. Since it is difficult to imagine how such images could be transformed . . . they need to be seen as injurious reflections and supports of a hierarchical social system, and excised from our religious vocabularies."[31]

Feminists seek to imagine God in a variety of roles and forms and to allow us to use the idea of God without being wedded to any *single* version. As victims of rigid theology and institutional hierarchy, feminist theologians almost always stress that multiplicity is not a threat to spiritual purity but is a development beneficial to the entire religious community. For instance, lesbian Episcopal priest Carter Heyward identifies God with, among other things, the erotic connection between loving partners. In doing so, she is not invoking the familiar concept of God and then asking (as it were) for God's approval of her lesbianism. Rather, she is expanding the ways in which we can think about God.[32]

This development can lead to dramatic reversals in the way familiar texts are understood. Rachel Adler, for instance, criticizes the prophetic image of the God-human relation as abusive and sexist. Yet, she continues, this image of the relation *also* humanizes God, showing a kind of vulnerability to human love.[33] To think of God as somehow in need of us is a relational, culturally female idea. Unlike the dominant theme of most masculine accounts, it moves away from the image of God as all-powerful and totally self-enclosed. In Noddings's words, "A fallible God . . . still struggling toward an ethical vision [is] lovable and understandable to women [but] may be unattractive to many men because he cannot make absolute claims on us for worship, obedience, and authority . . . A fallible god shakes the entire hierarchy, and endangers men in their relations to women, children, animals, and the whole living environment."[34]

In this search for a new language and new religious sensibility, the point, as Adler suggests, is to take the concept of God *seriously*, but not *literally*.[35] This orientation continues and develops Kierkegaard's point that definitions of and proofs for the existence and nature of God are really external to an authentic religious life and that one should focus on a personal relation to God, on sincerity and devotion, rather than on an "objective" description of divinity. Most, if not all, feminist theologians (consciously or not) are building on this perspective. However, they make the relation to God collective rather than purely personal. And they add the political principles of justice, mutual respect, fairness, and equality as markers of true faith, moving beyond Kierkegaard's painfully individualistic and culturally masculine perspective.

Some defenders of the patriarchal status quo argue that the feminist stance simply imports a foreign *political* viewpoint into religion. The Enlightenment values of democracy and rights may be fine for sustaining social peace in our inevitably pluralistic modern societies—in fact, that might be how they got there[36]—but they are inappropriate for religion. A critique of ideology might be appropriate for biased media. But ultimately, traditionalists often contend, there is such a thing as expertise: the legitimate authority of those who have been authorized to speak for God, to know the truth, and to instruct those who are less holy, knowledgeable, or competent. One no more needs democracy and equality in a church, their argument might continue, than one needs them in an operating room or the cockpit of a jetliner. For example, responding to the notion that each person might serve as his or her own spiritual authority, an Orthodox rabbi responds: "If you break a leg, don't go to a foot doctor to set that bone. Set it yourself!"[37] (Some joke!)

Feminist theologians reply that they are not turning their back on legitimate authority; they are rejecting the claim that male religious leaders have been legitimate authorities in the first place. Male religious "doctors," these critics maintain, have been systematically mis-setting the "broken bones" of women for a very long time. Their supposed expertise is deeply flawed; and the fact that they cannot see their failures is but one more indication that their inherited authority is illegitimate. Moreover, the analogy itself is mistaken from the start. Medicine that without reason forbade the training of women doctors would be for that very reason suspect; and in fact the rise of feminism and the increased number of women doctors and researchers have altered the diagnosis and treatment of women and the actual direction of a good deal of medical research. Medical authority is no more gender-neutral than any other kind.

More generally, the feminist point is that the religious context never was "purely" religious, if by that term we mean an immaculate and totally open response to the word of God (or to the kind of insightful experiences about consciousness that are the basis of Buddhism). It was *always* political, in the sense that it always reflected norms for the distribution of power, privilege, and collective respect. It was always political in that the community that experienced the original revelation (who stood at Sinai, who heard Jesus or Buddha speak)—and every community since that time—has rules about who can preach and who is to be silent, who interprets and who merely receives what has been decided. The feminist goal, in Adler's words, is to "constitute a new interpretive community," one more likely to hear the truth.[38] In that spirit, for instance, Rochelle Millen analyzed Talmudic passages in which women were exempt from time-bound commandments, thus guaranteeing their consignment to child care and their exclusion from central dimensions of Jewish religious life. She concluded that the actual rabbinic arguments were weak and were more aimed at reflecting and reinforcing the prevailing gender division of labor than carrying forward anything specifically Jewish. The broad point, she tells us, is that theology has always had, and can be seen to have had, a sociological basis.[39]

This basis is further reflected in the way the actual history of women's religious participation and authority has been ignored or forgotten. The tradition, some writers discovered, was not as "traditional" as contemporary traditionalists say it was![40] The closer we get to a modern society in which women's full participation could actually become normative, the more the historical precedents of such participation are denied. So it is not just the past sexism of the tradition that is at stake, but also the way accounts of the past are manipulated in order to preserve sexism in the present. For example, Elisabeth Schussler Fiorenze has done groundbreaking work on the role of women during early Christianity. Women have played, she argues, "an authentic history within biblical religions," and therefore they should reclaim their place in those religions rather than simply walk away.[41] Historian Tikva Frymer-Kensky found women with social power in the Biblical period and argues that Judaism's later misogyny was partly assimilated from Greek culture.[42] Or consider this pointed statement supporting women's rabbinical ordination: "There are those who say that the Halachah does not permit women rabbis because rabbis are judges, and women cannot be judges since women cannot be witnesses. But what about Deborah [who served as a judge in the Bible]? If a woman could serve as a judge then, she can serve as rabbi now."[43]

The overall question, then, is not whether religion should be touched by politics. It is, rather, what kind of politics will be doing the touching.[44]

In response to this question, Julie Greenberg asks, "How dare men claim the prerogative to define Judaism for us all [women as well as men]?"[45] The traditionalist reply is likely to be: "We aren't defining, we are recording, and at most tinkering with what others have recorded." Ultimately, there may be no way out of this disagreement, except to observe that once religion is seen as partly a human creation, and exactly to the extent that it is, a progression toward concepts of rights, equality, and the critique of ideology may be inevitable. To traditionalists who claim that religion is *not* a human creation or that their goal is to preserve the unchanging essence of the religion against the encroachments of modernity, it may only be possible to make the following reply. "Will you," we ask, "turn back the clock so that religion once again supports aristocracy against democracy; accepts racism; preaches violent misogyny and anti-Semitism; uncritically endorses modern industrialism; and—let's not forget—requires animal sacrifice?" If traditionalists are happy with these positions, little can be said. But if they are not, then they are open, at least in principle, to fundamental changes sparked by or including political principles. At that point the only question is whether they agree with the *particular* political demands of feminism, for they have already accepted, like it or not, that religion can be improved by politics.

Openness to change, feminists argue, and thus to politically motivated change, is part of what religion is. As Gross says about Buddhism, but in a statement echoed many times by writers from other traditions: "Buddhism is not a closed, finished, and unchangeable system, but like any living religious symbol system, changes and incorporates nontraditional elements into itself."[46]

In this respect, of course, religions are similar to other social practices that aim at some "good": from science and art to philosophy and anthropology. As Alasdair MacIntyre has convincingly argued: Traditions are actually constituted by the pursuit of some purpose that the tradition itself defines, and also by the continuing struggles over the precise nature of that purpose and what it will take to achieve it.[47] Religions seek God or enlightenment, just as artists seek beauty, chess masters seek excellence at chess, and car designers seek the best possible car. As long-standing historical traditions, religions are marked both by acceptance of some common revelation, text, or teaching and by continuing struggles over the meaning of those common elements. Whether male or female, Buddhists will continue to pursue enlightenment, Jews to serve God, and Christians to have faith in Jesus; but debates will rage (as they have from the beginning) on what all this means.

Accordingly, a Christian feminist may argue that the original intention of the gospel was not sexism but gender equality, and that later misogynistic developments were distortions of the original meaning. If the gender egalitarianism of the initial revelation was not seen, it was only because of the decidedly *un*-Christian sexism of the male-dominated church.[48] Buddhist feminists can argue that Buddha's assertions about how social role and the body are not essential to our identity imply that gender is irrelevant to spiritual life. In Rita Gross's words: "Perhaps the key element in the strategy for a feminist revalorization [i.e., reinterpretation along feminist lines] of any major world religion is to demonstrate that *the core teachings of the tradition do not permit bias or discrimination* on the basis of gender, and that they are essentially egalitarian in their implications, no matter how sexist some historical interpretations may have been."[49]

In this light, Gross has described many recorded teaching dialogues that either feature women as the source of knowledge or stress that enlightenment has no gender. Like the Christian feminist, the Buddhist feminist then argues that these texts contained the religious truth of the matter and that the many sexist aspects of actual Buddhist practice (e.g., rejecting women as institutional leaders, claiming that women had to be reincarnated as men to reach enlightenment, and so forth) reflected a systematic, unjust, and religiously incorrect development of doctrine. What was ignored is now given attention and respect. And what was taken as central is now pushed to the periphery.

———— • ————

Feminist religion has much to teach us about how secular political movements contain resources for religious life. However, what of the relation between feminist religious efforts and secular feminists' struggles for equal rights, attempts to end violence against women, and pursuit of a transformed, nonsexist society?

For a start, the feminist position leads to solidarity among women from different faiths. Just as conservative religionists have made common cause around issues such as church-state relations, pornography, and homosexuality, so feminists find themselves reading each other's work and reaching a position of spiritual mutuality. When Judith Plaskow speaks of the effort to find new names for God in Judaism, she invokes comparable efforts by Christian women.[50] When Christian Anne Clifford writes a book called *Introducing Feminist Theology*, she pays careful attention to the perspectives of Asian, African-American, Hispanic, and African Christians, having learned from secular political movements the dangers of privileging the experiences and beliefs of white Europeans.[51]

More broadly, feminist theologians generally view themselves as necessarily in solidarity with theologies from other oppressed groups: Third World peoples, disadvantaged minorities, gays, and lesbians. Once political criticism of religion is taken to be part of religion itself, religion must then turn its eyes to political realities outside the church, meditation hall, or synagogue. Realizing that they have been inspired by a secular movement to reimagine their faith, feminist theologians are impelled to see their now-politicized faith as an essential element in comprehending—and remaking—the world.

To the extent that feminist theology and spirituality challenge the dominant cultural devaluation of women, they cannot help but be part of the overall feminist political movement. It is hard, after all, to imagine women achieving equality in other spheres while their necessarily sinful or deficient nature is being taught—at least without being contested—in the churches. It is hard—or at least much harder than it need be—to imagine women in positions of secular authority if positions of religious authority are closed. Further, as I have argued above, religion itself offers certain "goods," the distribution of which can be morally and politically evaluated. In these ways the feminist transformation of religious life is itself a political event. To seek justice anywhere is to seek it politically; and that includes the prayer service and Bible interpretation as well as in the factory, the legislature, and the bedroom.

It is therefore interesting to note that within the women's movement itself, a tension between "political" and "spiritual" (or "religious") feminism has at times surfaced. This conflict is most evident in regard to those forms of feminist spirituality that reject traditional religion altogether, but it also applies to feminist theology in the context of the dominant religions.

On the political side, spiritual feminists were charged with being self-indulgent, narcissistic, apolitical, individualistic, and attached to world-denying metaphysical fairy stories. Spiritual feminists were much less likely to dismiss the activities or goals of the political side but defended their own feminist credentials by asserting that self-transformation was essential to political change, that spiritual resources were essential to sustaining activists through the long hard years of political struggle, and that politics without spiritual values were often marked by counterproductive anger and vindictiveness. In general, each side has been put off by the style of the other: sometimes with good reason, and sometimes because of irrational fears and prejudices.[52] In short, all the standard charges and countercharges described in Chapters 3 and 4 were repeated. All were to some extent true, and all, at the same time, false. That is, they were true to the extent that feminist world-making secular politics and feminist spirituality have valid criticisms of each other; and they were false to the extent that these criticisms cut both ways, and in no case invalidated the importance or value of either side.

What then is the meaning of the conflict, such as it has been, between religious and political feminists? For one thing, there are differences in temperament, vocabulary, and emphasis that, in a context of struggle against a long-dominant patriarchal system, lead to unnecessary conflict. Activists of all stripes are still people: people who feel more comfortable with those who talk, dress, think, and act like themselves. People oriented to religion or spiritual expression often have a different style than those who never developed this aspect of life or who have rejected the religious ties of their childhood. People who are trying to make the world anew are inevitably in a minority, always haunted by fears of isolation, failure, and irrelevance. They often reserve their sharpest criticisms for those closest, because it is those closest— other feminists, in this instance—whom they need the most and of whom they are most afraid when differences arise.

More particularly, Cynthia Eller observes, political activists tend to focus on short-term, immediate goals, whereas spiritual feminists think in "religious time." "Religious feminism," says Eller, "is not primarily interested in political successes that must be secured this year to the next. It is more interested in a vision that—once realized—will end forever the need for incremental political successes."[53] Such utopianism, say more politically oriented feminists, is both comforting and escapist. And it can, indeed, often mask self-indulgence and the creation of a cozy communal space at the expense of concern with pressing issues that face women on a daily basis. Less reasonably, there is a knee-jerk political rejection of some spiritual practices such as prayer, meditation, and ritual. These practices, political types have insisted, are "escapist ... focusing on inner subjective reality as opposed to external objective conditions." They are at best irrelevant and at worst a distraction from "the "real" political work that needs to be done."[54]

On the religious side, there has been some resistance to the emotional tone of anger and condemnation that almost always accompanies activist politics. There has also been a constant assertion that the psychic and spiritually energetic aspects of reality are no less central to women's liberation than issues of political rights or control of the economy and that the avowedly secular political feminists sometimes reproduce patriarchy's false divisions between matter and spirit, society and psyche, masculinity and femininity.[55]

Once again, all these complaints are both valid and limited. In each case, the side being criticized has much to learn from the criticism. Feminist politics, sadly like male-dominated politics, have suffered from narrow-mindedness, unnecessary conflict, an inability to sustain activists over the long haul, unnecessary sectarianism, and vituperative styles of interaction. Each of these might have been mitigated by the presence of authentic religious values of compassion, forgiveness, humility, trust in God, meditative awareness, and recognition of how the divine can be found within even the most misguided opponent. On the religious side, there unfortunately remains a tendency toward unjustified self-righteousness, escapism, and a desire to ignore the wider world in favor of simply reforming the "church" at hand.[56]

However, the spiritual-political conflict within feminism has always been a great deal less intense than in other contexts. There was much more mutual conversation, and even mutual criticisms that were actually listened to, than between, say, the Communist Party and the Catholic Church, or the Socialist Party and mainline Protestant denominations. Coming after the civil rights and the antiwar movements, feminism was able to take advantage of a political scene that had witnessed religious figures in the thick of demonstrations, manifestos, and civil disobedience. Martin Luther King Jr. is the most famous of these, but the list behind him was significant. Individuals like William Sloan Coffin, Daniel and Philip Berrigan, and Abraham Joshua Heschel, and organizations like Clergy and Laity Concerned About the War in Vietnam, achieved a vital national presence. Once America witnessed that presence, it was much harder for political radicals to dismiss religious values as irrelevant to social struggle and for religious figures to suggest that political struggles and spiritual life should be kept separate. Similar connections were made around the world. From the religious role in Europe's antinuclear movement to Archbishop Romero, from Latin American liberation theology to the role of religious activists in anti-apartheid struggles, the alienation of religion and progressive politics became harder and harder to take for granted.

The reconciliation of religion and politics is furthered for feminists by the fact that women working within established religions *had* to invoke political concepts like justice and equality to voice their criticisms. And their criticisms could not help but be attuned to the way men's self-interest masqueraded as universal religious truth. For such writers, it was typically impossible not to see religious sexism as a species of the sexism of the entire social order. As Sandra Wilson, a black Episcopal priest, writes, "I use the church as my case study, but what I have to say is, I believe, applicable to black women in institutions in all of society . . . At the top of the ladder is the . . . White Anglo-Saxon Protestant male . . . at the bottom . . . the black female."[57]

Thankfully, many feminists opposed simplistic, old-style oppositions between spirituality and political life. Charlene Spretnak has argued that "[b]oth politics and spirituality are concerned with power—power created, maintained, and utilized in alignment with a particular view of life."[58] Other writers have stressed the commonality of oppression women experienced in the spheres of religion and politics, pointing out that a rigid division between the two arenas was yet another manifestation of male dualistic thinking, not unlike those between male and female, spirit and matter, reason and emotions. In particular, violence against women, an early theme of the women's movement and chronicled in books like Susan Brownmiller's classic study of rape, was seen to have theological as well as secular roots. Religion, feminists argued, made male power seem natural. The struggle against theology was thereby political—just as religion itself always was.[59]

Similarly, for those women who pursued women's spirituality outside the bounds of the dominant religion, their "enemy" was patriarchal culture as a whole: thousands of years of hierarchy, exploitation, and misogyny. It was impossible for them even to frame their spiritual values without at the same time offering, at least by implication, a political critique of world culture.[60]

Further, because feminism necessarily bridges the gap between the private and the public spheres, the most intimate details of personal life come to be seen, by a woman whose consciousness has been raised, as political. Therefore, feminism undermined the tendency of more conventional progressive politics and conservative religion to accept a division between personal and political, private and public. It is hard for a feminist to accept the familiar religious negation of political life, "Change yourself before you change the world," when for women the "self" is so obviously bound up in the political structures of the world. A feminist religious spirit cannot be "private" or "personal" any more than a feminist assessment of marriage can be just about a relationship between two people. In both cases, the deepest longings of the heart are intimately related to social norms, cultural representations, collectively formed expectations, and a legally sanctioned distribution of power.

The deep connections between feminist politics and feminist religion show what can happen when world-making politics and religion are partners rather than enemies. The civil rights movement saw religious nonviolence provide the energy and direction to overturn segregation. Similarly, the feminist critique of unjustified male power offers a more coherent, fulfilling, and holy vision of religion. Without abandoning the quest to live by sacred values or God's truth, feminism has taught that these goals simply cannot be achieved if we do not attend to the justice of our human and spiritual communities alike.

7

Saving the World:
Religion and Politics in the
Environmental Movement

Christians are joining together to save the world's rainforests in Jesus'
name.

—Target Earth[1]

"Bishops Say Dealing with Global Warming a Moral Imperative"
—Boston Globe, June 16, 2001

We must learn to . . . recognize the interconnectedness of all living
creatures, and to respect the value of each thread in the vast web of
life. This is a spiritual perspective, and it is the foundation of all
Green politics.

—Petra Kelly, Thinking Green[2]

Two short stories:

March 25, 2000. Over 1,000 people crowded the halls of the urban
campus of Boston's Northeastern University. This was, in terms
reminiscent of the 1960s, a teach-in. It was called Biodevastation—
in ironic parody of the simultaneous Boston gathering of high-tech

151

entrepreneurs, scientists, and policy wonks of the genetic engineering industry. Public demonstrations and civil disobedience actions were planned for the next day. Calls would be made for an end to the commercialization of genetically engineered products, corporate control over food and health, and ownership of forms of life (patenting of seeds, and so on); and for tighter public regulations of potentially dangerous biotechnologies.[3]

As one of the day's many workshops, I had been asked to give a talk about the role of spirituality in environmental politics. Because the crowd seemed heavily political, I wasn't sure anyone would show up. Much to my gratified surprise, the medium-size lecture hall held a standing-room-only crowd, with bearded activists, student leaders, and passionate organizers sprawled on the floor and spilling out into the hallway. Although I would have liked to believe it was my vast fame that had brought folks to hear me, I was well aware that most of them didn't know me from Adam, but were drawn by the topic. Like me, they intuited that resistance to the interconnected issues of global environmental crisis, genetic engineering of organisms, and centralized international power of institutions like the World Bank and the International Monetary Fund necessitate a new spiritual and political vision. Concern for humanity's place in the cosmos will have to join resistance to the inequalities of race and class; a moral commitment to future generations of human beings will be matched by care for other species; a deep distrust in the wisdom of markets will be balanced by an emerging faith in ordinary people's knowledge of their own lands and lives.

March 1998. In my own community of Jamaica Plain, a racially and economically mixed section of Southwest Boston, people are banding together to protect our treasured Jamaica Pond: an actual lake—one and one-half miles around—within the city limits! The pond is bordered by a thin belt of trees and graced by seagulls, Canada geese, ducks, mysterious looking cormorants, snapping turtles, and imported swans. Its marvelously clear water attracts joggers, baby carriages, dog walkers, drummers on hot summer nights, old Chinese ladies doing Tai Chi, and couples of various sexual persuasions dreamily holding hands. On brilliant weekends in July or sweltering August afternoons, city-owned rowboats and sailboats allow the city dwellers to feel like they've gone away to their country estates.

When you stand at the little boathouse where popsicles and pop-corn are sold, you can look across the water and see the sun set over wooded hills. These hills, which border the park but are not actually part of it, had been sold to a builder seeking to replace the old trees with luxury condos—so that proud owners can enjoy the vista of the pond while the rest of us can view the sun setting over expensive apartments. On the coldest night of the winter of 1998, 350 people jammed a local church to express their disagreement. After a variety of audience members spoke their piece, I approached the mike and said, quite gently, that I was going to use a word rarely heard in polit-ical circles but that I hoped people would understand. "The pond," I declared quietly, "is sacred space."

Although this was not a particularly religious crowd, a stunned si-lence soon gave way to a rising murmur of agreement that soon swept the room and culminated in sustained applause. In thirty years of university teaching and of public speaking in a wide variety of con-texts, I had never sensed such an immediate, visceral, and heartfelt response. I had voiced my truth, and it seemed to serve virtually everyone in the room.

These two stories illustrate the theme of this chapter, that in the environ-mental movement there is a dramatic confirmation of the major ideas of this book. World-making politics and emancipatory religion have joined in envi-ronmental politics and ecological spirituality. Theology has been trans-formed by political awareness and action. And political ideology has tran-scended the constraints of individual rights and group self-interest. If the civil rights struggle shows religion transforming the world of politics and feminist theology demonstrates the political transformation of religion, then the environmental movement reveals the two working together in critically important ways, at times virtually fusing to form a historically unprecedented phenomenon.

———————

Modern environmentalism has challenged and changed religion throughout the world. Awakened by environmental activists, religious institutions have been moved by the seriousness of pollution, climate change, endangered species issues, resource depletion, and overpopulation. Religious leaders, the-ologians, and local clergy have signed on to the recognition that the earth as a whole is in an unprecedented predicament. Even if this response is not uni-form and absolute, it is still extremely widespread.

Using language that would not be out of place in a Greenpeace broadside, Rabbi Arthur Hertzberg, vice president of the World Jewish Congress, has warned: "Now when the whole world is in peril, when the environment is in danger of being poisoned, and various species, both plant and animal, are becoming extinct, it is our Jewish responsibility to put the defense of the whole of nature at the very center of our concern."[4] In 1990, Pope John Paul II spoke of the worldwide threat caused by "a *lack of due respect for nature* . . . the plundering of natural resources and . . . the widespread destruction of the environment."[5] The Dalai Lama, in his foreword to the first major anthology of writings on Buddhism and ecology, wrote: "The Earth, our Mother, is telling us to behave. All around, signs of nature's limitations abound. Moreover, the environmental crisis currently underway involves all of humanity, making national boundaries of secondary importance."[6]

Yet claims that we are in ecological hot water do not, in themselves, make for a particularly religious contribution to environmentalism. Part of what is so important about that contribution is that it brings to the context a new language, expressing a distinct point of view. For instance, Bartholomew I, ecumenical patriarch of the Eastern Orthodox Church's more than 100 million members, wrote in 1997:

> To commit a crime against the natural world is a sin. For humans to cause species to become extinct and to destroy the biological diversity of God's creation . . . to degrade the integrity of Earth by causing changes in its climate, by stripping the Earth of its natural forests . . . to contaminate the Earth's waters, its land, its air, and its life, with poisonous substances: these are sins.[7]

Conversely, as a Protestant theologian and environmental activist puts it: "The specter of ecocide raises the risk of deicide: to wreak environmental havoc on the earth is to run the risk that we will do irreparable, even fatal harm to the mystery we call God."[8]

A religious perspective applied to the earth, to a "nature" that because of human action has become the "environment," offers insights and prompts emotions that a purely secular story cannot. Spiritual language offers the environmental movement a means to express its passion, hope, and love, regardless of whether activists accept the explicit details of one theology or another. Instead of a large rock with vegetation growing on it, the world becomes "creation" or "the goddess." We experience the world as "holy"—and mean we believe in a God who created it, or that it is of "ultimate concern," or simply that it is heartbreakingly beautiful and infinitely worth cherishing and preserving. Commonplace processes—the co-evolution of a rain-forest plant with its pollinating insect partners, how wetlands clean water, the murmur of whale songs—become "daily miracles."

When religion engages in environmental concerns, the customary boundaries of "religious issues" in political life are decisively broken. Asserting that environmental degradation is not only a health danger, an economic catastrophe, or an aesthetic blight but also *sacrilegious, sinful,* and an *offense against God* catapults religions directly into questions of political power, social policy, and the overall direction of secular society. Religious organizations now take it as given that their voices deserve to be heard on issues such as energy, economic development, population, transportation, industrial production, and agriculture. These topics are, to put it mildly, a far cry from the usual public religious concern with abortion, school prayer, tax exemptions for churches, Holocaust memorials, national Christmas trees, or even pornography in the media.

For example, in March 2001, six senior Christian and Jewish religious leaders wrote to President George W. Bush asking for a meeting with him about his environmental policy, especially around issues of climate change. In a fascinating combination of scriptural references, quotes from the Environmental Protection Agency (EPA), and appeals to scientific expertise, representatives of conservative Judaism (the chancellor of its major rabbinical school), the head of the National Council of the Churches of Christ, and senior officers of the Presbyterian Church, the United Methodist Church, the Disciples of Christ, and the African Methodist Episcopal Church sought to use religious authority to influence national politics.

In another instance, we find that the World Council of Churches (WCC), an international Christian umbrella organization representing 340 churches in 122 countries, has tied its environmental concerns to a deep suspicion of globalization. In doing so, it has challenged the globe's dominant institutions, from the International Monetary Fund and the World Bank to corporations whose budgets are larger than most countries. Globalization is intimately linked to environmentalism because the new global institutions consistently preempt local efforts to control pollution or create sustainable economies. Their tribunals have ruled against clean air legislation in the United States, Canadian restrictions on toxic gasoline additives, attempts to protect marine mammals, European rejection of hormone-injected beef, and efforts to support indigenous, organic farmers rather than Chiquita bananas.[9]

Recent developments have reinforced our perception that issues of justice, peace and creation need to be seen together. One such development is globalization. Globalization impacts not only national and regional economies, causing ever-greater social and economic injustice. It also destroys relationships between individuals, groups, communities, nations, causing conflicts, wars and violence. And it affects the environment of our whole inhabited earth.[10]

The secular left, too, has begun to realize that religious organizations are part of the environmental movement. In the May 2001 issue of *The Nation*, environmentalist David Helvarg has listed actions by the National Council of Churches, the Evangelical Environmental Network, and the Jewish Council of Public Affairs in an article titled, "Bush Unites the Enviros."[11] Over the past several years, all of the major environmental magazines—including *Sierra*, *Audubon*, *Amicus Journal*, and *E Magazine*—have run features on the rise of religious environmentalism.[12] They have recognized that from the National Religious Partnership for the Environment, with constituent groups numbering 100 million Americans, to the New England Friends' recent collective commitment to "speak truth to power" in protecting human health and the environment, self-defined religious groups are now major players on the environmental stage.

On the religious side, the environmental crisis is seen by some thinkers as the critical test of their faith's contemporary relevance. As Catholic priest and cultural historian Thomas Berry, whose own attempt to offer a new understanding of humanity's place in the cosmos has been enormously influential, says: "The future of the Catholic church in America, in my view, will depend above all on its capacity to assume a religious responsibility for the fate of the earth."[13] Bearing this out, the web site of the Lutheran Church offers study material on "health and the environment." One situation offered for reflection asks what a "Christian response" would be to a family whose children are suffering from environmentally caused asthma and who cannot move because no one will buy their house, which is surrounded by polluting industries.[14] For Lutherans, in other words, the interlocking contexts of health, the economy, and pollution are now part of their ministry—as much as sexual ethics or the discipline of prayer.

These few instances of the extremely numerous meetings between religion and environmentalism further exemplify modern religion's political transformation. Historically, the dominant attitudes of religious leaders toward modern industrialism—that is, to the immediate source of the environmental crisis—was positive. Once it was clear that capitalism and democracy were here to stay, most churches saw increases in scientific knowledge and technical expertise as promising a better life. Provided that industrial workers achieved a reasonable standard of living, technology meant progress. Challenges to the modern economy came from poets like Blake and Wordsworth, anti-Communist Western Marxists like Max Horkheimer and Herbert Marcuse, philosophers like Martin Heidegger, and imaginative nature lovers like Thoreau and John Muir. As in the case of feminism, it was only after a political movement brought global ecological crisis to the fore of public discussion that religion jumped on board.[15] Yet jump on board it did, and with an energy and acumen that has, so far, outpaced corporations, organized labor, the academic community, and such professionals as doctors or lawyers.

Besides an acknowledgment of the severity of the crisis, new theologies have been devised in which the earth, or nature, or our fellow creatures are recognized as carrying a divine and sacred meaning. Such theologies are in stark contrast to what has been the dominant position of world religions, especially those of the West. Despite the presence of occasional dissenting voices, Western religions long stressed the gap between humans and the rest of creation, espousing ethical systems in which concern for the nonhuman was peripheral at best. Just as feminism has required a new valuation of women, so the ecological crisis has led to a new—or at least a revised—sense of our proper relationship to nature.

These new theologies sometimes originate in attempts to recover the few nature-respecting elements that can be found in tradition. Thus, Lynn White, whose 1967 essay criticizing the "anthropocentrism" (human-centeredness) of Western religions helped initiate a dialogue on the subject that continues to this day, did not suggest a total rejection of Christianity. Rather, he proposed St. Francis's love of animals and the whole of physical creation as an alternative to the reigning Christian attitudes.[16] Similarly, essayist and farmer Wendell Berry challenged dominant interpretations of the biblical passage often cited as divine justification for human dominion, God's command to Adam: "Go forth, subdue the earth, and master it" (Genesis 1:28). By stressing the importance of other passages of the Torah, especially Deuteronomy 8:10 ("Thou shalt bless the lord thy God for the good land which He has given you"), Berry teaches that biblical ethics requires us to live "knowingly, lovingly, skillfully, reverently" rather than "ignorantly, greedily, clumsily, destructively." In the first case, our use of Creation will be a "sacrament," in the latter, a "desecration."[17] Jewish writers have recovered biblical and Talmudic doctrines stressing the sinfulness of squandering resources (*bal tashchit* ["do not waste"]), holidays celebrating the birthday of the trees, and biblical restrictions on the exploitation of animals (if your ox is threshing your grain, you can't muzzle him, even if he ends up eating some of it!). These traditions are then applied to a host of contemporary ecological issues, such as recycling, carpooling, the disposal of toxics, the waste of food, factory farming, and the protection of old-growth forests.[18]

Buddhist teacher Thich Nhat Hanh has adapted the mindfulness practice of Buddhist *gathas* (short prayers or poems used to focus attention) to include ecological awareness. For instance, while planting trees, one may recite: "I entrust myself to Buddha;/Buddha entrusts himself to me./I entrust myself to Earth;/Earth entrust herself to me."[19] The National Council of Churches offers the following prayer to be included in First Sunday after Easter as part of a service called "Witnessing to the Resurrection: Caring for God's Creation":

> We pursue profits and pleasures that harm the land and pollute the waters.
> We have squandered the earth's gifts on technologies of destruction.
> The land mourns, and all who live in it languish; together with the wild animals and the birds of the air, even the fish of the sea are perishing.[20]

Or in the words of the general secretary of the United Methodist Church: "Our biblical tradition affirms that God calls people of faith to defend and protect all of God's creation, both human and non-human."[21]

———————

Feminist versions of Christianity and Judaism may, in good conscience, focus their efforts on creating inclusive God language, getting women into positions of power in religious organizations, and criticizing the sexism of past doctrine. By contrast, the new theologies of nature necessarily involve their adherents in political life. Once religions assert that "ecology and justice, stewardship of creation and redemption are interdependent"[22] or that "[w]here human life and health are at stake, economic gain must not take precedence,"[23] they are—like it or not—headed for a confrontation with the dominant powers of economics and politics.

In this confrontation, religious discourse has and will continue to play a significant role. If this is not a universal religious response, it is an extremely widespread one. As one journalist puts it: "More and more it appears religion and ecology are walking hand-in-hand. The sermon titles are the Kyoto treaty on global warming and endangered species protection."[24] For example, there is the 1997–1999 campaign of the "Redwood Rabbis," a group of rabbis and lay Jewish environmental activists who struggled to protect an ancient redwood grove in Northern California. Working with the local Sierra Club, the group invoked biblical principles and contemporary ecological values to try to influence Charles Hurwitz, a visible leader of the Houston Jewish community and head of the corporation that was clear-cutting the site. The Redwood Rabbis received backing from the Coalition on the Environment and Jewish Life—which is itself supported by mainstream Jewish groups such as Hillel, Hadassa, and B'nai Brith—and engaged in civil disobedience by planting redwood seedlings in defiance of Hurwitz's orders.[25]

Buddhists in both the United States and Japan have actively resisted the storage and transportation of dangerous nuclear material, while in Germany, Buddhists have challenged both the ethics and the environmental consequences of factory farming.[26] Christian groups have formed coalitions to reduce global warming, have held religious services to celebrate lakes, and have authorized study groups to reduce the environmental impact of church buildings. National and international organizations have formed to radically transform theological education to take account of the environmental crisis.[27]

In these and thousands more examples, it is clear that to be ethical in relation to environmental issues is also to be political. The economy, the government, the military, health care, transportation, and just about everything else are called into question. Believers may still pray for a pure heart and train their awareness mindfully, but environmental problems simply cannot be solved though individual action. In just this way, environmental issues are a direct confirmation of the claims I made in Chapters 1 and 3 about how the modern world politicizes ethics. Through the work we do and the taxes we pay, what we buy and what we drive, our personal moral lives have a global meaning. When any serious religious group talks about the environment, it necessarily expresses support for certain concrete political policies: for instance, the need to monitor and restrict market forces, limit the prerogatives of corporations, make the government responsive to the interests of ecosystems and the socially powerless, limit military expenditures, and direct technology toward sustainability.

As they confront the environmental crisis, many religious groups throughout the world advocate not only the values of "ecotheology" but the pursuit of "ecojustice," i.e., the seamless blending of concern for earth's creation and human beings, the biotically marginalized and the socially powerless, endangered species and endangered human communities. This blending includes issues of class, race, gender, and indigenous rights, alongside more familiar concern with "nature." It requires—and is achieving—a comprehensive understanding of political life that joins religious visionaries with the most sophisticated and principled of secular political movements.

Consider the comprehensive notions of environmental racism and environmental justice, phrases that refer to the fact that racial minorities and the poor in the United States, just like indigenous peoples worldwide, are exposed to a great deal more pollution than are the racially and economically dominant groups. Lacking social power, their lives are held as less valuable; the environmental crisis is written on—and in—their bodies.[28] During the last thirty years, a comprehensive concern with environmental justice developed with the constant input of black religious social activists.[29] The historic 1987 report *Toxic Wastes and Race*, the first comprehensive account of environmental racism, was researched and written by the commission for racial justice of the United Church of Christ.[30] This report detailed the fundamental racial and class inequality in the siting and cleanup of hazardous wastes in the United States. Its lead investigator, Reverend Benjamin Chavis, was instrumental in connecting the civil rights, religious, and environmental communities of the South. Four years later, in 1991, the very first principle of the historic National People of Color Environmental Leadership Summit proclaimed that "environmental justice affirms the sacredness of mother Earth, ecological unity and the interdependence of all species, and the right to be free from ecological destruction."[31] A few years later, President Clinton ordered government agencies to take environmental justice issues into account in their programs.

Alongside racial and class issues, an ecojustice perspective focuses on the ways in which Western thought has historically equated women and nature and devalued both. The initial justification for this dual subordination was found in the claim that both lacked the holiness or closeness to God of men. Later, it was men's (self-proclaimed) rationality that was thought to justify masculine social privileges. In terms of concrete social policy, contemporary Western schemes of economic development for poor countries often have disastrous effects on Third World women, whose lives and livelihood are tied to their immediate surroundings. For example, in poorer countries men plant cash crops, but women plant subsistence crops. When export agriculture promoting a single agricultural commodity takes over, women in the local community are hurt more than men. Awareness of the combination of the cultural devaluation of women with their economic subordination helps create an "ecofeminism" that has powerful religious and political implications.[32]

The religious presence in environmental politics, like a good deal of the entire environmental movement, not only breaks barriers between religion and politics, theology, and social activism but also helps develop a world-making *political* agenda that may avoid being limited to one or another particular social group. Religions have a powerful contribution to make here. Insofar as they have a mandate, it is, after all, from God: a God who is not tied, one hopes, to the valid but inevitably partial concerns of one political group or another. Of course, in the past much of traditional religion was rabidly sectarian, racist, colonialist, or just downright nasty. But religions that have been deeply affected by the liberal and radical politics of the last two centuries have moved beyond those moral failings, or at least are trying to.

Ecojustice is, thus, a comprehensive political and spiritual vision. In the words of the Ecojustice Ministries, a Denver-based Protestant activist organization, part of that vision involves "Confronting Power Relationships":

> Faithful and ethical living is not confined to personal choices. Moses and the prophets all spoke to, and about, the power structures of their communities. Jesus and Paul dealt with the realities of political power. An eco-justice perspective recognizes that the power relationships of each situation must be analyzed and addressed. In our globalized economy, it is absurd to suggest that personal choices alone can address the crises we face. Various forms of power—economic, political, military, intellectual and personal—must be taken into account in the ways that we understand the world and live within it.
>
> Eco-justice is not one "issue" out of the many from which congregations can pick and choose: hunger, housing, guns, abortion, militarism, morality, globalization, families, wilderness, affirmative action, civil rights, economic justice, education, immigration, hunger, health care—and the list goes on and on. Rather, eco-justice is a theological perspective that shapes the way that we approach each of these issues.[33]

The religious participation in the environmental justice movement is not simply a matter of pious statements. There are many places where religious organizations play an active role in the movement itself. For instance, The White Violet Center for Eco-Justice of Indiana is staffed by Catholics and focuses on a range of justice and environmental issues, including wetlands preservation, organic agriculture, and preservation of endangered bird species. It "exists to foster a way of living that recognizes the interdependence of all creation" and "seeks to create systems that support justice and sustainability, locally and globally."[34]

The Social Action Organization of Queensland, Australia, is also centered in the Catholic Church. It has an annual budget of $A160,000 and employs one full-time coordinator and four part-time employees. One of its main areas is "ecojustice," in the pursuit of which it prepared a detailed and technically sophisticated account of the human and environmental affects of a prospective development of the Brisbane harbor. It also encourages readers to boycott Exxon, and its web site provides links to both church statements on environmental issues and secular political groups like Greenpeace.[35]

When in 2001 a Boston coalition was formed to confront environmental justice issues in the local distribution of toxic materials, the Greater Boston

Coalition on the Environment and Jewish Life played a critical role.[36] When the first resistance to dumping of PCBs in predominantly poor and black Warren County, North Carolina, got underway in 1982, it was the black religious community that took the lead. Worldwide, indigenous peoples resist environmentally destructive "development" of their land in part because they have religious bonds to the land that are essential to their culture and community.[37]

These examples are a tiny fraction of the whole picture. But the essential point is clear. It is simply no longer true of religions, as political radicals have been claiming for nearly two centuries: "They concentrate on the individual and not social institutions; they are unwilling to envision radical social changes; they cannot see the links among different moral and political concerns; they seek changes in attitudes or values rather than in basic social institutions; they are unwilling to learn from the insights of world-making political theory." Such criticisms may well continue to apply to some groups, but they have become completely inapplicable to others. The great divide between religion and progressive politics, weakened by Protestant abolitionism, the social teachings of the Catholic Church, and the social gospel of the late nineteenth century, cracked by Gandhi and King and the religious presence in the peace and anti-apartheid movements, has in the global environment movement finally been decisively overcome.

If religions have to some extent turned Green, Green politics are in some important ways religious. In the contemporary environmental movement, even those groups totally unconnected to religiously identified organizations are often practicing a new kind of politics, one in which a religious or spiritual sensibility is present. It is this simultaneous transformation of both religion and political activism that helps make environmental politics dramatically new and historically important.

The politics I have in mind here include but are not limited to government programs and laws. Politics, as political scientist Paul Wapner says, also "takes place in the home, office, and marketplace."[38] At one end of the spectrum of activities and concerns that make up Green politics, we find direct actions aimed at stopping some particular instance of "development" or some concrete industrial practice. When the women of India's Chipka movement physically encircle the trees of their beloved forest (which provides herbs, fodder for animals, and firewood) to prevent them from being chopped down, when Greenpeace plugs the outflow pipe of a chemical factory, when thousands protest "free trade" agreements that would cripple communities' rights to limit ecological degradation, environmental politics means putting your body on the line to protect both other species and human beings. At the other end of the spectrum, we find attempts to influence world culture through teaching, writing, films, Internet sites, poetry, and art. In between these two poles are a host of governmental and nongovernmental policies, institutions, and activities: from government regulation of pesticide use to the creation of wildlife refuges, from lobbying to protect wetlands to resisting environmental racism, from researching the duplicity of the chemical industry to organizing neighbors to clean up a local river. In this light, nongovernmental organizations like transnational environmental groups "contribute to addressing global environmental problems by heightening world-wide concern for the environment. They persuade vast numbers of people to care about and take actions to protect the earth's ecosystems."[39]

What gives this wide spectrum of Green politics a religious or spiritual dimension? Well, in some cases this dimension will not be present. If we seek to preserve a forest so that we can hunt big game in it (one of the original motivations for wildlife preservation efforts)[40] or if our sole concern with pesticides is their effect on human health, then our approach to environmental issues is purely "instrumental." It is, we might say, simply a continuation of the "anthropocentric" attitudes that have marked Western culture for at least 3,000 years, attitudes resting on the belief that only human beings are morally valuable. In this form, caring for a river or an endangered species is little different from concern over auto safety or tennis elbow—valuable and important, to be sure, but not historically new or spiritually significant.

If however, we are at least partly motivated by "ecocentric" or biocentric values, if there is an element of "deep ecology" in our passion, if we see nature as a mother, a lover, or a partner, then the situation is different[41]—for then we are expressing a distinct vision of the value of our surroundings and a new and powerful sense of the meaning of human identity itself.[42] When environmental politics are motivated by a concern for life as a whole or ecosystems above and beyond the human, I believe, they are profoundly spiritual and, in a deep and general sense, *religious*.

Whether known as deep ecology, ecofeminism, bioregionalism, the land ethic, or simply the special place that some beach, forest, or mountain has in our hearts, this sensibility involves a passionate communion with the earth. What is "deep" about this perspective is the experience—and the conviction—that our surroundings are essential to who we are. And this is not just because they are useful, but because we are tied to them by invisible threads of inspiration, memory, esthetic delight, emotional connection, and simple wonder. Sky and earth, bird and fish, each leaf on each tree—without them, we could not be ourselves. As one of the architects of modern environmental politics, David Brower, wrote: "To me, God and Nature are synonymous."[43] Poisoning nature thus not only leads to the concrete suffering of soaring cancer rates and our children's asthma but creates the emotional and spiritual crisis comparable to what would happen if our families were murdered, our cathedrals bombed, or our holy books burned.

In contrast to the precisely formulated content of ecotheology, with its biblical references, new models of God, and creative applications of traditional concepts to environmental issues, some of the new environmental spirituality is diffuse and at times hard to capture. As Christopher Childs, longtime Greenpeace activist and spokesperson says, "[T]here is broad acceptance among Greenpeace staff that the work is quintessentially spiritual, though definitions of what is meant by the term vary."[44]

When this sensibility enters environmental politics, it takes a variety of forms. One element is the simple faith in the political power of a moral statement. For instance, the Quaker-inspired practice of "bearing witness" is "central to Greenpeace's well-publicized actions in the face of pollution or mammal killing."[45] The goal is to reveal the damaging actions to the world and to help encourage an alternative perception of reality that might lead to massive resistance or at least a shift in public sentiment. Similar elements can be found in Buddhist and feminist resistance to the production and transport of radioactive materials. In these settings ecoactivism calls on a quasi-religious sense of the ultimate imperative of moral action, a sense that hopes for victory but does not depend on it. As I indicated in Chapter 4, it is one of religion's gifts to assign to moral acts an abiding importance in and of themselves, an importance that can keep us going even when (as almost always seems the case in environmental politics) we have no certainty of getting the results we seek.

This spiritual vision of environmental politics also provides a crucial alternative to the destructive values of the global marketplace, values that privilege economic growth, rising exports, and individual autonomy above all else. The "religion" of modernity demands control over nature and a model of development that turns every meadow and village into the same old mall. Nature is thought of as a thing, an element to be used. Selfhood is defined by consumption, and there is a widespread attempt to broadcast excessive styles of consumption throughout the world.

Sulak Sivaraksa, Buddhist environmental activist from Thailand, writes that "Western consumerism is the dominant ethic in the world today . . . The new 'spiritual advisors' are from Harvard Business School, Fletcher School of Law and Diplomacy, and London School of Economics. . . . The department stores have become our shrines, and they are constantly filled with people. For the young people, these stores have replaced the Buddhist temples."[46] The drive toward globalization, says a Third World Christian theologian, is often seen as a sort of new religion: "it has its God: profit and money. It has it high priests: GATT [General Agreement on Tariffs and Trade], WTO [World Trade Organization], IMF-WB. It has its doctrines and dogmas: import liberalization, deregulation . . . It has its temples: the super megamalls. It has its victims on the altar of sacrifice: the majority of the world—the excluded and marginalized poor."[47]

Referring to the conflict between native peoples and economic development over the proposed building of a massive, ecosystem-destroying and native-people-uprooting hydroelectric dam in James Bay, Ontario, David Kinsley argues:

> If hunting animals is a sacred occupation among the Mistassini Cree, building dams to harness power for electricity is equally sacred for many members of modern industrial society. . . . the conflict between the Cree and [Ontario political leader] Bourassa, then, is not so much a conflict between a religious view and a secular view as it is a conflict between two contrasting visions of the nature of human beings and human destiny, that is, two conflicting myths about the place of human beings in the natural order, two contrasting ecological visions.[48]

Charlene Spretnak describes the difference between these two visions: "Modern culture . . . is based on mechanistic analysis and control of human systems as well as Nature . . . nationalistic chauvinism, sterile secularism, and monoculture shaped by mass media. . . . Green values, by contrast, seek a path of 'ecological wisdom' and attempt to integrate freedom *and* tradition, the individual *and* the community, science *and* Nature, men *and* women."[49] To accomplish that goal, said leader of the German Green Party Petra Kelly, "We must learn to . . . recognize the interconnectedness of all living creatures, and to respect the value of each thread in the vast web of life. This is a spiritual perspective, and it is the foundation of all Green politics."[50] Or as Earth First! activist Mark Davis said, in explaining why he broke the law in trying to prevent the further expansion of a ski resort into mountains revered by the Hopi and Navajo, "[T]he bottom line is that those mountains are sacred, and that what has occurred there, despite our feeble efforts, is a terrible spiritual mistake."[51]

In fact, spiritual values in general and the value(s) of nature in particular give us a way out of the ecocidal cul-de-sac of the endless mall. They help us to develop an alternative sense of self that acknowledges dependence, mutuality, and happiness *without* requiring endless "development," soulless gadgetry, and the elimination of other life forms. This alternative allows the withdrawal of psychic energy from a cultural and economic system that threatens the earth and people alike. In the same vein, a spiritual relationship with the natural world allows us to orient political struggle in a direction not tied (or at least less tied) by psychic addiction to the very social system that destroys us. Greens have, some observers believe, "moved beyond materialist values while at the same time embracing some preindustrial values derived from indigenous non-European cultures. These value shifts have been tied to specific issues that are crucial for the Greens but often ignored by the Democratic Left."[52] The interface of spiritual and Green values has helped create the emerging discipline of "ecopsychology," which is oriented to understanding the psychic costs of our alienation from the rest of the earth, and the psychologically and spiritually healing experiences that come from lessening that alienation.[53]

Sociologist Manuel Castells describes a deep Green perspective as one in which:

> The holistic notion of integration between humans and nature . . . does not refer to a naive worshipping of pristine natural landscapes, but to the fundamental consideration that the relevant unit of experience is not each individual, or for that matter, historically existing human communities. To merge ourselves with our cosmological self we need first to change the notion of time, to feel "glacial time" run through our lives, to sense the energy of stars flowing in our blood, and to assume the rivers of our thoughts endlessly merging in the boundless oceans of multiform living matter.[54]

Such a perspective, Castells believes, leads environmentalism to be in fundamental opposition to the dominant values of multinational corporate power, transnational economic institutions like the IMF and the World Bank, and placeless cultural and economic icons like MTV and Nike. When Green values inform the best of Green politics, "we are a long way from the instrumentalist perspective that has dominated the industrial era, in both its capitalist and statist [i.e., socialist] versions. And we are in direct contradiction with the dissolution of meaning in the flows of faceless power that constitute the network society."[55]

It is environmentalism, more than any other political setting, that unites the "cultural creatives" described in Chapter 2; the nonviolent spiritual resistance of the civil rights movement, feminist theology, and spirituality of Chapter 6, and in fact the comprehensive notion that religion has something specific and precious to add to political life. In environmentalism, liberal support for individual rights and the socialist concern with economic rationality can meet each other and join forces with the non-Western emphasis on community and responsibility.

Environmentalists can be dramatically different from each other. They include those who long nostalgically for a hunter-gatherer lifestyle, those who support Aldo Leopold's call for "an individual responsibility for the health of the land,"[56] as well as hard-headed city planners eager to replace cars with bikes, integrate communities with an ecofriendly Internet, and design apartment complexes with organic rooftop gardens. Yet the comprehensive values referred to by Spretnak, Kelly, and Castells resonate throughout much of the movement. These include a distrust of uncontrolled economic growth and thoughtless technological innovation, in combination with the belief that both the market and technology should serve collective rather than narrowly human interests. There is a corresponding belief that has clear spiritual overtones: the idea that human life has other purposes than the acquisition of power and wealth. It is stressed, rather, that we live for the development of wisdom, peacefulness, harmonious coexistence with the earth, and the quiet (itself a radical demand in these deafening times) enjoyment of life. Journalist Mark Dowie suggests that despite the enormous diversity of the environmental movement, a number of common principles can be found. Along with familiar political goals, these include an ethical and spiritual redefinition of human beings as part of nature and not its master or the only part that really matters.[57]

What applying these values would mean is often far from clear. Since the ecological crisis is a product of our entire civilization, broader in scope and more universally threatening than any other form of political injustice or collective irrationality, the transformation called for is correspondingly large. We might take as a hopeful example the enormous social success of Kerala, India's southernmost state, which has dramatically increased literacy and education, reduced infant mortality, raised life expectancy to nearly Western levels, improved women's social position, and cultivated a culture of intellectual and artistic engagement *without* high levels of industrialization or the raising of per capita income. We might consider Columbia's village of Gaviotas, where appropriate technology has led to a sustainable life in the midst of a formerly barren wasteland, sustainable crops help regenerate a rain forest, and children's swings power the water pumps.[58] We might notice how the citizens of Maine, who suffer each year through several weeks of highly annoying and virtually impossible-to-stop black flies, reject the use of potentially dangerous chemical pesticides, even if it will cost them tourist income. "If people can't live with the flies," some say, "they just shouldn't come here."[59]

We can see the new sensibility expressed in political campaigns aimed at inclusive goals of protecting endangered species, preserving the culture and ecosystems of indigenous peoples, and preventing industrial pollution. In one powerful example, international activity mobilized in response to the Narmada River Valley Project in India.[60] Called by critics the "world's greatest planned environmental disaster," the project envisaged thirty major, 135 medium, and 3,000 minor dams throughout Central India. If completed as planned, it would have displaced close to 400,000 people, destroyed wildlife habitat, and flooded some of the last remaining tropical forests in India. As early as 1977, local opposition formed when people realized that there was in fact no land available for the residents who were to be displaced—that they would simply join the tens of millions of other "refugees from development." During the next decade and a half, opposition grew and took a variety of forms: road blockades, hunger fasts, demonstrations at state capitals, and massive gatherings at sites that were to be flooded. A ring of international solidarity formed. Japanese environmentalists persuaded their government not to advance money to it, while American activists pressured the World Bank. The San Francisco–based International Rivers Project organized financial and technical aid. In 1992, facing reports that the entire project was marked by fraud and incompetence, legislators in Finland, Sweden, and the United States asked the World Bank not to lend any more money. In this heartening case, the more familiar dimension of human rights mixed with concern for other species; citizens of different countries and continents gave time, energy, and money to support those of another. A vital mix of personal and group self-interest, abstract political principle, and transpersonal celebration of the earth took shape.

Such principles can be found anywhere environmental struggles emerge. In an attempt to protect their village from predatory commercial fishing, a Brazilian group stresses values connected to Catholic liberation theology: "group solidarity, the participation and inclusion of all in . . . group decisions and . . . a suspicion if not of material wealth itself at least a distrust of what wealth acquisition requires in terms of . . . oppressive and unjust structures."[61] In resistance to ecologically damaging mining and timber practices in India, local groups have combined concern for health, local communities, and the sacred status of forests or rivers.[62]

In all these struggles, environmentalism is not simply interest-group politics applied to forests and toxic incinerators. Rather, it is informed by a comprehensive vision of human identity and of how that identity is interrelated with the universe as a whole. This vision deserves to be considered, in the broadest sense, religious.

———————

When the United Church of Christ talks about racism in citing toxic waste sites, when religious organizations instruct the president of the United States on global warming, when Buddhist monks protest globalization, they show how contemporary religious and spiritual voices have adopted some of the conceptual tools of progressive political theory. Broad orientations toward human identity (we are kin to the rain forest); or to moral values (we have obligations to other species and to humans injured by our industrial practices); or to the meaning of life or the cosmos (our task is to be part of life, we are to be loving stewards to the earth) have always been part of religion. However, when the critique of dams, the diagnosis of racism in the placing of Superfund sites, and analysis of the economic and human costs of globalization are added in, something new is afoot.

For example, consider the Dalai Lama's suggestion that "[w]hen we talk about preservation of the environment, it is related to many other things. Ultimately, the decision must come from the human heart. The key point is to have a genuine sense of universal responsibility, based on love and compassion, and clear awareness."[63] This statement correctly points out that each person who opposes the juggernaut of industrialism must make a personal commitment, with no guarantee of "success," to a daunting task. However, the statement ignores the fact that *personal* awareness, love, and compassion are extremely limited if they are not joined by an understanding of—and an attempt to change—our collective institutions. The Dalai Lama—exactly like the author of this book and, in all probability, the reader as well—plugs into the same electronic grid as everyone else, burns fossil fuels to fly from place to place, and employs the resources of our environmentally unsustainable society in his struggle to save some vestige of his people's national identity. His personal love and compassion, in short, do not keep him from contributing to the mess! Understanding the problems, criticizing them fully, and offering alternatives requires a "social" ecology whose nuts-and-bolts account of the economic and political sources of ecocrisis take their place alongside appeals to personal love, compassion, and awareness.

To take another example, one of the most ambitious descriptions of what an ecological society might look like, *For the Common Good: Redirecting the Economy Toward Community, the Environment and a Sustainable Future* is—significantly—the joint product of a Protestant theologian (John Cobb) and a professor of economics and former senior economist for the World Bank (Herman Daly). Daly and Cobb propose a rich combination of policy and value changes. They challenge existing economies of scale and current trade policies, suggest new ways to cultivate local communities, and redesign educational priorities. And they address the cosmic meaning of human existence and the ethical standards that should guide it. Similarly, when theologian Dorothy Soelle confronts the prospects of religion in the twenty-first century, she must diagnose the political ills of globalization along with the more familiar problems of Christian complacency or arrogance.[64]

What we are witnessing, then, is a double movement: the entry of spiritual values into world-making political perspectives and religion's assimilation of analytic tools for understanding the logic of ecological destruction. Here, despite the moral, political, and economic institutional failures of Communist nations, it is not hard to see how much of Marxist theory is in fact extremely useful. And despite the fact that many claim to have left Marxism in the dustbin of history, its general understanding of capitalism is widely used.

Marx's original theory correctly predicted much of the economic future of capitalism: the expansion and development of productive technology, the ascendancy of corporate power in politics and culture, the evolution of larger and more concentrated forms of wealth, and the worldwide spread of social relationships based on money. Since Marx, theorists under his influence have described an economy dominated by national and global megacorporations, the role of the government in organizing and stabilizing the economy, and the manner in which the international market economy leads to the internationalization of poverty and ecological destruction. We have not "outgrown" Marxist insights in our age of global capitalism, corporations larger than many nations, and frequently unrestrained state power in the service of big business.[65]

Let us examine, for example, the replacement of subsistence agriculture with large plantations producing a single crop for export. This pattern has been repeated countless times throughout Asia, Latin America, and Africa, almost always with disastrous results. Basic Marxist premises provide a straightforward explanation. Land oriented toward local production for use has been converted to production for profitable export. Because the land is no longer directly connected to a self-subsistent community, its distant owners have no compunctions about using techniques that degrade both land (now overburdened by unsustainable pesticides, chemical fertilizers, and water use) *and* the human community (now turned into poverty-stricken "masses," usually forced to join the unemployed in overburdened urban centers). If enough profits are made, it does not matter whether much is left of the land (or people) when the capital is transferred to some other investment. In this way international *trade* in sugar and bananas, coffee and cotton, degrades agricultural *communities and land* throughout the world. And the situation is only made worse when genetic engineering further reduces the diversity of seeds, farming techniques, and input from traditional farming communities.[66]

Another problem that can be easily understood in broadly Marxist terms concerns the way corporations can treat the pollution they cause as "external" to the cost of the commodities they sell.[67] Production, sale, and profits are typically the business of the company in question; cleanup and health costs are borne by society—and the ecosystem—as a whole. What looks like "freedom of the market" is really the privilege to acquire wealth while impoverishing the human (and nonhuman) community.

In cases such as these, abstractions about our "attitudes toward nature" may be relevant, but not nearly so much as is an understanding of the capitalist globalization of agriculture or the vital need for some collective control of productive life.

For a Marxist political orientation, the ultimate question is whether this control can be realized. Even though most religious environmentalists do not call for complete nationalization of the forces of production, the vast majority of them do demand serious social constraints on the productive activity of private corporations. This Marxian goal, though rarely acknowledged as such, is common to all but the most timid and conservative forms of religious environmentalism. In many other instances, more direct condemnations of the imperatives of capitalism are present.

What I have just described in reference to Marxism could be repeated in relation to religious environmentalists' use of a feminist critique of patriarchy, antiracism theory, and postcolonial perspectives on the pernicious effects of globalization. The United Church of Christ report, after all, was about a structural racism that had little or nothing to do with emotional racial antagonism, traditional segregation, or minorities refused jobs or mortgages. Religious voices concerned with environmental justice focus on contrasting real estate values, differences in the capacity of communities for self-defense, and lack of personal connections to motivate institutional concern.

Whether those who use such language to describe social problems needing religious attention are ministers, professors of political science, or paid organizers, the language itself is the stuff of progressive political theory and originates in secular political movements. Without these perspectives, the new values of environmental theology simply cannot comprehend the real world.

——— · ———

Just as the pressure of a historically unprecedented environmental crisis transforms traditional religion and nondenominational spirituality, so political theory has had to change as well. For a start, Western liberals and radicals, like their religious comrades, have had to question their own anthropocentric premises. Democratic theory, rooted in the notion of the autonomous, "rational" individual, has been extended to discussions of the rights of animals, trees, and ecosystems. Marxism, in many ways functioning under the same human-centered premises as liberalism, has similarly had to ask whether the liberation of the working class and the fulfillment of human goals were the sole purposes of political movements. All progressive political positions have been challenged to answer new questions about what they mean by happiness, freedom, justice, and human fulfillment. As Andrew MacLauglin has argued, and many Greens have agreed, the problem is not simply capitalism, but an "industrialism" that privileges human consumption, unchecked technological innovation, and a mindless popular culture over tradition, community, and ties to other species.[68] If traditional religion was not up to the demands of the environmental crisis, most world-making political theories weren't either. Just as the nonviolent activists of biodevastation were eager to think about the spiritual roots of their passion for the earth and my Jamaica Plain neighbors understood the pond as sacred, so it is that many hardheaded accounts of the death of forests or toxic air quality indicate a fundamental concern that is spiritual in terms of its transcendence of purely instrumental interest.

I've argued throughout this book that the religious spirit can add something to political life. In particular, we often find in world-making religious social activists certain values typically absent in the secular left. These values include compassion, empathy even for the guilty, self-awareness, and some reflective distance from the typical pursuit of status and power within the movement.

Such virtues are especially important for environmentalism. One reason this is true is that the universality and severity of the ecological crisis offer environmental activists an enormous range of potential allies. Harshness, unforgiving self-righteousness, and uncontrolled anger will alienate many who might join the cause. Self-destructive infighting, arrogance, aggression, name-calling, and factionalism can—once again—only lead to failure. These were, according to its most well-known leader, the source of the downfall of the once-powerful German Green Party.[69]

For environmental politics, simple pieties like those of Thich Nhat Hanh about how it is important to smile, breathe, and be pleasant to adversaries become critically important. The spiritually rooted practice of moral self-examination, the awareness of the near-universal tendency toward egotism (or "sin"), and the trust that others act badly only out of ignorance can lead spiritual social activists to a more human, inclusive, and ultimately successful politics. Often, environmental struggles involve fundamental shifts in community life: Jobs are at stake, freedom to use private property is curtailed, cultural values such as hunting are challenged. In the face of the inevitable emotional pain such struggles create, activists need all the resources of empathy and compassion that spiritual traditions—at their best—can offer.

Similarly, the environmentalists' concern for nature is a value that can provide the basis for a new kind of social solidarity. We might remember that whatever else divides us as human beings, we all need air and water; and virtually all of our hearts rejoice in the sounds of spring. These commonalties may save us when the divisions of race, class, gender, ethnicity, or sexuality leave us deeply suspicious of each other. Emphasizing what we share is a particular gift of spiritual social activists.[70] Such activists cultivate respect for each person's essential spiritual worth and not just condemnation of the "bad guys"; and this attitude is stressed as much within the movement as on the outside. As an example of detailed thought on this matter, consider the "Fourteen Precepts for the Order of Interbeing," which Thich Nhat Hanh wrote as a kind of guidebook for Buddhist social activists. These precepts stress humility, peacefulness, and integrity in the pursuit of political change. "Do not force others," one precept teaches, "to accept your views, whether by authority, threat, money, propaganda or even education. However, through compassionate dialogue, help others renounce fanaticism and narrowness."[71] Of course, one person's peaceful pursuit of ecological wisdom might be another's fanaticism. Guidelines of this kind cannot end all the tensions of political life. However, even a casual examination of the history of world-making political organizations reveals how much more successful political groups might have been if they had even been aware such principles existed! The environmental movement has had its share of bitterness, infighting, careerism, and energy wasted on internal hostility. We might remember how the career of David Brower, perhaps the single most important architect of modern activist environmentalism, was marked by situations of unnecessary conflict.[72]

Because activists are struggling against a system in which they themselves take part, spiritual values of humility and self-awareness seem particularly appropriate. In the more familiar contexts of racism or sexism, one can overcome prejudicial attitudes, refuse to support stereotyping or discrimination, and promote the interests of the oppressed group; and, in the case of men and feminism, a man can do his share of the housework and make respect for women a basic masculine virtue. However, when it comes to the environment, it is unlikely that we will stop using electricity, consuming food transported from thousands of miles away, or driving. To be sure, everyone is not equally responsible. Only a tiny percentage of us control energy policy, displace peasants to create pesticide-drenched export farming, or support political candidates who will lessen restrictions on automobile fuel efficiency. But we all consume the fruits of industrial civilization and contribute to the mess.

Also, environmental movements from developing nations, particularly those of Asia, offer an emphasis on collective well-being and communal values that is an important counterweight to the Western stress on individual rights. Having been catapulted into a global economy without the centuries-long development of extreme forms of individualism, Buddhist and indigenous groups can remind the rest of us that concern for the village, the tribe, the community, the clan, and the people are as essential to the creation of a just and rational social order as is the "individual." These are political concerns that focus on peoplehood, on shared culture, and on ties to a particular place rather than on issues of economic class or generalized race or ethnicity.[73]

Further, unlike movements keyed solely to economic gain or group interests, environmentalism must counter the reigning belief that the "good life" is defined by high consumption. It must propose alternative models of human goodness, fulfillment, and happiness.

Most secular political viewpoints have ignored this task. Liberalism, after all, was concerned with untrammeled personal freedom in social and economic life. Marxism sought to liberate exploited classes. Most of the dominant social movements of the last two centuries have focused on equal treatment for their constituents and raising standards of living. As products of the Enlightenment, they carried its strengths and its weaknesses.

Although certain elements of the 1960s counterculture and feminism did challenge some of modernity's basic principles, these elements have come to full flower in environmentalism—especially environmentalism that is infused with some spiritual values. These radically new perspectives ask: What is the ultimate worth of this construction project, these jobs, that commodity? Whose needs or wants deserve to be satisfied? Which desires are or are not healthy? Rational? Spiritually fulfilling? How might they be altered? If we truly suffer, as writers from David Abram to Stephanie Kaza have insisted, from a great loneliness for the "more-than-human," what do we need to change to encounter its mystery once again?[74] Asking these questions goes to the core of both our broad cultural values and our hard-edged institutions. They allow us to confront inner-city toxic incinerators and wildlife preservation, the commodification of agriculture and saving the redwoods. For example, deep ecology's emphasis on the value of the nonhuman offers a measure of and a limit to what we are seeking when we pursue an improved "standard of living." The notion of a "sustainable" form of life begins to condition what we are after, becoming an essential defining element along with "justice," "freedom," and even "community."

Buttressing these challenges to our way of life with a religious vocabulary gives us a leg to stand on when so much that is familiar is being criticized. Perhaps only the divine right of God is a powerful enough to challenge what many take to be the divine right of the economy! As Max Oelschlaeger suggests:

[R]eligious discourse, expressing itself in the democratic forum, offers the possibility of overcoming special interest politics—especially those which are narrowly economic—on environmental issues . . . Biblical language has been a vital part of our nation's public debate over the structure and texture of the good society. There is no reason that it cannot play a role in determining an environmental agenda.[75]

In this line of thought, there is a clear overlap between ecological activists and the religious traditions, for many elements of both share a love of simplicity, an appreciation for life, and a long-term, nonmonetary definition of "success."[76] As world-making movements, religion and politics now converge.

Finally, as I argued at the end of Chapter 4, religious traditions can offer social activists the practical techniques of moral and emotional self-transformation found in prayer, meditation, and ritual. Such resources are particularly needed in the environmental movement. The scope of the problem, the daunting resources of the adversary, the awareness of how much has been lost already—all these make ecological activism rife with grief, anger, and despair. Yet as the Dalai Lama said, when asked why he did not hate the Chinese for what they had done to Tibet, "They have taken so much else from me, I will not give them my peace of mind."[77] In fact, a spiritual perspective on our successes and failures can help sustain us in hard times. Prayers of thanksgiving, beseeching pleas to a Great Spirit (of whatever form) to help us along the way, rituals to mourn for the dead and take joy in what remains—all these are the common stuff of religion, easily adapted to the great task of coming to a sane and sustainable relation with the rest of the planet. As necessary counterbalances to a constant focus on rising cancer rates, clear-cut ancient forests, and extinguished species, rituals of celebration and joy allow activists to feel some happiness no matter what. Such rituals, however, do not come easily to most great traditions of social struggle. The lifestyle of secular radicalism rarely has a place for moments of silence, prayers for peace, candles lit in memory of the fallen, or—as Thich Nhat Hanh puts it—moments of delight in the trees that have not yet been stricken by acid rain.

———

We can now return to the question of religious pluralism, of how politically oriented religious groups can function in modern society without undermining the enlightenment values of religious freedom, free speech, and a reasonable separation of church and state.

Religious participation in environmental politics, it seems to me, has solved this problem: if not by addressing it theoretically then—more important—in practice. The common bond of love of the earth and the use of the vocabulary of divinity, sacredness, and ultimate concern far outweighs the names of gods, the holidays celebrated, or the precise form of prayer. In interfaith partnerships for environmental reform and programmatic statements, religious environmentalists have realized the goal I described in Chapter 2: to hold fast to ethics while allowing for a pluralism of metaphysics.

Consider, for example, these excerpts from a remarkable statement on global warming and climate change by the North Carolina Interfaith Coalition on Climate Change:

> As witnesses of the serious climate changes the earth is now undergoing, we leaders of North Carolina's *various spiritual traditions* join together to voice our concerns about the health of the planet we share with all species. We acknowledge the need to commit ourselves to a course of action that will help us recognize our part in the devastating effects on much of our planet brought about by increasingly severe weather events. We declare the necessity for North Carolina's *spiritual communities* to be leaders in *turning human activities in a new direction* for the well-being of the planet . . .
>
> We believe that global warming is a challenge to all people but particularly to the spiritual communities that recognize the *sacredness of preserving all eco-systems* that sustain life . . .
>
> Global warming *violates that sacredness*. Already we see people dying from extreme weather conditions exacerbated by climate change, including record-breaking storms, heat waves, floods, and droughts. The burdens of a degraded environment fall disproportionately upon the most vulnerable of the planet's people: *the poor, sick, elderly*, and those who will face still greater threats in future generations . . .
>
> We pledge ourselves to . . . organize our communities to meet with local and state political leaders, and members of Congress, to encourage their participation and support.[78]

The thirty-six signers listed on the group's web site include rabbis, Buddhist priests, Roman Catholic and Episcopal bishops, and ministers from the Lutheran, Unitarian Universalist, Quaker, Baptist, Methodist, and United Church of Christ denominations. If we examine the language of the document, we see what appears to be a self-conscious attempt to put in practice a conception of religious life that prizes finding common ground on which different groups can work together. The frequent use of the term "spiritual" signals an acceptance of the variety of paths to God; the acknowledgment of the sacredness of the earth announces an end to theological anthropocentrism;

naming the special vulnerability of the poor opens the way for an account of irrational and unjust social institutions and for common work with secular liberal to leftist organizations. The challenge to existing political and economic arrangements is direct and serious.

In another example, we find that in 1986, the World Wide Fund for Nature celebrated its twenty-fifth anniversary by bringing together representatives of five major world religions to focus on how their respective faiths understood and could respond to the environmental crisis. Catholic priest Lanfranco Serrini declared: "We are convinced of the inestimable value of our respective traditions and what they can offer to re-establish ecological harmony; but, at the same time, *we are humble enough to desire to learn from each other*. The very richness of our diversity lends strength to our shared concern and responsibility for our planet earth."[79]

In these two illustrative cases, the Gordian knot of pluralism—how religions can coexist despite their different beliefs—is undone. And if that is undone, then our fear that any serious religion is necessarily fanatical and undemocratic should be similarly assuaged. Facing the enormous implications of the environmental crisis, believers have shown that they are capable of actively working with people whose theologies are different from their own. But that was always the key question: Could the faithful function respectfully with people who held contradictory beliefs? Contrary to the secular left's belief that religion is inherently antidemocratic, religious environmentalists have shown both a broad spiritual openness and a deep civic concern. More than this, surely, is not necessary. Religions become—like the AFL-CIO, the World Trade Organization, General Motors, and Ralph Nader's Green Party—one more group that seeks to realize its particular vision in social life. Each vision promotes certain values and institutions rather than others—whether those are the rights of private property, higher wages, the SUV, or sustainable agriculture. The demands of religion are no more irrational, partial, or exclusive than those of any other group in our uneasy democracy. That some leaders or groups are bigoted or tyrannical may be true, but which secular movement doesn't have its share of the same? Given this similarity, the task is to oppose bigotry and tyranny, and not world-making religion or politics.

Religions now enter the modern world as legitimate and authentic partners in the political drama of making—and remaking—the world. Further, their values now color the world's most important political movement. Surprisingly, as time progresses it is getting harder and harder to tell the two of them apart.

8

Beyond Our Private Sorrows: Spirituality and Politics as Responses to Breast Cancer and Disability

My scars are an honorable reminder that I may be a casualty in the cosmic war against radiation, animal fat, air pollution, McDonald's hamburger and Red dye No. 2.

—Audre Lorde, The Cancer Journals[1]

"I" am disabled, then, only from "your" point of view . . . Whoever gets to define ability puts everyone else in place, which . . . then becomes other, outside, a cheerless and chilly spot.

—Nancy Mairs, Waist-High in the World[2]

I could choose to interpret my son's disability as I wanted. Will it be a burden, a challenge, or an opportunity?

—Charles A. Hart, "Life's Illusions"[3]

World-making politics and religion, I believe, must encompass more than government programs, conventional ideas of justice, or the rewards of prayer. They should also have something to say about how, at the heart of life's deepest sorrows, social relationships and individual experience affect each other.

179

In all likelihood, every reader of this book will be personally acquainted with someone who has breast cancer and will know of people who have—or whose children have—disabilities. If, that is, it is not their own lives that have been touched. The power of these examples lies in the fact that they are at once intimate and impersonal. How they affect us has everything to do with who we are, both in our most private selves and in our most public, unchosen, collective identities. Therefore, breast cancer and disability are a crucial test of the perspective developed in this book. If politics and religion are to help us remake the world, addressing these kinds of issues must be part of the project. I will argue here that without political understanding and action, our response to the trials of either cancer or disability will be individualized, personalized, and blind to the larger contexts of cause and cure, justice and discrimination. Without religious—or at least "spiritual"—resources, we will be dreadfully hard put to make our peace with the heartache that these challenges inevitably cause.

———— • ————

My forty-eight-year-old friend Sally works as an accountant for a company that makes computer hardware. Seventeen years ago, her mother, then fifty-eight, died after a difficult struggle with breast cancer. An initial biopsy had proved cancerous. Despite a mastectomy of her affected breast, the cancer reappeared. Despite radiation and chemotherapy, it spread to her lungs. Sixteen months of steadily declining health ended in an excruciatingly painful death.

Sally is educated and informed. She knows that as a woman whose periods started early, who has never had children, and whose mother died from the disease, she is at extra risk. She does weekly breast self-exams and has a mammogram each year. She eats a low-fat diet, keeps her weight down, and gave up smoking the day she heard her mother's diagnosis. She sometimes wonders if she should take the new drug Tamoxifen as a precaution—even though she has shown no symptoms and Tamoxifen has serious side effects. She knows women with cancer in their families who have had their breasts removed rather than choosing to face waiting and worrying about finding the telltale lump.

For Sally, watching her mother die was a wrenching experience only slightly soothed by her participation in a support group for victims' families. More than anything, she wants a cure to be found. A runner since her teens, she is an active participant in the Race for the Cure, a distributor of material at her workplace during Breast Cancer Awareness Month (BCAM), a voter who wants to know if political candidates support increased funding for breast cancer research. Since her mother's death, she lives under a dark cloud of fear, one that marks her as different from all those who have miraculously escaped whatever combination of bad luck and bad genes afflicted her mother—and may be waiting to afflict her.

Sally is a composite figure, drawn from what many women say about the meaning of breast cancer. What is most important to notice is that her experience, while deeply *personal*, is in crucial ways not *individual*. In several senses, as I will now show, breast cancer is a social product. Its predominant causes do not lie in either fate or genes. Therefore, medical expertise understood as a form of purely technical knowledge will not cure it.

To begin with, there is the question of genetic causation. As Zillah Eisenstein points out, even the highest estimate would have only between 5 and 10 percent of breast cancers caused by inherited genes. And even for those cases, it is often forgotten that genetic traits can emerge only if certain other conditions are present. The body does not develop normally, no matter what its genes, without nutrition and comfort in the womb and a hospitable environment after birth. The same is true for the "maldevelopment" of cancer. "Genetic mutations are dispositions awaiting triggers. And the triggers may be as significant as, or more significant than, the genetic site itself."[4]

Further, the vast majority of cancers are not hereditary. For the most part, cancer occurs not because of what the genes were when a woman was conceived but because of what happens to her genes throughout her life. As biologist and cancer survivor Sandra Steingraber puts it, "Our genes are less an inherited set of teacups enclosed in a cellular china cabinet than they are plates used in a busy diner . . . Cracks, chips, and scrapes accumulate. Accidents happen."[5]

What are these accidents? To a very great extent, the stresses and strains of living in a polluted environment. By pollution I mean human-made substances that can fundamentally damage the human body, including but not limited to our genetic makeup and immune system. When we think genes, we think of factors that cannot be changed, that we are stuck with. This view places all the emphasis on cancer cures. When we think pollution, we think of causes that are produced by people and hence capable of being eliminated, and therefore of cancer prevention. Between those two viewpoints, there is a world of difference.

According to the World Health Organization, as many as 80 percent of the world's cancers are a product of environmental factors.[6]

Within the broad demographic picture, there is a distinguishable relationship between the rates of breast cancer and the general use of man-made chemicals. The highest rates of breast cancer are found in the industrialized nations of North America and northern Europe, and the lowest are in Asia and Africa. Researchers who looked at the 339 U.S. counties with hazardous waste sites and contaminated groundwater found consistently higher rates of breast cancer than in counties without such contamination . . . People who move to industrialized countries from countries with low breast-cancer rates soon develop the higher rates of the industrialized country. Young women who emigrate to the U.S. from Asia, where the rate is lower by four-to-seven times, undergo an 80 percent increase in their risk within the span of a generation. A generation later, the rate for their daughters approaches that of U.S.-born women.

An estimated 75,000 synthetic chemicals are in commercial use today, two-thirds of which have never been tested for their effects on human health. It is a well-documented fact that chemicals persist in the environment, accumulate in body fat and are carried by women in their breast tissue. Studies have identified the presence of dozens of synthetic chemicals in women's breast milk. Indeed, the modern breast has been characterized as a "toxic waste site."[7]

Why isn't there a larger cry for more research into the cancer-causing properties of humanly produced substances? Why was Rachel Carson's 1962 call for a systematic investigation of the effects of chemicals repeated, almost word for word, by the National Cancer Institute in 1995?[8] Why are chemicals considered innocent until proven guilty, when any rational social policy would require that their safety be proven first? Why is it that when they *are* regulated, the corporations that produce them exercise frightening control over how the regulations are observed (or eluded) and can authorize biased research, bribe regulators, pay off legislators, or end up getting asked to write the regulations themselves?[9] Why, when Sally thinks of what is necessary to improve her chances and those of other women, does she think: "more money for research on drugs, more mammography, more individual choices"?

The most important answer to such disturbing questions is that these are the dominant messages and policies of an enormously powerful cancer establishment of foundations, treatment hospitals, and research centers. Our responses to the breast cancer plague, feminist journalist Ellen Leopold writes, are colored by "Prevailing biases in the research agenda" that "reflect the influence of powerful interest groups in society."[10]

This provocative and perhaps even frightening statement leads to more questions. "Why," asks physician Janet Sherman, "is our primary well-funded National Cancer Institute not devoting its efforts to primary prevention?

Has breast cancer, like so many aspects of our culture, become just another business opportunity?"[11] Her answer is:

> There is a massing, in a few hands, of the control of production, distribution and use of pharmaceutical drugs and appliances; control of the sale and use of medical and laboratory tests; the consolidation and control of hospitals, nursing homes, and home care providers. We are no longer people who become sick. We have become markets. Is it any wonder that prevention receives so little attention? Cancer is a big and successful business![12]

Let us consider Breast Cancer Awareness Month (BCAM). This event was initiated and designed by Imperial Chemical Industries, a British giant that gave rise to Zeneca Pharmaceuticals in 1993 (which later merged to form AstraZeneca). "Now the principal corporate sponsor of BCAM, AstraZenaca retains authority to approve or disapprove all printed material used in BCAM." And so women are told, "Early detection is your best protection—get a mammogram now."[13] Zeneca sells the cancer drug Tamoxifen, to the tune of nearly $500 million a year. It has also sold pesticides and herbicides, including (for another $300 million) the carcinogen acetochlor. This dual role resembles that of GE and DuPont, whose dumping practices place them among the leaders in Superfund toxic sites and which also sell mammography machines (GE) and mammogram film (DuPont). As historian Robert Proctor observes, "Companies such as these profit, so to speak, from both ends of the cancer cycle."[14]

Mammograms are not prevention. They are, at best, doorways to early treatment. They have limited accuracy, failing to detect the disease in 20 percent of women over fifty and 40 percent of women under fifty.[15] And mammograms are certainly not an attractive option for younger women, since there is real controversy over whether or nor mammograms themselves cause cancer. But when a 1997 National Institute of Health task force recommended leaving the decision of whether to have a mammogram up to individual women in their forties, a political firestorm preempted consideration of their reasons or evidence. "Special interest groups within the medical community—especially radiologists—and members of Congress were dominant. The case illustrates that the mammography debate is inherently political."[16]

Sally, and the rest of us, might of course not be surprised that an individual congressman could make political hay out of a widely important women's health issue (as Pennsylvania senator Arlen Specter, trying to recover from his markedly anti-woman tone in the Anita Hill hearings, did in the mammogram controversy). Beyond that, we might not be surprised that large corporations would have the chutzpah to sell both the cause and the "cure" of a disease.

What, however, about basic research? What of the National Cancer Institute, the American Cancer Society, the Sloan-Kettering clinic? Sadly, their research agenda is no more independent of the basic political and economic structures of society than is Breast Cancer Awareness Month or the professional interests of the American Society of Radiologists—and this for the simple reason that in modern society, science in general is virtually always integrated into corporate and governmental institutions. Sophisticated research is simply too expensive to conduct without support of groups that have particular social interests in the results. And such support for research comes in the main from corporations or the government. Thus, the choice of problems, the basic direction of research, the kinds of solutions that are sought—all these necessarily bear the imprint of the interests of those funding the research.

It will seem less strange that roughly 98 percent of cancer research is oriented toward cure rather than prevention when we consider that the directors of major cancer institutions are often managers of polluting industries. One of the medical directors of prestigious Sloan-Kettering, perhaps the most respected cancer treatment and research center in the country, was Leo Wade. Before he was on the Sloan-Kettering board of directors, Wade had been the medical director for Standard Oil of New Jersey, a member of the Manufacturing Chemists Association, the American Petroleum Institute (a lobbying group for oil companies), and the National Association of Manufacturers. Is it then any surprise to hear Wade ridiculing efforts to control chemicals in the environment as "both futile and suspect"? In the same vein, many of the carcinogens ignored by the American Cancer Society are "byproducts of profitable industries in which its directors have financial interests."[17] When Occidental Petroleum CEO Armand Hammer chaired the National Cancer Advisory Panel, a group with direct access to the president, his appeal for $1 billion in funds contained precisely zero percent for study of the carcinogenic effects of the oil industry.[18]

Finally, there are the doctors and scientists themselves. As historian Robert Proctor writes:

[T]he sad truth is that cancer prevention is low prestige. Prevention is impoverished in an age of heroic medicine, where the reward structure is heavily biased in favor of last-ditch, quick-burst, high-tech interventions and high-profile, Nobel Prize potential basic science. In ... research, this means exorbitant funding for therapies and molecular genetics, and a more penurious approach to epidemiology, nutrition, health education, occupational health and safety.[19]

For all these reasons, public health and environmental policy are way down on the list of priorities.

But, Sally might reply, after all the money spent, all the research by all the white lab coats, we are winning the war on breast cancer, aren't we? This belief is encouraged by propaganda from the cancer establishment—and is highly doubtful. In fact, despite a small decline in breast cancer mortality among white women, "the death rate is still higher than it was when Rachel Carson died of the disease in 1964, and the proportion of women developing the disease at all remains at the highest level ever recorded."[20] To put numbers to it: "More than 175,000 women were diagnosed with invasive breast cancer in 1999, and approximately 44,000 died."[21] (Similarly, in the 1990s the rates of colorectal, brain, testicular, and kidney cancer continued to rise.)[22] In general, as Harvard Medical School professor Jerome Groopman writes in a recent article surveying the politics and overinflated rhetoric of public cancer policy:

> [T]he high expectations of the early seventies seem almost willfully naive. This year alone, more than a million new diagnoses of major cancers will be made and about five hundred and fifty thousand Americans will die of cancer, an average of fifteen hundred a day. In the course of a lifetime, one of every three American women will develop a potentially fatal malignancy. For men, the odds are one in two.[23]

Beyond biases in research and false publicity about the "successes" of the war on cancer, there are also biases in treatment. Once again we find a combination of established powers in medicine, pharmaceuticals, and government restricting consumer choices, harassing alternatives, and failing to report on the limitations and disastrous side effects of accepted "scientific" cures. The fifty-year persecution of the Hoxsey herbal cancer therapy by the American Medical Association and the government is but one case in point. Outlawed without being tested in the 1950s, it was used by tens of thousands with some dramatic results, while legal action was taken against those who administered it. Recently, tests have confirmed that all of its active herbal ingredients have some anticancer properties, and a panel of experts has recommended that it be systematically evaluated.

Yet because the Hoxsey treatment is herb-based it cannot be patented and sold for the enormous profits drug companies are used to. With global sales of chemotherapy drugs at over $30 billion a year, pharmaceuticals have little interest in something that cannot be patented, and their influence on the Food and Drug Administration helps create the fact that "the FDA has yet to approve a single nontoxic cancer agent or one not patented by a major pharmaceutical company."[24] Herbal treatments are way down on the list of priorities.

In general, according to Dr. Susan Love, advocate of better breast cancer treatment, the accepted treatment mode is to slash (surgery), burn (radiation), and poison (chemotherapy).[25] And the effectiveness of these treatments is often questionable. Of the women who are diagnosed with breast cancer without lymph node involvement, fewer than 10 percent will benefit from chemotherapy, "but many will suffer the consequences of side effects"[26]

And so Sally is told to get a mammogram and to exercise, to cut down on red meat and eat more vegetables. Eating organic foods will not be stressed, at least not by the American Cancer Society and the National Cancer Institute, even though the carcinogenic effects of chemical agriculture are hardly a secret. Few (if any) conventional authorities will tell Sally to avoid dioxins, PCBs, pesticides in city parks, radiation, or the effects of plastic on her endocrine system. And even if they did, the advice would have little effect, *for these things she simply cannot do as an individual.* These are social problems, demanding a collective response that will alter some of the basic structures of social life. So she is told that if she gets cancer, it is nobody's fault but is simply a matter of her individual genes or her "lifestyle." She may be counseled to come to terms with her "fate"; but she will rarely be encouraged to give voice to rage against those who have polluted our world and made us sick.

Death from breast cancer—afflicting young women in their prime of life, middle-aged women with families, active grandmothers—is always a personal tragedy. But however deeply personal the anguish to the person afflicted, however intimately painful to her friends and family, breast cancer is not just individual. From causes to treatment, from budgets for research to laws on "acceptable" treatments, it is also a social, and therefore a political, reality.

Truths that run counter to the dominant social institutions can only be accessed and known by politically defined groups that resist those institutions. In this case, an activist movement combining the efforts of feminists and environmentalists enables us to recognize the political nature of all dimensions of breast cancer and that, as Eisenstein puts it, "Breast cancer is both an individual and a socially and politically constructed experience . . . intimate and public; personal and political; genetic and environmental; economic and racialized; local and global."[27]

Concerns over women's treatment by a male-dominated medical profession were an essential part of the women's movement from the start. Poet and essayist Audre Lorde, who died from breast cancer in 1992, wrote of the bizarre pressure to wear a breast prosthesis in her doctor's office to protect "morale" in a place where every woman "either had a breast removed, might have to have a breast removed, or was afraid of having to have a breast removed." Yet, she noted scathingly, any woman "attempting to come to terms with her changed landscape and changed timetable of life and with her own body and pain and beauty and strength . . . is seen as a threat to the 'morale' of a breast surgeon's office!"[28] As early as 1975, a critic of the then prevalent procedure of doing mastectomies while women were still anesthetized for their biopsies wrote: "No man is going to make another man impotent while he's asleep without his permission, but there's no hesitation if it's a woman's breast."[29] Growing from scattered local support groups to a national movement, women have demanded access to information, choice in treatment, a reevaluation of the distorted cultural meaning of women's breasts, simple respect from medical personnel, and changed research priorities. Also, "issues of racial and economic diversity and of the links between breast cancer activism and social and political efforts directed at social change have begun to surface."[30]

On the side of environmentalism, four decades of ecological concern from Rachel Carson to Theo Coburn have stressed the relationships between pollution and illness. The environmental movement has insisted that breast cancer is a public health problem, not one of individualized disease, that it is a social, and hence a political, matter.

In recent years, the two streams have come together. From the Breast Cancer Fund to the National Organization of Women, from the Sierra Club to the Women's Community Cancer Project (one of their slogans is "Breast Cancer and the Environment: MAKE THE CONNECTION"), a political alternative to the dominant understanding is being fought for.[31] The Breast Cancer Fund demands the reduction or elimination of "toxic chemicals that are omnipresent in the lives of so many women in the modern industrialized world."[32] The president of the National Organization of Women told Congress and the president that "the environmental links to breast cancer must be researched. We are poisoning the earth, and women are dying because of it. Politicians must look past the bags of money the corporate lobbyists carry and look into the eyes of women with breast cancer."[33] The International POPs (Persistent Organic Pollutants) Elimination Network, an alliance of 100 nongovernmental organizations, advocates a worldwide ban of at least twelve of the most hazardous chemicals known to science. All of these "dirty dozen" chemicals are organochlorines that can travel thousands of miles through the atmosphere, linger in the environment, and concentrate in the fatty tissues of wildlife and humans.[34] And in *The New Our Bodies, Ourselves*, a

1992 updating of the classic feminist self-help book on women's health, a detailed section of the book links environmental hazards to illnesses and cancers of all kinds.[35]

Because these movements exist, Sally can see breast cancer in a new way. Although the United States continues to lose more people to breast cancer than the number lost in all the wars we've fought in the last sixty years, we no longer have to despair that this is due to some mysterious, uncontrollable genetic fate or some inexplicable "plague" that will be cured by the magic of science. When Sally thinks of her mother, she can ask not only about their common genes but about what was in their shared water, air, food, and home. She can join with others not in a "race for the cure" but in an attempt to change social life so that prevention, not treatment, is the goal. To do so, she will have to challenge the accumulated power of the chemical and drug companies and the entrenched "expertise" of the cancer establishment's bureaucrats, doctors, and scientists. Fortunately, as part of an international political movement, she will not have to do so alone.

If, as Tolstoy tells us, each happy family is alike but each unhappy one different, the same is true—in spades—for disabilities. Each disability has its own profound and particular effects on body, mind, and soul. Each person with disabilities and each set of their caretakers face distinct challenges, griefs, and opportunities for growth. Although a great deal has been written about these issues in recent years, much of what I write here will draw lessons not only from our collective situation but from my own family.

My fifteen-year-old daughter, Esther, suffers from an undiagnosed neuromotor disability. Her difficulties include developmental delay, extremely weak muscles, severe scoliosis, easily dislocated joints, breakable bones, mild hearing loss, seizure disorder, and tendencies to anxiety and perseveration. She attends a special school and has been seen by (at least) 250 doctors, therapists, alternative healers, and consultants. She requires help with many of the activities of daily living, cannot be left alone in our home, and cannot go out by herself. Managing her medical, educational, and therapeutic help takes enormous amounts of research, strategizing, phone calls, and coordination. Because she has no diagnosis and because alternative treatments not covered by medical insurance often make a highly significant difference in her general health and quality of life, we spend many thousands of dollars each year on out-of-pocket medical expenses.

In some ways, Esther is one of the happiest people I know. An extremely loving person, she has with our help found people and places where she feels welcome and at home: her school, our temple, the community music center where she has had music therapy for eight years, her summer camps. At the same time, in many ways her life is extremely limited and difficult. And she is smart enough to know, as she said to me once, that "I have special needs; and I'm sick of it. I want to be normal, like everyone I know. I'm tired of being so slow, and having a hard time reading, and trying to help my back. It's not fair."

Most of all, Esther lacks friends, peers, other kids to hang out with. She has her family, social activities into which we have worked quite hard to integrate her, and the TV set. But the simple fact is that she lacks the social skills to make friends with "normal" kids her own age. When she engages with adults, who will compensate, she is a charming conversationalist. But most kids don't compensate, and Esther cannot keep up with their banter, their easy laughter, their quick minds shifting from subject to subject. (At the same time, she has a surprisingly creative ability with language—once calling toasted marshmallows "fire ice cream" and describing a windy day as one in which "the wind is purring.") This problem is the source of a great loneliness for those with mental disabilities, and of an enormous pressure to compensate for that loneliness on the part of caregivers.

Disability issues and breast cancer have at least one political dimension in common. For Esther and millions of other children born with mysterious birth defects, what is presented as a private "tragedy" may in fact have a good deal to do with social life. The same chemicals that alter cell structure to promote cancer can cause birth defects as well. We have just begun to examine how the 75,000 largely untested chemicals that permeate our surroundings are damaging our children; but we already know that dioxins, lead, and PCBs have harmful effects on the developing nervous and endocrine systems.[36] In this sense, Esther's disabilities may be an effect of collective arrangements that allow dangerous chemicals into the environment. What has happened to her and our family may be, thus, a *political* fact.

Since there is so much overlap, I need not go into detail here, except to say that (once again) seeing this dimension of disability, like comparable insights in regard to breast cancer, is itself a political accomplishment. The national toxics movement, with struggles typically initiated by uneducated mothers and housewives, began when these women reflected on clusters of mysterious illnesses among their own and their neighbors' children. Made famous by *A Civil Action* and *Erin Brockovich*, this movement has challenged the role of environmental toxins in cancers, birth defects, and countless other illnesses. As Lois Gibbs of Love Canal fame, who was one of the first leaders of the movement, recalls: "I got involved because my son Michael had epilepsy, and my daughter Melissa developed a rare blood disease . . . I never thought of myself as an activist or an organizer. I was a housewife, a mother, but all of a sudden it was my family, my children, and my neighbors."[37] Trying to understand the causes of these illnesses led these women into battle with dishonesty and paternalism from professionals, corporations, and the government, and with widespread sexist and classist resistance to working-class women speaking out on public policy. They often found themselves up against a good deal of the political and cultural power structure. But they also discovered that their worst fears were justified: Something in the air or water had poisoned their children.[38]

Although the *causes* of breast cancer are a social matter, most would agree that the diagnosis, once achieved, is a straightforward matter of medicine. For disability, on the other hand, the very idea of what it is to *be disabled* is in many ways a social and political issue. In fact, many people have questioned the whole idea that "being disabled" is a simple, natural fact about a person, comparable to their height or eye color. To counter this notion, disability activists introduced the distinction between an "impairment" and a "disability" (and some formal agencies, including the Word Health Organization have adopted this). An *impairment* is some restriction on the normal functioning of a limb, organ, or mechanism of the body. A *disability*, by contrast, is a kind of disadvantage or restriction caused by the particular way in which society is organized.[39] To understand the point, consider that 500 years ago, I, with poor vision bordering on legal blindness, would have been seriously disabled. In our society, I need merely put on my glasses to see almost perfectly. My *impaired* vision is, in contemporary America, no *disability* at all. Severe dyslexia causing an inability to read is a big deal today; but in a peasant village in which almost no one was literate, the concept of "someone who has trouble learning to read" would not even exist.

If we focus on Esther's impairments, the central explanation for why it is not safe for her to walk around the block alone is that there is something wrong with her. Her impairments are the cause of the problem. This viewpoint gives rise to her—and at times her parents'—sense of humiliation and marginalization. When these feelings predominate, the disabled and their caregivers become demoralized: endlessly aware of their limitations, unable to think that they deserve rights. If, however, we examine the social patterns that are as much at the root of Esther's inability to go out for a walk by herself as her own developmental delay and motor weakness, then we are led in a different direction. Then we see that while Esther is *impaired* because she is less strong, coordinated, and socially savvy than the norm, she is *disabled* because we live in a society in which the unwary or frail are preyed upon in public, where masculinity is often bound up with violence, where severe economic inequalities breed frustration and crime, and where women are often viewed as sexual prey. We can then wonder: What is the real problem: Esther's motor weakness and emotional immaturity or these sicknesses of our culture?

Journalist Joseph Shapiro makes the point in describing a wheelchair-bound disability rights activist:

> To Jones, there is nothing tragic about the childhood polio that resulted in her needing a wheelchair or a three-wheeled motorized scooter to get around in. Disability becomes a tragedy only when she and her husband . . . who also uses a wheelchair, cannot get into a restaurant or are kicked out of a movie theater because the manager decides their scooter and wheelchair make them a "fire hazard."[40]

Of course it might be argued that the problem with Esther—and it is a problem—is that she cannot be normally "autonomous" because she lacks normal "intelligence." But these concepts too are socially constructed, and the manner of their construction tells us as much about what our society lacks as it does about how Esther is deficient. In this and the following section, I will show how even these familiar concepts of intelligence and autonomy have a political dimension.

We all seem to have a pretty clear idea of what intelligence is: how it is assessed from an early age. How our schools streamed us as very bright, bright, ordinary, or dull. How we had that sinking nervous feeling in our stomachs before we opened the letter with our College Board scores, and how we might have hit our own mental wall at calculus, irregular French verbs, or Hegel. We all know that getting into Harvard means you're smarter than if you get into Ohio State, that doctors and lawyers and scientists are smarter than housecleaners, cab drivers, and car salesmen. But most important, we all know that there is a poorly defined but terribly real line that says: This person is of normal intelligence, and this person isn't. Of course, in a time when a disturbing (and increasing) percentage of children are diagnosed with learning disabilities, the line is becoming less and less clear; and there are all sorts of confusing boundary cases about which we can argue. Yet the image of the person who is "slow," "developmentally disabled," or "retarded" remains.

But what is the meaning and value of this intelligence? An MIT scientist once suggested that we respond to global warming by covering the oceans with white Styrofoam chips to reflect the sunlight. Before ozone-depleting CFCs were introduced, they were tested for their effects only up to 40,000 feet—as if they would somehow know to stop there and not go up higher to where the ozone level is; even after the damage that CFCs cause was known beyond the shadow of a doubt, they were still being produced and sold.[41] I personally—with my doctorate and list of books—have repeated certain spiritual errors over and over again. And not unlike many other folks, I spend a good deal of my adult life very, very slowly unlearning misguided ways of dealing with grief or fear.

If these are the products of "normal" intelligence, why are we so unreflectively eager to have it, display it, and reward it—and to feel superior to those who have less? Of course, it is true that the MIT scientist had to have the brainpower to get a Ph.D.; and whatever the environmental effects of CFCs, it is quite a technological feat to create home freezers and cars that can be cool on the hottest summer days. And it is also the case that Esther's asthma medicine and leg braces had to be designed by "smart" people.

But surely it is one of the critical questions of our time to ask: What is the deeper meaning of intelligence *beyond* technical competence?[42] Living in a global society that combines enormous technical accomplishments with enormous practical and moral failures—the Internet with mass starvation, for instance—should make us realize that our collective intelligence is, not unlike Esther's, very strong in some places and disabled in others. Esther lacks many mental abilities that she needs. But she would not, for example, allow her house to be filled with poisons if she could help it. And she is highly accomplished at extending emotional support to people who are upset. Who has more problems with their cognitive capabilities: the child who cannot learn to read or the nations that supported the threat of nuclear war for forty years? The child who has trouble chatting with peers or the larger society whose enthusiasm for war, racial conflict, overconsumption, and toxic spectacles is making us all sick?

It might be suggested that the failures here are moral, not cognitive; that people act in these destructive ways because they seek profit or power, not because they lack intelligence. It can be replied, again, that these acts are not performed in a vacuum: They are allowed, tacitly supported, or openly encouraged by the larger society. If those in power act badly not out of a lack of intelligence but out of a lack of character, what is the nature of the collective failure of the rest of us who allow them to run the show?

It is true that Esther cannot read the *Times*, do long division, or understand the nature of representative government. But could it also be that focusing on what Esther lacks is a distraction from our own limitations? Could it be that "normal" society is riddled with such monumental obtuseness that singling out the developmentally delayed as being the ones who are deficient in intelligence is itself an act of monumental chutzpah? And perhaps a reflection of our accommodation to the social and political status quo?

Then there is the other key issue, that of autonomy. The great advantage of modern society—that we can choose how we will live (where, with whom, and under whatever ideological, religious, or lifestyle banner our hearts desire)—is not for Esther. In her daily life, she is extremely dependent. Because of her motor problems, lack of understanding of her own body in space, poor balance, and muscle weakness, the sheer number of things she cannot do for herself is daunting. This issue is very much at the center of my concerns for her, and many other parents I've met feel the same way.

Yet I remember an internal dialogue I once had about her situation, one in which I was asking myself, as directly as possible, just what it was that tormented me about the effects of her impairments. "I don't care if she doesn't go to medical school," I reflected. "It is just how *dependent* she is. How different she is from the rest of us."

Then, however, I began to question this last thought. It was a pretty cold February day in Boston—and I remembered that the oil delivery was due that afternoon. Without that delivery, just exactly how was I going to keep warm when the temperature dipped below 10° at night? It was also rather late in the week, and I needed to make my usual shopping trip to our local mega–health food store for the $100-plus of organic vegetables, imported seaweed, grains, Brazilian orange juice, Chilean fruit, and obscure nutritional supplements that make up the diet of my nutritionally correct family. Where in fact would we be, I realized—all of us and not just "dependent Esther"—without the vast reaches of the modern food system? These examples, so obvious when thought about, could be multiplied indefinitely. We are all dependent on countless anonymous individuals for our food, energy, clothes, transportation, and medical care. We need emotional connection with parents, siblings, lovers, and friends. We need the energy of the sun and the work of the nitrogen-fixing bacteria in the soil, not to mention the billions of friendly microbes that service the interior of our own digestive and immune systems. In these and countless other ways, "autonomy" is to a great extent a myth.

Further, imagining ourselves as fully autonomous often goes along with forgetting that the body is essential to who we are and that our bodies are only temporarily "able." As Martha Nussbaum writes, when we identify with our rational, independent intellects, or our temporarily able bodies, we forget that we are subject to accident and luck and that we change with age.[43] The truth is that reason and intelligence depend on the state of our bodies, often diminishing when we are least ready. Once again, the stress on Esther's differences obscures certain truths about our sameness. This is a social convention, a widespread belief, with powerful political consequences.

———————

The idea of intelligent (or, as philosophers often say, "rational") autonomy as central to human identity is usually represented as a neutral picture of human nature. That it leaves out the very young, the sick, the old, and the disabled has until recently not bothered political philosophers very much. If we examine the political implications of this omission, one that often also applies to critics of individualism, we will see some of the central ways in which the conditions of the disabled and their caretakers are politically rather than medically determined.

In its initial version, this image of human nature, for all its faults, had a positive aspect. By imagining the rational, autonomous individual, Enlightenment philosophers created an alternative to the reigning oppressive norms. The new perspective enabled world-making political thinkers to justify knowledge, morality, and political power without appealing to tradition, inherited authority, and religious dogma. As an individual knower, I could subject church teachings to rational science. As a free citizen, I could ask whether political arrangements violated my personal rights, rights that legitimately took precedence over decisions by those in power. As an autonomous moral agent, I could enter into equal and reciprocal relationships with other moral agents.

Yet when individualism of this kind is examined from the perspective of the real spectrum of human capabilities, its failures emerge. In particular, the dependent or disabled do not fit the model of the autonomous individual. They may require others' help for the most basic of bodily needs and be unable to reciprocate in kind for what they receive. They may be incapable of fully voicing their own interests in the realm of politics. Some cannot freely enter into contracts, exercise personal freedom, or form adequate conceptions of social life. How then will they exercise their rights? How then can they receive "justice"?

On the flip side of the situation, those who care for the extremely dependent carry a burden far in excess of the normal subjects of political struggle. In many cases, they do not have the time, energy, or money to organize, represent themselves in the public sphere, or reshape social life in terms of their interests. When the labor of dependency is poorly paid and assigned to minorities and when doing it well requires a unique blend of personal involvement and moral commitment, how will dependency workers have the time, energy, or resources to represent their personal interests in a public sphere designed for autonomous individuals? Even political improvement based in other struggles may well not be adequate to this one. For instance, even women who can vote, own property, and become brain surgeons will lack real social equality if they are expected to take primary responsibility in the care of their own children, their aging parents, their paraplegic sister.

Much of political philosophy of the last century and a half has been highly critical of individualism, yet it also slights the disabled and their caretakers. Hegel and Marx argued that social life was shaped by collective action; feminist theory asserts that connection rather than autonomy is basic to both ethics and psychology. And politically, there are times in our society when a collective concern supersedes individual interests. Workers, women, and racial minorities came to the fore in law and politics when they learned to argue collectively on their own behalf.[44] The problem, however, is that some of the extremely dependent, especially the aged or the developmentally challenged, cannot achieve their rights or organize to have their needs met in the same way. In some cases, at least, they need to have others organize *for* them. Although the disability rights movement has won tremendous gains for those with disabilities, there remains a hierarchy both in the movement itself and in the broader society, in which those with "normal" intelligence have status and position that the developmentally delayed do not.

Thus the dominant political views, including those of liberals and progressives, need some work in this area. As philosopher Eva Kittay writes, models of equality for women that simply envision women being allowed into men's roles will not do. She forcefully argues that unless dependency needs are met in a different way than they are at present, every "successful" woman with a family will need the services of some other women to deal with the dependency needs of the rest of the family.[45] Although this might be workable for the comparatively short time and limited scope of what nondisabled children need, it is quite another matter to deal with one who is permanently disabled or to care for an adult who is stricken with a long-term illness.

> The world we know is one fashioned by the dreams of those who, by and large, consider themselves independent. Their self-understanding as independent persons is generally purchased at a price—one set so low and considered so inevitable that few have traditionally considered it pertinent to considerations of social justice. The purchase price of independence is a wife, a mother, a nursemaid, a nanny—a dependency worker.... Those who do dependency work ... become vulnerable to economic deprivation, lack of sleep, disruptions of their own intimate life, loss of leisure and career opportunities.[46]

And by a diminished ability to represent their—and their charges'—interests in the realm of politics.

——— • ———

To take dependency needs seriously, our society would have to profoundly change its politics, economics, and culture. The notion that social relations outside the home are to be based on reciprocity—I do for you if, and only if, you do for me—would have to be replaced by some large-scale commitments to care and human dignity. We would have to move beyond exchange as the central principle of human relations and beyond "rights" thought of as fences to keep us from interfering with each others' exchanges and preferences.

In such a society, perhaps I would not have been delayed promotion by my employer for missing department meetings, because my employer would realize that I take Esther to forty to fifty doctors and therapy appointments a year and spend countless hours helping her with activities of daily living. I simply have a lot less time for meetings than people without such responsibilities. Similarly, it would not be taken for granted that poor, uneducated, and often nonwhite women are the ones who will tend our parents and grandparents in nursing homes. Esther's needs—or those of people in wheelchairs, or those who cannot speak, or those who have trouble relating—would be understood as part of the human condition, and those who have them as part of our human community. Such a community might resemble, surprisingly, Marx's definition of communism: "From each according to his ability to each according to his needs." It would also remind us of religious values from Moses and Jesus to Buddha and Muhammad: "Do unto others as you would have them do unto you." And here one needs only think, as Alasdair MacIntyre[47] has pointed out, how one would like to be treated if "it"—paralysis, blindness, brain damage—had happened to oneself.

Making these values effective in social life would fundamentally alter the experience of disability. In some cultures, the developmentally challenged are thought to be special messengers of God, and thus people's attitudes toward them and their own quality of life are very different than in our society. In our own time and place, we need a new story, an altered perception, for us all.

In recent years, we have made some movement in that direction, largely because of a political movement for disability rights. The movement begins with a description of the social conditions faced by those with disabilities, leading from that description to the claim that a good deal of their suffering is a result of social injustice. In general, says disability rights activist Evan Kemp, society sees the disabled as "childlike, helpless, hopeless, nonfunctioning and noncontributing members of society."[48] James Charlton's *Nothing About Us*

Without Us chronicles the common oppression faced worldwide by the disabled, including marginalization, poverty, humiliation, paternalism, secondary legal status, cultural stigmatization, and violence.[49] He also describes how, in response to oppression, disability activists have organized for "rights, not charity," by challenging precisely those cultural presuppositions and political arrangements that turn impairments into disabilities. Struggles have included issues of public access, right to employment without discrimination, and the availability of services.

In 1990, decades of struggle and preliminary legislation culminated in the passage of the historically unprecedented Americans with Disabilities Act. Through it, the disabled received civil rights recognition and protection, similar in some ways to African-American advances gained through the Civil Rights Act of 1964.[50] Its passage was a victory over the prevailing legal climate. This climate, according to a Philadelphia public-interest attorney:

> Reflected common stereotypes of disabled persons as dependent and inferior. Laws characteristically excluded handicapped persons from services, benefits, and protections provided, as a matter-of-course to all persons. Specialized legislation enacted to protect the disabled was premised on notions of charity rather than entitlement and implemented so as to segregate the disabled and suffocate their ability to participate in society.[51]

Individuals with disabilities must overcome this generalized cultural meaning. Jean Stewart, confined to a wheelchair by a rare muscular condition, compares people with disabilities to other oppressed groups, all engaged in the "self-abuse trade." "The social worker who warned me to stay away from 'handicapped groups' knew perfectly well what she was doing . . . she was trying to keep us apart, by convincing each of us that our disabilities were our own personal problems." Everyone was eager to tell her how to get special services at home, but not to encourage her to go out into the public world. "No one spoke of civil rights . . . And no one, nope, *no one*, in my world anyway, tried to name the problem: whose fault was it we were 'homebound?' *Who bound us?*"[52]

Grassroots disability groups seek a new perspective. In Connecticut, People First represents the mentally handicapped, who, despite their impairments, demand a fundamental change in their treatment. "Close down all state institutions for people with retardation. Give us paid sick leave, vacation time, and holidays at our job sites and at sheltered worships. Recognize our right to have relationships, even to have sex with those we choose in our institutions and group homes." Self-advocacy groups have engaged in a variety of activities, from picketing the Department of "Mental Retardation" in Massachusetts for an end to the demeaning label to demanding decent wages for their labor in Denver.[53] In a way, the claim of those with disabilities returns us to the theme of making knowledge democratic that was raised in the feminist critique of traditional religion. Just as women asked, "How can you know what God's will is if you don't allow women to study God and speak their truth?" so the disabled ask: "How can we know what limitations our impairments cause, if we are not granted the rights, support, and respect to make as much of our lives as we can?"

As Esther's father, I know that we have a long way to go. Political rights and cultural acceptance are far from complete. But in a comparatively short time, the lives of those with serious impairments are, at least in some countries, dramatically different from what they used to be. Because we have made some strides toward a society of collective support and recognition rather than competition and power, being in a wheelchair or having less than normal intelligence just do not mean what they once did. Just as I am a different person in a society that makes eyeglasses, so shaping lives through care and dignity make a different Esther. To the extent that this is a political difference, what Esther is—the meaning of her strengths as well as her weaknesses—is a matter of politics.

———————

And yet.

No matter what political changes occur, cancer and disability will still give rise to much suffering; and many of the needed changes are not yet even on the horizon. The anguish these conditions cause, both to those who suffer and to their families and caregivers, will remain for the foreseeable future. If we are not to live in despair over our own fate—a despair worsened when we realize that our sufferings could be dramatically improved by social change—we need the virtues of compassion, awareness, love, and transcendence of the ego that can be found both in traditional faiths and in eclectic spiritual perspectives.

In a society dominated by images of autonomous accomplishment, consumption, and pleasure, cancer and disability represent only loss, tragedy, and despair. In conventional terms, such lives are defined by an untimely death after a debilitating illness or by limitations, physical pain, dependence, and social isolation. As one friend said to me—actually trying to be supportive!—having a child like Esther is "every parent's worst nightmare." Occasionally, of course, we see a TV drama in which there is a heroic triumph over all odds. The one-legged boy who runs the marathon, the cancer survivor with a miraculous cure, the charming boy with Down's syndrome. These images only emphasize how bereft are all the others who are not special, who don't beat the odds, who are not at all cute. When (it seems) the whole world is celebrating Mother's Day, we can only feel the ache of loss for the one who is not there. When youth, physical beauty, career success, and a neat portfolio are the ideal, children who cannot read or walk seem simply to be a loss. Acquaintances casually talk about how I will feel "when your kids finally go away to college." It is a small but painful matter to remind them that my older daughter will go, but Esther will not. The awkward silence that follows only emphasizes that those of us with disabled children—no less than those whose mothers were lost to cancer—inhabit a different country, a different universe, than the norm. As the mother of a developmentally delayed son in the poignant documentary *Best Boy* says: "If you want to know heartache, have a retarded child."

It is here that spiritual resources are most needed. A political understanding, we have seen, teaches us that suffering we thought inescapable is in many ways socially created and that we can struggle for rights as well as hope for charity. Conversely, a spiritual understanding enables us—on our good days, at least—to live in the face of death, physical pain, and impaired lives without denial, escapism, bitterness, or despair.

In the context of breast cancer, the central issue is a death that comes painfully early, wrenching women out of their lives.[54] One familiar religious response is to say that the death of the body is not the death of the person. But although the prospect of heaven or reincarnation can be enormously soothing to some, it is not such metaphysical claims that I focus on here. The heart of religious teaching for a modern age, I believe, comes from its psychological insight and moral wisdom, not its promises about Other Realms. In any case, I want to describe resources that can be meaningful to people no matter what their beliefs (or lack of belief) about life after death.

Is there any way to deal with the terrible sense of unfairness, isolation, and defeat aroused by an untimely death from cancer? I am not saying without grief. Both for the dying and those who love them, grief is the natural response to death. But the bitter sense of loss that comes when we lose our forty-six-year-old-mother or confront our own life being cut short at fifty-three and imagine the effects on husband and children—that is not the same as the more normalized sorrow that accompanies someone who has had a full term of life.

We can begin a response to this question by remembering the work of Elisabeth Kübler-Ross, who introduced the simple but (sadly) at the time unheard of practice of counseling terminal cancer patients in hospitals by talking directly to them about the fact that they were dying. Her gift was to encourage

people to face the imminent end of their lives, to directly experience the fear
and rage that end was provoking, to finish whatever they could in the time remaining, and, thus, to be able to achieve some kind of clarity and peace as the
end approached.[55] Remembering Tolstoy's character Ivan Ilyich, who
lamented that the most painful part of his ever-worsening illness was how
people around him kept pretending that he was not dying, we can appreciate
how enormous Kübler-Ross's contribution was.

Although this might sound more psychological than religious, its success
depends, I believe, on a fundamental reorientation toward the meaning of
life. Such a reorientation is in a broad sense spiritual. The central value is
first on facing reality directly, surely a nearly revolutionary stance in a society
so bound up in denial and illusion as ours is. Contemporary culture, driven
by images of unending consumption and medical expertise, treats death as a
stranger, an enemy, an obscenity or, equally unreal, as a spectacle. Religions
teach us, in the words of Solomon, "There is a time to live, and a time to
die." Students of Buddhism have long been instructed to meditate on corpses
or on what their own body will look like in a hundred years. Every traditional
Jewish prayer service includes a prayer to be said by mourners. And there is a
wonderful story in which a famous rabbi tells his followers that repentance,
which traditionally one is supposed to do for more than a month before the
critical holiday of Yom Kippur, needs be done for one day only, the day before one's death. "But Rabbi," asked a confused disciple, "how are we to know
which day it will be?" "That," the rabbi replied quietly, "is the point."

Stephen Levine adapted Kubler-Ross's work to a Buddhist framework. His
inspiration is the traditional Buddhist belief that pain can be endured and
overcome best when it is looked at directly, without resistance or judgment.
He suggested that for the dying and those around them, the task was to seek
openness to whatever the present moment contains, including the realities of
pain and imminent loss, and to allow the bounds of separate identity and ego
involvement to fade in the process. He writes: "Resistance to the pain about
us causes the heart to wither. Allowing that pain to enter into us tears our
heart open and leaves us exposed to the truth." The truth Levine finds is that
when we fully open our hearts to the pain, we find a wellspring of compassion—for ourselves and others.[56]

It is a discovery of this kind that makes the pain bearable and that for some
breast cancer "victims" makes the experience into something of enormous
personal benefit. As one of the coauthors of *Speak the Language of Healing*, a
book about how to face cancer without "going to war," writes: "It is the very
transience of life that makes it precious. If we all expected to live forever, life
would not amount to much. It would become very cheap . . . Given the real-

ity of death, how do I find peace of mind? . . . Knowing that I will die—perhaps in a year or two, perhaps this afternoon—is exactly what makes me savor life."[57] Or as many spiritual writers have said: Time is an illusion. The fantasy future is just an image in the mind, a "shorter" life only a product of thought that compares one mental image to another. To fully engage in *this* moment is to take all that we could ever really have. In that full engagement, neither past nor future exist, because we no longer compare the reality of what we have with the thought of something else. In that time without comparison or limit, we can find joy no matter what the state of our cancer. As another author in *Speak the Language of Healing* says: "I believe we arrive in this life as spiritual beings, and one of our tasks here is to learn to be human. For me, cancer has been my greatest teacher and my greatest gift. In four difficult years following the diagnosis, my heart embraced a life lesson that Adrienne Rich shared in her poetry: 'I came to see the damage that was done and the treasures that prevail.'"[58]

A woman with breast cancer lists the lessons of her illness, her "treasures that prevail": to accept the reality of her limits and imperfections, to face her fear, to fulfill her own need for nurturance. Having learned these lessons, she can tell us that the "real measure of my healing would not be about a cure in my body. No, healing would happen in my heart and soul." When that happens, she is ready to say, "I do not yearn for the old breast, the old life. If cancer was the price I had to pay to make the transition to a place of peace, I would do it again in a heartbeat."[59]

Of course, a committed secularist or devoted skeptic might look askance at such revelations. "What are these stories," they might say, "but people screwed by environmental pollutants and bad luck clutching at illusions?" My reply would be that in the end *everyone* is telling a story, and all we can do is decide which ones we like better. Saying that breast cancer is only a tragedy, a loss, and a defeat is just as much a "story" as saying that it is a spiritual teacher. Each account is equally compatible with the facts; neither can be "proved" as more rational than the other. However, it is not hard to see which one will give us a meaning that we can live—and die—with, and which one is more likely to leave us bitter. None of the women quoted above are appealing to faith in Heaven. Neither are they denying the reality of their pain. However, they have found ways to think about their experiences that allow them some real happiness despite their troubles. If such achievements are "illusions," they may work too well to be cast aside.

And, of course, none of the spiritual responses to cancer rule out legitimate political anger at its causes or diminish the wrenching loss of care a woman might have given to her family. As a survivor of breast cancer who constantly confronts the possibility that it may return, Carol Osborn tells us that for her the spiritual meaning of her illness is a simple question: "What do I need to do next to live as much life as I can fully, wholly, and deeply?" Also, however, she refuses to surrender her anger at the "military-industrial complex, fueled by greed, machismo, and selfishness, that has polluted the environment and raised to unprecedented levels the risk for developing cancers."[60] Here, spiritual insight and political critique are comrades, equally part of a full and constructive response to the rigors of life.

In the context of disability, there is the spiritual struggle of those with impairments, and those faced by their caregivers. As Eva Kittay says, we live in "nested dependencies," in which the needs of a person with disabilities radiate outward in concentric circles of care. Although this is true for a wide range of people it holds, I believe, a special weight in the case of parents. Since this enormous topic deserves it own book—which it won't get here—I abandon any pretense to painting a balanced picture and simply concentrate on my life with Esther.

As a father, it is my enduring grief that I cannot heal Esther of her weaknesses, limitations, and pain. I cannot straighten her twisted spine without submitting her to a life-threatening operation, and I cannot enable her to understand complicated abstractions. Fears and frustrations of this kind have been particularly significant in her case because, lacking a diagnosis, it has never been clear how much she could accomplish or develop if we found just the right therapy or healing technique. Yet even with home-study programs, searching for gifted but unconventional healers, making her exercise before she gets to watch TV, purchasing thirty-seven overpriced computer learning programs, and doing Hooked on Phonics together, there is only so far she can go, and only so much my wife and I can do. And the older she gets, the less Esther (in this she is normal) wants to learn from either of her parents. Her best efforts are reserved for her teachers and therapists.

Even worse in some ways, I can do little to shield her from the casual cruelties of the surrounding society. I can pave the way for her at Hebrew school, her music center, her summer camp. But then I will simply have to hope for the best. I cannot make friends for her, get her invited to birthday parties, or make sure she will not be sexually abused in later life. As I age, and consider what will happen after my wife and I die, I can only hope that other people will see the beauty of her soul and take care of her. Political insights about how this society could be different, and her life easier, don't compensate for the way things actually are right now.

In *conventional* terms, Esther's impairments make her a kind of failure, and me a failed—or at least dreadfully unlucky—father. She will have few of the standard forms of happiness. Neither career nor a nuclear family is in her future. And she will not give me very many of the usual types of parental pleasure either. Virtually every aspect of *my* life—marriage, friendships, professional life, travel, finances—is severely contracted to meet her special needs.

Thus, I cannot control what I seek to control, and I will not get that for which I had hoped. If I am to value my parenting and my child, it must be through the development of a different perspective than the one most parents use to look at themselves and their children. I must remake my own approach to fatherhood in spiritual terms—as well as hope that in the future the world will be remade politically.

For a start, I must see my parenting dilemmas as a ceaseless reminder that what I can accomplish is really very limited. For me, this is a spiritual test of the highest order, for it requires that I overcome my narcissistic interpretation of Esther's fate: that it was given to me to save her life. Yet who, after all, told me that I was God and had the power to heal what is broken in the world? At the same time, I cannot walk away from the obligations that have been placed before me. I must do what can be done, even while knowing that a good deal of what I do may accomplish little. Returning to a theme introduced in Chapter 4, isn't this dilemma precisely what much of the world's spiritual teachings focus on? The warrior Prince Arjuna, hero of the Hindu religious poem *Bhagavad Gita*, is instructed by the god Krishna to fulfill his social duty but release his attachment to the results of his actions. Buddhists counsel us to realize that the problem is not that the world is uncontrollable, but that we don't accept this fundamental truth. And, they add, it is also essential that we live with compassion for all who suffer. Kierkegaard said flatly that if we are to avoid despair, we must give up our attachment to "world-historical" accomplishments and concentrate on the passions of our religious subjectivity, making sure to lead principled ethical lives at the same time. The Talmud, stressing the integrity rather than the accomplishments of love, teaches us that "to save one person is like saving the whole world." And it also suggests that even if we cannot save the one person, our efforts make a difference in "other realms." Countless traditional and nontraditional spiritual voices have said that whatever healing, helping, and social improvement we perform is God working through us, not the fruits of our own individual abilities or powers.

In the end, the only aspect of Esther's life that I can control is the part in which I offer her love and give up my desperate attachment to "results." Spiritually, the central task is not to change her, but myself. For if I am to love her even though she is not cured, I must accept the value of my own love even if I cannot cure her. I cannot use *her* progress as a measure of *my* adequacy. This means that her sweet smile, her genuine joy in the happiness of others, her jokes, her courage, and her emotional wisdom can shine for me at least as much as the career in environmental law or four grandchildren that I will not get from her. In spiritual terms, of course, my tasks are not really that different from other people. Having Esther simply means I've got a built-in teacher in this area. Because she is what she is, I cannot evade what other people are more able to hide from.

A spiritual understanding of my situation, when I can manage it, helps makes life in a disabled family possible, bearable, and also beautiful. As Eva Kittay writes, "Sesha" (her multiply handicapped daughter who cannot walk or speak) is a "teacher of love."[61] Michael Berube argues that the ultimate value of mainstreaming his son, Jamie, who has Down's syndrome, is that the other children will learn to understand and value difference, and thus develop their humanity. And that in this sense Jamie has as much to offer the "normal" school setting as it has to offer him.[62] In several collections of writings by parents of children with disabilities, the same message is repeated.[63] When we love, and when we see clearly, it is all right. The pain is not erased. But it has a different meaning.

For in the end, it is only love that we can control. And thus the value or goal of love is the one sure ticket out of the cul-de-sac of despair that disabilities can cause. As Miriam Greenspan writes, despair is different than other painful emotions because to a greater extent it has a moral dimension that asks us to make meaning out of suffering. Despair leads us to ask: Why has this happened? What is the point of struggling against it? What do I gain for all my labor, for all my loneliness? In the context of disability, these questions abound. If we are to find a way out of despair, says Greenspan, it can only be through listening to its insistent message that we must change our expectations, attachments, beliefs, and dreams. We must find some new way in which to live.[64] The father of a child with autism writes, "The sorrow, although unwelcome, can be a pathway to an unconditional love that grows from a realization of the intrinsic beauty of each child's existence. We parents of children with disabilities can feel fine about ourselves when we grasp this and give up superficial achievement-based values."[65] This process is complex and multifaceted, marked by pain that cannot be discounted. As the mother of a child with multiple handicaps says, "Sometimes I feel burned out, other times, completely inspired . . . I realize that I am a better person for having gone through this struggle. But I also know that my lost innocence was the price I paid for this enrichment as a human being."[66]

This need to face and understand our suffering, and to change toward new values, is perhaps the basic spiritual narrative—the common core of world spirituality. The Jewish experience of slavery and liberation, the crucifixion of Jesus, the acetic wanderings of the Buddha, Muhammad's flight through the desert—all these may well be read symbolically as well as literally. They are all, in a sense, about a kind of death and rebirth, about a profound loss and suffering that makes possible a life deepened by love, broadened by compassion, and illuminated by appreciation for the miracles of daily life. These stories are not about finding a form of life in which nothing is lost. Jesus had his moments of despair on the cross. The Jewish patriarch Jacob was able to carry on the covenant only after he wrestled with an angel, an encounter that left him with a permanent limp, "disabled." "Suffering," C. S. Lewis declared after his wife died of cancer, "is God's wake up call."[67] But what is it we are to wake up to? To accepting that a life that we cannot control, that may be enormously painful, is still a life worth living.

From a spiritual point of view, each person is of infinite value, because each person, if looked at properly, can help us with the infinite task of finding our true nature, loving God, or reaching enlightenment. In this context, unlike the SATs, football games, law school, or the stock exchange, disability is no handicap. If we pay attention, anyone can be our teacher. That is one reason human beings deserve love—and the respect and care that love entails. The theme of the healing, transformative power of love is also basic to religious traditions. The Torah lists among God's attributes several different terms denoting care and compassion. The New Testament proclaims that God sacrificed His son out of love for human beings. In Hindu Bhakti Yoga, loving devotion to the guru is the path to enlightenment. In these kinds of love, we both lose and find ourselves. We know—with a knowledge that will sometimes give way to fear and despair but which, having arisen, is never fully lost—that despite everything our lives are precious.

What of those who have the disabilities? What of their spiritual path? In ways similar to what I have sketched, and echoing the rallying cries of the disability rights movement, they must first resist our culture's typical understanding of their condition. That meaning centers on loss, frailty, inertia, lack of autonomy, and helplessness. Susan Wendell, a philosopher suffering from extreme chronic fatigue syndrome, writes in terms that apply to science and beyond: "In the societies where Western science and medicine are powerful culturally, and where their promise to control nature is still widely believed, people with disabilities are constant reminders of the failures of that promise, and of the inability of science and medicine to protect everyone from illness, disability, and death. They are 'the Others' that science would like to forget."[68] Wendell, like those struggling with breast cancer, must work through despair if she is to make sense of her life. This she does by valuing what she has, rather than simply missing what is gone forever.

> When I look back on the beginning of my illness, I still think of it, as I did then, as an involuntary violation of my body. But I now feel that such violations are sometimes the beginning of a better life . . . The state of my body limited the possibilities in new ways, but it also presented new kinds of understanding, new interests, new passions, and projects. In this sense, my experience of illness has been profoundly meaningful.[69]

This struggle has at times been against the dominant interpretation of religion as much as against that of secular culture. Religion too has cast disability in a dark light, at times characterizing it as a consequence of sin, identifying suffering with virtue, or ignoring disability rights in favor of charity. As one example: In 1986, the American Lutheran Church, revoking a commitment to disability rights from five years before, explicitly excluded people with "significant" physical or mental disabilities from being ministers. Pastors, the church taught, needed to be mobile and ambulatory to fulfil their mission.[70] Yet over the last ten years or so, the disability rights movement has changed much of organized religion's interpretation of the issue, much as feminism and environmentalism did during the previous two decades.

Spiritually speaking, people with disabilities—like those of us who do not have the marriage, career, family, waistline, or friends we would have liked—*can* nevertheless find ways to have a meaningful life. It will be harder for them, if only because they must resist the dominant social understanding of their condition. But struggling against that extra difficulty can give rise to inner strength, self-satisfaction, pride, and tranquillity. Of course, none of this is guaranteed, and positive feelings are often likely to coexist with periods of depression, rage, and grief. Once again, those of us who are honest will admit that in experiencing this range of emotions about their lives, those with disabilities are just like the rest of us—if only a bit more so.[71] As many spiritual teachers have said, if we have the courage to fully experience our painful emotions, we can move through them to a life that is meaningful. It may even be, as Miriam Greenspan tells us, that the emotions themselves contain a kind of special wisdom. Grief, fear, and despair, if experienced mindfully, openly, and with courage, can lead to gratitude, joy, and faith.[72]

And Esther, what of her spiritual life? She regularly goes to temple with me. When she prays, she prays with all her heart. At her Bat Mitzvah she commented on a passage in Numbers 20, about yet another time when the

Jews lost confidence in their journey. "I think this story basically means that you should not complain because it only makes the journey harder. You should just keep going and try hard and not complain. Just do what you have to do to get where you're going. When the Jews were losing confidence, I think they should have breathed and said to themselves 'It's okay, we'll make it.'" Her own life, she went on to say, is that way, too.

Another time, as part of a talk she gave to 500 people at a Friday night service to mark our temple's commitment to inclusion, she said:

> To parents that have kids with special needs: You need to learn to be patient because it's not your fault that your kid was born like this. If your child is having a hard time, you can give them a hug and say "Everything's going to be okay," and put your arms around them and be loving to them . . . Having special needs, I have been able to deal with it in a way that has been calming most of the time. For me, I have been able to be closer to God because of having special needs.

On the other hand, Esther is perceptive enough to see the differences between herself and her able-bodied sister, the other kids on the street, the teenagers in the sitcoms she watches. She knows that they are smarter, faster, more adept, and have less physical discomfort. And, amazingly, she is wise enough to know how to voice her disappointments not only to her parents or friends but to God as well. "Now is the time to scream at God," she once said, when I told her she probably couldn't be a counselor at her beloved day camp. "God, why did you give me this body, why did you give me special needs?" she will cry out, sometimes in the middle of shooting baskets in our driveway. And then, having demanded an accounting from the Source of Meaning, having voiced the anguish that she cannot deny, she will return to her normal, often anxious, incredibly loving self. When asked, at age twelve, what the meaning of life was, she answered without hesitation: "to love people." She will not become a professional or own a house in the suburbs, will never run a marathon or a hundred yards, will never "fit in." But those lacks do not erase what is beautiful about her and her life. And she knows it.

9

Toward Hope, Together

Let Justice roll down like water, Righteousness like a never-ending stream.

—Amos 5:24

———— • ————

In the end, it may only be our songs in praise of God that make God real.

In the end, it may be only our willingness to live as if a truly moral society is possible that can bring such a society into existence.

———— • ————

Sometimes the very boundaries between politics and religion move toward each other, blur, and even dissolve, leaving the religious and the political as two sides of one deeper, all-inclusive vocation of seeking to heal both the world and the self.

Consider the life of Vietnam veteran Ron Kovic, as told in his memoir, *Born on the Fourth of July*, and (somewhat differently) in the film of the same name.[1] Kovic was a red-blooded American boy, a natural athlete, and a politically conservative Catholic. Attracted to the heroic mystique of war, gung ho to stop communism, he volunteered for the marines. Yet the Vietnam War betrayed his ideals. He took part in the shooting of unarmed women and children and in the confusion of battle killed a fellow marine (a mistake his superiors willfully ignored). Then Kovic himself was wounded and paralyzed. During a painful and difficult rehabilitation, he went through a period of profound depression and semi-alcoholism. He came to question his earlier conventional patriotic understanding of the war, wrestled with guilt for those he killed, and despaired that life could be meaningful in a wheelchair.

A war veteran in the world's richest country, Kovic did not suffer from the poverty that afflicts paralysis victims throughout most of the world. Yet he had

209

clearly internalized the generalized social meaning of disability: that it creates a useless life; that along with the ability to get an erection, it destroys manhood; that it ends the possibility of love. In a heart-wrenching narrative, Kovic overcomes his depression and is eventually propelled toward political activism against the war.

His political transformation is, in the broad sense, simultaneously a spiritual one. Deeply troubled by his neglect in a veterans' hospital, he attends an antiwar demonstration. The speakers, the energy, and above all the violent treatment by the authorities move him to an antiwar position. He then progresses from opinion to activism. His veteran's income gives him a certain amount of freedom, but when he hears about a group of vets throwing away their medals in protest of the war, he realizes that "my easy life could never be enough for me. The war had not ended. It was time for me to join forces with other vets."[2]

By transcending a narrative in which he is nothing but a pathetic victim, Kovic is able to change. Echoing a famous prayer from St. Francis, he learns to think: "When I am in need, let me turn to the needs of others"; and in giving to others, he comes to terms with his own pain. Like Holocaust survivors who kept themselves alive in concentrations camps out of a relentless hunger to tell the story of those who perished, Kovic recovers his own life through a desire to let the country know the truth about that part of himself that was broken. The process of emotional resurrection centers on his realization that even from a wheelchair, he can make his voice heard in the struggle to end the war. But to make his voice heard, he has to move beyond his own sorrows to political activism. That is why he put his wheelchair-bound body into the streets of Miami in demonstrations against the 1972 Republican Convention.

Acting politically enabled him to accept his disability. Even more, he could now view his body, which to most other people was useless, as an asset. He found it could serve him in his newfound commitment to ending the war. His wheelchair and his medals gave him legitimacy in the antiwar movement and American society as a whole. In 1976, as one of the leaders of Vietnam Veterans Against the War, he gave a nationally televised address to the Democratic National Convention.

In his memoir, Kovic wrote:

> I went totally into speaking out against the war. I went into it the same way I'd gone into everything else I've wanted to do in my life . . . but this was something that meant much more . . . I could see that this thing—this body I had trained so hard to be strong and quick, this body I now dragged around with me like an empty corpse—was to mean much more than I had

ever realized. . . . I was a wounded American veteran. They would have to listen. Every chance I had to get my broken body on the tube in front of an audience I went hog wild.[3]

Here, politics is not simply a way of understanding how society controls our lives, or of the mass structures of injustice, or even of large-scale movements of change. It is a way of coming to terms with loss, moving beyond the self, and finding meaning in the midst of a difficult fate.[4] In just these ways, political activism itself becomes a kind of spiritual journey—and spirituality a kind of politics, because both can lead a person away from conventional, constricted, and ultimately unfulfilling ideas about happiness, value, and meaning. Kovic's spiritual transcendence toward concern for others was his way out of the loneliness and shame that marks the conventional understanding of disability. And his commitment to changing the foreign policy of the world's most powerful nation joined him with people whose personal energies had fused into a world historical force.

Consider another story of personal collapse and regeneration, told by Buddhist deep ecologist Joanna Macy. Macy was emotionally overwhelmed by the horrors of the Vietnam War, so much so that she entered a period of profound depression. Her normal life started to fall apart; she could barely function. Her therapist was convinced that such a powerful reaction could not be related to a political event and sought to find its roots in her early childhood. On the basis of some as yet unformulated inner wisdom, Macy resisted this privatization of her pain, realizing (and, later, teaching) that there is an intimate connection between our deepest emotional lives and our sense of the moral condition of the world. What we feel and what we see in the world at large are intimately linked. Facing the pain, says Macy, requires spiritual practices: meditation, prayer, openness to the truth, the spiritual virtue of being able to look directly at what is, and models of devotion and love. Simultaneously, however, our inner peace requires outward action to resist injustice and madness, and to express our solidarity with the victims. In this world, she emphasizes, psychological health, spiritual development, and political activism cannot be separated. Without openness to the pain we feel for the world, we will fall prey to depression, numbness, or addiction. Without spiritual resources, we will not be able to endure the pain that openness produces. Without politics, our spiritual lives will be escapist and superficial.[5]

In these examples we have come full circle, back to the original discussion of religion and politics as two ways of world making. The message is simple: to remake the world we need simultaneously to remake ourselves, and we stand little chance at remaking our selves without at least the attempt to remake the world. The spiritual journey beyond the confines of the individual ego, the political journey toward fundamental social change—either one undertaken without knowledge of the necessity of the other has scant chance of success. Religious passion without political understanding slips all too easily into the errors of historical ignorance and personal narcissism. And political activism without the gifts of religion may well be blind to our own humanity and that of those we wish to reach.

What then is to be done? Where shall we start? These are perhaps impertinent questions, for many readers of this book will no doubt already be engaged in rich religious and political lives and certainly will need no direction from me.

But for those who are perhaps unsure about what to do next, I would quote Elie Wiesel. When asked by someone, "Where should I start to make the world better?" Wiesel replied, "Start anywhere."[6] And anywhere it can be: a neighborhood, an office, a school; global movements for ecological sanity and indigenous rights; resisting sexual harassment and protecting the earth from pesticides; challenging the media, the government, the World Bank, a colleague's casual racism. There are so many causes, all of which are critically important, that the important thing is to join in wherever and whenever you can.

And the same is true for religious life. From formal services in established churches to tender moments when we appreciate the energies of sky and water, from the poetry of the Psalms to the eloquence of regular periods of quiet meditation, from celebrating the birth of Jesus or the liberation from Egypt to the painful examination of our own sins, religious belief and practice can make our lives more sustainable, moral, and politically aware.

In terms of the larger social forces that move mountains and make history, I believe that we now possess an unprecedented opportunity for the ethical passions of religion and the social vision of world-making politics to work together. In feminism and environmentalism, movements for peace between ethnic groups and social justice for the poor, religion's ethical force and progressive politics' commitment to change will continue to shape the world. How much they do so will depend on a multitude of factors that few of us can envision and none of us can control. Collectively, each person, each group, and each movement can play a vital part.

As I write these concluding words, the world is still reeling from the horrible terrorist attacks on the United States on September 11, 2001. Like the violent and hateful components of the Christian religious right, Islamic terrorism has its own vision of the unity of politics and religion. The values and beliefs that inspire that vision—the suppression of women, death for those who disagree, the dismissal of peace, the rejection of democracy and human rights—are a threat to those who seek a world of justice and care. At the same time, Western-based forces of globalization lead us toward increased poverty, ecological devastation, and cultural vacuity. Those of us who believe that political life can be more than the quiet imposition of a deadening globalization, and that religious passion is more than private ecstasy or public despotism, have a responsibility to share our vision with others and try to put it into practice.

———

Ultimately, if religion and politics are to remake the world, they both require a kind of hope. Yet hope, let us be clear, is not certainty. It is not the dogmatic confidence with which religious true believers know that they will go to heaven because they followed the rules. Nor is it the old Marxist certitude that the laws of history would insure the triumph of the working class. Certainty of heaven breeds contempt for the earth, and for those who are not as saved as we are. Certainty of revolution breeds contempt for anyone who gets in our way.

The kind of hope I have in mind has to do with a willingness to act in the face of sorrow and loss, a willingness to look clearly at what must be changed and to act without surety of success. The crucial role of hope is, perhaps, simply to admit that one doesn't know what will happen. Clearly, after a century that included the Holocaust, the nuclear arms race, two world wars, and the devastation of nature, cheerful optimism may be a little out of place. Yet history is nothing if not ambiguous. The same century saw the end of colonialism, successful struggles for democracy, and feminism. Humanity produced an international environmental movement as well as ever more deadly weapons, Gandhi and King as well as Richard Nixon and Saddam Hussein. If looking at the past is supposed to tell us whether we can hope, the answer is clear: yes and no.

We will have to be satisfied with that answer. But as important as any assessment of history or "human" possibilities is, there are quiet moments of faith during which those who seek to change society for the better hold on to a single image, one clear thought, a simple shining possibility. It may take the form of a phrase from a poem or speech—such as when John Lewis had his life transformed by hearing Martin Luther King Jr. talk of the "beloved community." It may be something evoked in a work of art: the simplicity of John Lennon's "Imagine," the openness to nature of Gary Snyder's poetry, the soulful promise in the narrative visions of Toni Morrison. It may be found in the moral character of one person: a Hannah Senesh who left Palestine for Nazi-occupied Europe to die trying to save some remnant of the Jewish community during the Holocaust; or a Dorothy Day, who for forty years combined an austere and loving faith in God, service to the poor, and bold public stands for peace and justice. We may recognize it in wheelchair-bound men and women refusing to be shunted to the sidelines of life, in courageous Afghan women risking death to teach their daughters how to read, in Nigerian tribes resisting the oil companies poisoning their homelands. Or in any one of us who makes peace by seeking to understand the pains and passions of those with whom we are at war.

In such instances, we see realized—if only for a moment, or only in imagination—something of the world we seek to make. And as our own spirits are raised by these glimpses of a better world, we need only remember our own passion to believe that there is hope. The love and care these images inspire in us—we must believe—can reach others as well.

Will such inspiration reach enough people—and in time? We cannot know; and that ignorance may be our richest source of hope. All we can be sure of is that in living out what is most sacred to ourselves, we choose the path that is most likely to take us all to that new world, the one where justice and righteousness "roll down like a never ending stream," and where human beings, together, heal both the earth and their own hearts.

Notes

INTRODUCTION

1. Joan Vennochi, "Cardinal Veers into Politics—Again," *Boston Globe*, May 15, 2001; "Ashcroft Criticized on Prayers," ibid.

2. Stephen L. Carter, *God's Name in Vain: The Rights and Wrong of Religion in Politics* (New York: Basic Books, 2000), p. 171. My emphasis.

3. Charles Marsh, *God's Long Summer: Stories of Faith and Civil Rights* (Princeton, NJ: Princeton University Press, 1997), p. 3.

4. Senator Joe Lieberman, speech at Notre Dame University, October 24, 2000, "Vision for America: A Place for Faith," Religion News Service web site, www.religionnews.com.

5. Commenting on the proposal to use federal funds to allow religious groups to provide welfare services, Rev. Dr. C. Welton Gaddy, executive director of The Interfaith Alliance (a "grassroots faith-based organization dedicated to promoting the positive and healing role of religion in public life") argued: "There are numerous questions about how this federal initiative will treat religious groups and whether it is even possible to claim a commitment to equity. After all, religion is not a generic idea and the substance of each faith is very specific. There is a big difference between Evangelical Christianity and Hinduism or The Church of Scientology and Buddhism. In a politically charged environment like the White House, religious minorities from unknown or ridiculed faith traditions that could spark controversy are highly unlikely to receive federal support . . . Ultimately, there can be no effective guarantee enforcing fairness because the decision-making process will be inherently subjective—reflecting both bias and preference." From the Interfaith Alliance web site, www.interfaithalliance.org.

6. Some readers may recognize the influence of Alasdair MacIntyre here. Beyond MacIntyre, there is a book that influenced us both: W. B. Gallie, *Philosophy and the Historical Understanding* (London: Chatto and Windus, 1964).

7. Carter has a very limited conception of religion, which he initially defines in such a way as to exclude Buddhism and Taoism, and which in any case cannot accommodate the more individualistic forms of spiritual searching that have now become widespread. Or, at least, he seems not to realize that people can engage in personal spiritual seeking while seeing themselves as part of a larger community of such seekers, even if that community has no fixed institutional expression. Spiritual seeking, that is, can be social and political without necessarily being part of traditional ongoing "church" institutions.

8. Ellen Willis, "Freedom from Religion," *The Nation*, February 9, 2001.

215

9. See, for instance, a letter to President Bush from the Coalition Against Religious Discrimination, January 3, 2001, which sought assurance that the president would "not tolerate religious employment discrimination in any programs funded with taxpayer dollars." It was signed by nineteen organizations, including the ACLU, the Baptist Joint Committee on Public Affairs, Hadassah, and the Unitarian Universalist Association.

10. Terms and account from David P. Gushee, "The Bush Proposal and the Place of Religion in Public Life." From Religion News Service web site, www.religionnews.com; and editorial in *Tikkun*, May–June 2001.

11. Willis, "Freedom from Religion." My emphasis.

12. John Lewis, *Walking with the Wind: A Memoir of the Movement* (New York: Harcourt and Brace, 1998), p. 189.

13. For a range of thinkers here, see Staughton Lynd and Alice Lynd, eds., *Nonviolence in America: A Documentary History* (Maryknoll, NY: Orbis Books, 1995).

14. Francis Schussler Fiorenza, "Justice and Charity in Social Welfare," in Mary Jo Bane, Brent Coffin, and Ronald Thiemann, eds., *Who Will Provide? The Changing Role of Religion in America Social Welfare* (Boulder: Westview Press, 2000).

15. Ronald J. Sider, "Faith-Based Organizations and Community Foundations: They Should Develop a Closer Partnership," president, Evangelicals for Social Action, January 28, 2000, www.esa-online.org.

16. Stanley Hauerwas, *Wilderness Wanderings: Probing Twentieth-Century Theology and Philosophy* (Boulder: Westview Press, 1997), p. 197.

CHAPTER 1: TWO WAYS OF WORLD MAKING

1. Quoted in Isaac Deutscher, *The Prophet Outcast: Trotsky 1929–1940* (New York: Vintage, 1963), p. 479.

2. Edgar Snow, *Red Star over China* (New York: Grove Press, 1973); Thich Nhat Hanh, *Love in Action: Writings on Nonviolent Social Change* (Berkeley, CA: Parallax Press, 1993), pp. 42–43.

3. Paul Tillich suggested we understand God as "man's ultimate concern." See *The Courage to Be* (New Haven: Yale University Press, 2000).

4. Abraham Joshua Heschel, *I Asked for Wonder: A Spiritual Anthology* (New York: Crossroad, 1983).

5. For an account of how the distinction sometimes plays out in American life, see Robert C. Fuller, *Spiritual but Not Religious: Understanding Unchurched America* (New York: Oxford University Press, 2001).

6. Karl Marx, "Contribution to the Critique of Hegel's *Philosophy of Right*: Introduction," and *Manifest of the Communist Party*, both anthologized in many places, including Robert Tucker, ed., *The Marx-Engels Reader* (New York: Norton, 1972).

7. R. Scott Appleby, *The Ambivalence of the Sacred: Religion, Violence, and Reconciliation* (Lanham, MD: Rowman and Littlefield, 1999).

8. David Tracy, *Plurality and Ambiguity: Hermeneutics, Religion, Hope* (Chicago: University of Chicago Press, 1987), pp. 83–84. My emphasis.

9. The best treatment of this theme is still Michael Walzer, *Exodus and Revolution* (New York: Basic Books, 1991).

10. Nahum M. Sarna, *Exploring Exodus: The Origins of Biblical Israel* (New York: Schocken, 1986), pp. 15–26.

11. James H. Cone, *A Black Theology of Liberation* (Philadelphia: J. B. Lippincott Co., 1970); *Black Theology and Black Power* (New York: Harper and Row, 1969).

12. My emphasis. See also Leviticus 19:9 and 23:22.

13. W. Gunther Plaut, *The Torah: A Modern Commentary* (New York: Union of American Hebrew Congregations, 1981), p. 1500.

14. In this respect, the ethical and political message of the Exodus story bears a striking—and surprising—similarity to the norms of scientific knowledge, for what distin-

guishes scientific knowledge from tradition or convention is precisely its capacity for self-criticism. No particular theory is essential because any theory can be damaged by limited data, poor instruments, observational error, or the social and political biases of the researchers and those who fund them. What is fundamental, rather, is the way the scientific community is rooted in a commitment to unending free inquiry. Any theory considered true today can be refuted tomorrow; any lauded scientist can be proven wrong next week. A profound skepticism is built in.

15. Abraham J. Heschel, *The Prophets: An Introduction* (New York: Harper, 1955), p. xv.

16. Desmond Tutu, foreword to Lawrence Boadt, ed., *The Hebrew Prophets: Visionaries of the Ancient World* (New York: St. Martin's Press, 1997), p. 8.

17. Foreword to Nancy L. Eiesland, *The Disabled God: Toward a Liberatory Theology of Disability* (Nashville, TN: Abingdon, 1994), p. 11.

18. Joan D. Chittister, "The Power of Questions to Propel: A Retrospective," in Mary Hembrow Snyder, ed., *Spiritual Question for the Twenty-First Century: Essays in Honor of Joan D. Chittister* (Maryknoll, NY: Orbis Books, 2001), p. 172.

19. That is why Michael Lerner claims that the Torah contains two distinct voices—one of liberating compassion and another that repeats pain and oppression from generation to generation. See Michael Lerner, *Jewish Renewal: A Path to Healing and Transformation* (New York: Putnam, 1994).

20. Some will say that the Israeli treatment of the Palestinians reveals a similar process.

21. Steve Bruce, *Religion in the Modern World: From Cathedrals to Cults* (Oxford: Oxford University Press, 1996), p. 100.

22. There are now dozens of excellent surveys of Buddhism, each with its advantages and limitations.

23. Edward Conze, ed., *Buddhist Texts Through the Ages* (New York: Harper, 1954), p. 131.

24. Ibid., p. 128.

25. Claude Whitmyer, ed., *Mindfulness and Meaningful Work: Explorations in Right Livelihood* (Berkeley, CA: Parallax Press, 1994).

26. Edward Conze, *Buddhism: Its Essence and Development* (New York: Harper, 1959), pp. 125–126. My emphasis.

27. This formulation is indebted to liberal contract theory from John Locke to John Rawls.

28. For instance, Alasdair MacIntyre and Amitai Etzioni.

29. Of course, insofar as a community is shaped by tradition, it cannot be accepted at face value but will be at least potentially subject to criticisms of lingering forms of injustice.

30. A helpful point made directly to me by David Barnhill.

31. Karl Popper, *The Open Society and Its Enemies*, vols. 1, 2 (Princeton, NJ: Princeton University Press, 1972, 1976).

32. Francis Fukuyama, *The End of History and the Last Man* (New York: William Morrow, 1993).

33. It is a fascinating general question to ask: What leads believers to change from conservative to world making in their religious understanding? I have no general answer, but my account of religion and social movements in Part 2 provides some tentative answers for particular settings.

CHAPTER 2: THE TIME IS RIPE

1. "Citizens and Believers: Always Strangers?" in M. L. Bradbury and James B. Gilbert, eds., *Transforming Faith: The Sacred and Secular in Modern American History* (New York: Greenwood Press, 1989), p. 64.

2. *Boston Globe*, September 19, 2001.

3. Theda Skocpol, "Religion, Civil Society, and Social Provision in the U.S.," in Bane, Coffin, and Thiemann, eds., *Who Will Provide?* p. 46.

4. Bruce, *Religion in the Modern World*.

5. It was espoused by classic sociologists of modernity like Marx and Weber and noted by contemporary theorists like Peter Berger. See Max Weber, *Economy and Society* (Berkeley: University of California Press, 1978); Peter Berger, *The Sacred Canopy: Elements of a Sociological Theory of Religion* (New York: Doubleday, 1967). As Cox observes ("Citizens and Believers," Bradbury and Gilbert, eds., *Transforming Faith*) the thesis has taken a variety of forms of late.

6. For the United States, see summary in Bruce, *Religion in the Modern World*, p. 129.

7. In less-developed nations, religion may be an alternative form of nationalism or a national resistance to secular, class-based modernization, as in Iran.

8. Albeit, of course, at different rates among Europe, Japan, and North America.

9. Bruce, *Religion in the Modern World*, p. 232.

10. John Rawls, *Political Liberalism* (New York: Columbia University Press, 1996), pp. xxxix–xl. For this discussion I am indebted to Timothy Samuel Shah, "Making the Christian World Safe for Liberalism," in David Marquand and Ronald L. Netter, eds., *Religion and Democracy* (London: Blackwell, 2000); J. Judd Owen, *Religion and the Demise of Liberal Rationalism: The Foundational Crisis of the Separation of Church and State* (Chicago: University of Chicago Press, 2001); Monique Deveaux, *Cultural Pluralism and Dilemmas of Justice* (Ithaca, NY: Cornell University Press, 2000); Robert Audi and Nicholas Wolterstorff, *Religion in the Public Square: The Place of Religious Convictions in Political Debate* (Lanham, MD: Rowman and Littlefield, 1997); Kent Greenwalt, *Religious Convictions and Political Choice* (New York: Oxford University Press, 1988).

11. A related but distinct failure haunts the efforts another famous philosopher, Richard Rorty. Unlike Rawls, Rorty doesn't believe that any universal rules can be found. The liberal belief in autonomy, freedom, natural science, and rights is just one more ethnocentric habit, no more "rational" than fundamentalist Islam or alchemy. The best we can hope for is that we'll tolerate each other's idiosyncratic beliefs, while trying to develop some compassion for each other's suffering. We won't try to convince each other of our truths, we'll share our stories. Religion, like art or extreme forms of any philosophical belief, will simply be part of our personal self-development. Yet Rorty, no less than Rawls, wants to keep religious (and philosophical) passion private. His inconsistencies here are pointed out very well by Owen, *Religion and the Demise*.

12. Michael J. Perry, *The Idea of Human Rights: Four Inquiries* (New York: Oxford University Press, 1998).

13. Jeffrey Stout, *Ethics After Babel: The Language of Morals and Their Discontents* (Princeton, NJ: Princeton University Press, 2001), p. 341.

14. This view is found in countless writers. One classic formulation was that of H. Richard Niebuhr, who distinguished between "Christ," or the essential but never fully or finally found heart of Christianity, and "culture," which is the historically and socially relative way Christianity is practiced at a particular time. It is our task, said Niebuhr, always to be aware of thinking that the former had been encompassed by the latter. See H. Richard Niebuhr, *Christ and Culture* (New York: Harper, 1951), as well as the works of Reinhold Niebuhr. This theme is developed throughout Amanda Porterfield, who refers to a late-twentieth-century "awakening to the social and psychological construction of religion," in *The Transformation of American Religion: The Story of a Late-Twentieth-Century Awakening* (New York: Oxford University Press, 2001), p. 230.

15. See the discussion in Porterfield, *Transformation of American Religion*, pp. 39–40.

16. John B. Cobb Jr., *Transforming Christianity and the World* (Maryknoll, NY: Orbis Books, 1999), p. 75.

17. Søren Kierkegaard, *Concluding Unscientific Postscript* (Princeton, NJ: Princeton University Press, 1968), p. 219. This position is developed throughout the book.

18. The fundamentally different attitude toward verbal theology in Eastern religions makes this problem rather different there.

19. Quotes in Bruce, *Religion in the Modern World*, p. 67.

20. It would be interesting to compare religion in this respect to science, whose absolute claims have been severely criticized of late but which continues to be of central importance and authority nevertheless.

21. Robert Wuthnow, *After Heaven: Spirituality in America Since the 1950s* (Berkeley: University of California Press, 1998).

22. See chaps. 1 and 2 of Roger S. Gottlieb, *A Spirituality of Resistance: Finding a Peaceful Heart and Protecting the Earth* (New York: Crossroads, 1999). For other voices, consider Matthew Fox, Bernie Glassman, Christopher Titmuss, Marianne Williamson, E. F. Schumacher, Luisah Teish, Paul Gorman, Ram Dass, and Starhawk.

23. Robert Booth Fowler, Allen D. Hertzke, and Laura R. Olson, *Religion and Politics in America: Faith, Cultures, and Strategic Choices* (Boulder: Westview Press, 1999), p. 258.

24. Religion without passion tends to drift into irrelevance or serves simply as another form of conformism. During the 1950s, as America built new suburban churches and synagogues at a breakneck pace, it was noticed that worship was becoming increasingly banal. "Our services are conducted with pomp and precision," complained famed Jewish writer Abraham Joshua Heschel. "Everything is present: decorum, voice, ceremony. But only one thing is missing: Life" (quoted in Edward S. Shapiro, *A Time for Healing: American Jewry Since World War II* [Baltimore: Johns Hopkins University Press, 1992], p. 164). While a large percentage of Americans claimed that the Bible was the word of God, "a majority could not name any of the four gospels in the New Testament" (Will Herberg, *Protestant-Catholic-Jew: An Essay in American Religious Sociology* [Chicago: University of Chicago Press, 1983], p. 2). For an interesting discussion of religious change during this period, see Maurice Isserman and Michale Kazin, *America Divided: The Civil War of the 1960s* (New York: Oxford University Press, 2000), pp. 241–260.

25. See the account in Shah, "Making the Christian World Safe."

26. Jim Wallis, "Renewing the Heart of Faith: A Prophetic Convergence of the People of God," *Sojurners* (February 1993):13.

27. Wuthnow, *After Heaven*.

28. Fowler, Hertzke, and Olson, *Religion and Politics in America*, p. 251.

29. Reinhold Niebuhr, *Moral Man and Immoral Society* (New York: Scribners, 1953), pp. 276–277.

30. For a brief but illuminating commentary on its history, see Plaut, *The Torah*, pp. 892–893.

31. For a discussion of such a project, see Bruce Rich, *Mortgaging the Earth: Environmental Impoverishment and the Crisis of Development* (Boston: Beacon Press, 1993).

32. Gustavo Gutiérrez, *Theology of Liberation* (Maryknoll, NY: Orbis Books, 1988), p. 116.

33. Hannah Arendt, *Eichman in Jerusalem: A Report on the Banality of Evil* (New York: Viking, 1964); Gottlieb, *Spirituality of Resistance*, chap. 3.

34. Thomas Merton, 1962, quoted in Murray Polner and Jim O'Grady, *Disarmed and Dangerous: The Radical Life and Times of Daniel and Philip Berrigan* (Boulder: Westview Press, 1997), p. 107.

35. "The Problem of a Protestant Social Ethics," *Union Seminary Quarterly Review* (November 1959):11. Quoted in D. B. Robertson, ed., *Love and Justice: Selections from the Shorter Writings of Reinhold Niebuhr* (Louisville, KY: Westminster John Knox Press, 1957), p. 18.

36. For an account of how American religion has become oriented toward "humane standards and human flourishing," see Porterfield, *Transformation of American Religion*, especially chaps. 3 and 5.

37. Diana Eck, quoted in the *Boston Globe*, September 20, 2001.

38. For a survey of several different contexts, see Peter Ackerman and Jack Duvall, *A Force More Powerful: A Century of Nonviolent Conflict* (New York: St. Martin's Press, 2000);

Daniel L. Smith-Christopher, *Subverting Hatred: The Challenge of Nonviolence in Religious Traditions* (Maryknoll, NY: Orbis Books, 1998).

39. Lukacs, *History and Class Consciousness: Studies in Marxist Dialectics* (Cambridge: MIT Press, 1971).

40. Wilhelm Reich, "What Is Class Consciousness," in *Sex-Pol* (New York: Vintage, 1972).

41. Critiques of the identification of "reason" with limited, instrumental rationality are at the heart of the Frankfurt School of anti-Communist neo-Marxist theory. See Theodor Adorno and Max Horkheimer, *Dialectic of Enlightenment* (New York: Seabury, 1974); Jurgen Habermas, *Knowledge and Human Interests* (Boston: Beacon Press, 1968).

42. Michael Lerner, *Spirit Matters* (Charlottesville, VA: Hampton Roads, 2000); see also *The Politics of Meaning: Restoring Hope and Possiblity in an Age of Cynicism* (Reading, MA: Addison-Wesley, 1997).

43. André Gorz, "Reform and Revolution," in Roger S. Gottlieb, ed., *An Anthology of Western Marxism: From Lukacs and Gramsci to Socialist-Feminism* (New York: Oxford University Press, 1989), p. 218.

44. Ronald Inglehart, *Culture Shift in Advanced Industrial Society* (Princeton, NJ: Princeton University Press, 1990).

45. Paul H. Kay and Sherry Ruth Anderson, *The Cultural Creatives* (New York: Harmony Books, 2000). Sponsored at *Mother Jones* conference.

46. Philip Wexler, *The Mystical Society* (Boulder: Westview Press, 2000), pp. 2–3.

47. Leviticus 25. See the discussion by Arthur Waskow, "From Compassion to Jubilee," *Tikkun* 5 (March–April 1990):78–81.

48. Manuel Castells, *The Information Age: Economy, Society, and Culture*, vol. 1, *The Rise of the Network Society* (Oxford: Blackwell, 2000).

49. "During calendar year 2000, Facing History continued to offer our professional development programs, services, and resources to more than 13,000 educators throughout the United States and in Europe. Over 2,000 educators were introduced to the Facing History program. Over 1,400 attended 77 one- or two-day workshops and over 750 attended 32 weeklong institutes," www.facinghistory.org.

CHAPTER 3: POLITICS TEACHING RELIGION

1. James I. Charlton, *Nothing About Us Without Us: Disability, Oppression, and Empowerment* (Berkeley: University of California Press, 1997), p. 64.

2. Oscar Romero, *The Violence of Love* (Farmington, PA: Plough Publishing House, 1998), p. 124.

3. John B. Cobb Jr., *Reclaiming the Church* (Louisville, KY: Westminster John Knox Press, 1997), p. 64.

4. This way of understanding the limitations of religion once again bears an interesting resemblance to claims about the limitations of natural science. Thirty years of what has been called "post-empiricist" philosophy and history of science have identified the many ways in which scientific knowledge, whatever its ultimate source in the structures of the physical world, is *also* dependent on the social position and interests of those doing the research—or paying for it. Thus, at any given time scientific claims are *both* the best available knowledge and also beliefs that may well need to be reconsidered in the light of future evidence. This evidence, in turn, will often reflect the subsequent realization that certain social relationships were distorting our beliefs about the physical world. For instance, if military interests fund research, we are more likely to learn about weapons than renewable energy sources. If corporations are in charge, then whatever we find out about is likely to be something that can be sold. Scientists' approach to Nature, just like theologians' approach to God, always reflects the community of which they are a part.

5. For the history of the change, see David J. O'Brien and Thomas A. Shannon, eds., *Catholic Social Thought: The Documentary Heritage* (Maryknoll, NY: Orbis Books, 1992).

6. Taylor Branch, *Pillar of Fire: America in the King Years, 1963–65* (New York: Simon and Schuster, 1998), p. 611.

7. Joanna Macy, *World as Lover, World as Self* (Berkeley, CA: Parallax Press, 1990).

8. Adin Steinzaltz, *The Thirteen Petalled Rose* (NY: Basic Books, 1980), pp. 103–104.

9. David Steindl-Rast, *Gratefulness, the Heart of Prayer: An Approach to Life in Fullness* (Mahwah, NJ: Paulist Press, 1991).

10. Stanley Hauerwas and William H. Willimon, *Resident Aliens: Life in the Christian Colony* (Nashville, TN: Abingdon Press, 1989), p. 46. They are adopting the concept from John Howard Yoder.

11. Karl Marx and Friedrich Engels, *The Communist Manifesto* (Chicago: Gateway, 1964).

12. Kusum Nair, *Blossoms in the Dust: The Human Element in Development* (London: Duckworth, 1961).

13. Bill McKibben, *Hope, Human and Wild: True Stories of Living Lightly on the Earth* (New York: Ruminator, 1997).

14. Polner and O'Grady, *Disarmed and Dangerous.*

15. Rita Nakashima Brock, "And a Little Child Will Lead Us: Christology and Child Abuse," in Joanne Brown and Carole Bohn, eds., *Christianity, Patriarchy, and Abuse: A Feminist Critique* (New York: Pilgrim Press, 1990), p. 43.

16. Marie Dennis, Renny Golden, and Scott Wright, *Oscar Romero: Reflections on His Life and Writings* (Maryknoll, NY: Orbis Books, 2000); Oscar Romero, *Voice of the Voiceless: The Four Pastoral Letters and Other Statements* (Maryknoll, NY: Orbis Books, 1985); Romero, *The Violence of Love.*

17. Dennis, Golden, and Wright, *Oscar Romero*, p. 103.

18. Ibid., p. 73.

19. Cone, *Black Theology and Black Power*, pp. 151–152.

20. An excellent survey of Niebuhr's enormous body of work is: Langdon Gilkey, *On Niebuhr: A Theological Study* (Chicago: University of Chicago Press, 2001). For a collection with an excellent introduction, see Larry Rasmussen, ed., *Reinhold Niebuhr: Theologian of Public Life* (Minneapolis: Fortress Press, 1991).

21. Niebuhr, *Moral Man and Immoral Society.*

22. Valerie Saiving, "The Human Situation: A Feminist View," in Carol Christ and Judith Plaskow, eds., *WomanSpirit Rising: A Feminist Reader in Religion* (San Francisco: Harper SanFrancisco, 1992).

23. Also, Niebuhr doesn't really recommend any *spiritual practices* to make us more humble. Buddhism, for instance, has a whole repertoire of meditations designed to aid us in becoming less attached to our opinions, forgiving our enemies, dealing with our greed, and distancing us from our fear or anger. For Niebuhr, as for most Protestant theologians, developing these virtues is a matter of intellectual insight or the grace of faith. (That is perhaps why, as he later admitted, he was unaware of how his own vanity led him to ignore his wife's pleas that he spend more time at home and less giving public lectures.)

24. Niebuhr, "Ideology and the Scientific Method," in Robert McAfee Brown, ed., *The Essential Reinhold Niebuhr: Selected Essays and Addresses* (New Haven: Yale University Press, 1986), p. 215.

25. Robert Ellsberg, ed., *Dorothy Day: Selected Writings* (Maryknoll, NY: Orbis Books, 1998), p. 62.

26. The Dalai Lama and Howard C. Cutler, *The Art of Happiness: A Handbook for Living* (New York: Riverhead Books, 1998), p. 2.

27. Tony Campolo, *Revolution and Renewal: How Churches Are Saving Our Cities* (Louisville, KY: Westminster John Knox Press, 2000).

28. Dalai Lama and Cutler, *Art of Happiness*, p. 257.

29. For a highly sophisticated analysis of pacifism in international affairs, see Duane K. Friesen, *Christian Peacemaking and International Conflict: A Realist/Pacifist Perspective* (Scottsdale, PA: Herald Press, 1986).

30. Appleby, *Ambivalence of the Sacred*, p. 121.

31. Stanley Fish, *The Trouble with Principle* (Cambridge: Harvard University Press, 2001).

32. "If you're against abortion don't have one" is a popular bumper sticker that embodies this confusion.

33. Appleby, *Ambivalence of the Sacred*, p. 213.

34. Thich Nhat Hanh, *Love in Action*, pp. 143–145. My emphasis.

35. Marcia Prager, *The Path of Blessing: Experiencing the Energy and Abundance of the Divine* (New York: Bell Tower, 1998), pp. 53–54.

36. Ellsberg, *Dorothy Day*, p. 174.

CHAPTER 4: RELIGION TEACHING POLITICS

1. Jim Wallis, *The Soul of Politics: Beyond "Religious Right" and "Secular Left"* (New York: Harcourt Brace, 1995), p. xviii.

2. Thich Nhat Hanh, *Love in Action*, p. 65.

3. It is also true that many of these gains are partial and might be reversed. Contemporary Afghanistan has subjected women to social repression far worse than anything they suffered there in the past; and China seems a very long way from tolerating dissent of any type. Throughout the world, global corporations dominate both the global market and national governments, typically seeking profit at the expense of collective well-being or ecological reason.

4. Jean Hardisty, "Dispatches from Durban," *Sojurner* (October 2001):6.

5. Ira F. Stone, *Reading Levinas/Reading Talmud: An Introduction* (New York: Jewish Publication Society, 1998), p. 25.

6. Ibid.

7. Kierkegaard, *Concluding Unscientific Postscript*.

8. I regret that I cannot remember the source of the Eckhart quote. The Hasidic quote is from Arthur Green and Barry W. Holtz, eds., *Your Word Is Fire: The Hasidic Masters on Contemplative Prayer* (New York: Schocken Books, 1987), p. 7.

9. Readers wanting to know what I think that account looks like can consult my book: *Marxism 1844–1990: Origins, Betrayal, Rebirth* (New York: Routledge, 1992).

10. Quoted in Tony Smith, *Thinking Like a Communist: State and Legitimacy in the Soviet Union, China, and Cuba* (New York: Norton, 1987), p. 94.

11. Arthur Koestler, *Darkness at Noon* (New York: Bantam, 1984).

12. For the first insider's account of just how tyrannical and irrational the Stalinist regime was, see Roy Medvedev, *Let History Judge* (New York: Vintage, 1973).

13. Ellsberg, *Dorothy Day*, p. 213.

14. Sadly, the even more demanding notion of "loving" one's enemies seems to be so far from current social reality as not even to be a candidate for serious discussion.

15. Gordon Fellman, *Rambo and the Dalai Lama: The Compulsion to Win and Its Threat to Human Survival* (Albany: State University of New York Press, 1998), p. 25.

16. Thich Nhat Hanh, *Being Peace* (Berkeley, CA: Parallax Press, 1987), p. 79.

17. Medvedev, *Let History Judge*.

18. Todd Gitlin, *The Sixties: Years of Hope, Days of Rage* (New York: Bantam, 1987); and Stephen B. Oates, *Let the Trumpets Sound: A Life of Martin Luther King, Jr.* (New York: Harper, 1994).

19. Jean-Paul Sartre, *Search for a Method* (New York: Vintage, 1963), p. 23. For the exchange, see www.thenation.com.

20. Edward H. Carr, *The Bolshevik Revolution* (New York: Norton, 1985); Isaac Deutscher, *Trotsky: The Prophet Unarmed* (New York: Vintage, 1959); Robert Daniels, *A Documentary History of Communism*, vols. 1–2 (New York: Vintage, 1960).

21. Louis Fischer, *Gandhi: His Life and Message for the World* (New York: New American Library, 1991).

22. Thich Nhat Hanh, *Being Peace*, p. 93.

23. David Kahane recommends a secular version, which he terms "civic friendship," as a way to combine moral solidarity with social diversity. My point is that such friendship is often likely to benefit from a (suitably modernized) religious or spiritual worldview. David Kahane, "Diversity, Solidarity, and Civic Friendship," *Journal of Political Philosophy* 7 (3) (September 1999):243–262.

24. Colman McCarthy, "Peaceful Conflict Resolution Is Teachable: Nine Steps Provide the Key to Resolving Disputes Peacefully," *Fellowship* 66 (11–12) (November–December 2000):19.

25. Leah Green, "Learning the Language of the Heart," *Fellowship* 66 (11–12) (November–December 2000):6. My emphasis.

26. *Plough Reader* (Winter 2001):5.

27. From Jim Forest, Merton biographer. Quoted in Polner and O'Grady, *Disarmed and Dangerous*, p. 209.

28. I am indebted to Richard Schmitt for this point.

29. For an excellent survey, see Appleby, *Ambivalence of the Sacred*.

30. Ibid., p. 149.

31. Besides Appleby's survey, there are dozens of sources. Consider: Walter Wink, ed., *Peace Is the Way: Writings on Nonviolence from the Fellowship of Reconciliation* (Maryknoll, NY: Orbis Books, 2000); Friesen, *Christian Peacemaking and International Conflict*; Aung San Suu Kyi, *The Voice of Hope* (New York: Seven Stories Press, 1997).

32. James W. Douglass, *The Nonviolent Coming of God*, quoted in Lynd and Lynd, *Nonviolence in America*, pp. 328–329.

33. Herbert Marcuse, *An Essay on Liberation* (Boston: Beacon Press, 1969).

34. For a brief but illuminating account of how these two might work together, see Stephanie Kaza, "Keeping Peace with Nature," in David W. Chappell, ed., *Buddhist Peacework: Creating Cultures of Peace* (Boston: Wisdom Publications, 1999).

35. For a fuller discussion of a concept of the dominated self, see Roger S. Gottlieb, *History and Subjectivity: The Transformation of Marxist Theory* (Philadelphia: Temple University Press, 1987), chap. 10.

36. Michael Lerner, *Surplus Powerlessness* (Atlantic Highlands, NJ: Humanities Press, 1995).

37. Lukacs, *History and Class Consciousness*.

38. This is, actually, a dead end spiritually as well as politically. This is one of the dominant themes of Roger S. Gottlieb, *A Spirituality of Resistance: Finding a Peaceful Heart and Protecting the Earth* (New York: Crossroad, 1999).

39. Dayan Grunfeld, *The Sabbath: A Guide to Its Understanding and Observance* (Jerusalem: Feldheim Publishers, 1981).

40. Abraham Joshua Heschel, *The Sabbath: Its Meaning for Modern Man* (New York: Farrar, Straus, and Giroux, 1951).

41. Lerner, *Spirit Matters*, pp. 300–301.

42. Jurgen Habermas, "Technology and Science as Ideology," in Gottlieb, *Anthology of Western Marxism*, p. 317.

43. Herbert Marcuse, *One-Dimensional Man* (Boston: Beacon Press, 1964).

44. Marx, *Economic and Philosophical Manuscripts of 1844*, in Robert Tucker, ed., *The Marx-Engels Reader*.

45. For a concise account of this relation, see Philip Shabecoff, *Earth Rising: American Environmentalism in the 21st Century* (Washington, DC: Island Press, 2000), pp. 66–69.

46. Any history of communism would provide examples. For a fascinating case, see the description of Socialist-Zionist communes in Nora Levin, *While Messiah Tarried: Jewish Socialist Movements* (New York: Schocken, 1977). "Failing that, invent," comes from the radical feminist classic by Monique Wittig, *Les Guérillères* (Boston: Beacon Press, 1985), p. 3.

47. The Buddhist approach here differs from simple awareness of these tendencies as they might arise in psychotherapy. Buddhism, unlike secular psychology, provides an image

of egolessness, psychic freedom, and fulfilling involvement with the moment-to-moment flow of life

48. Aung San Suu Kyi, *Voice of Hope*, p. 35.

49. Gerald Shenk, "Global Conflict," in Carolyn Schrock-Shenk and Lawrence Ressler, eds., *Making Peace with Conflict: Practical Skills for Conflict Transformation* (Scottsdale, PA: Herald Press, 1999), p. 191.

50. For sources, one might begin with Wink, *Peace*; Catherine Ingram, *In the Footsteps of Gandhi: Conversations with Spiritual Social Activists* (Berkeley, CA: Parallax Press, 1990); and Ellsberg, *Dorothy Day*.

51. Of course, these are always understood and experienced in socially shaped ways. But some degree of universality exists in them nevertheless. This can be measured, at the least, by how easily people from different times and cultures can empathize with each other's experiences in these areas.

52. At the same time, however, we need to remember that illness can be environmental as well as inevitable; death may be met with community resources or in isolation; the aged can be honored or shelved in bleak nursing homes. Even these most human of pains are political as well as universally human.

53. For a development of this perspective on emotions, see Miriam Greenspan, *Healing Through the Dark Emotions: The Other Side of Fear, Grief, and Despair* (Boston: Shambhala, 2002).

54. Ellsberg, *Dorothy Day*, p. 192.

CHAPTER 5: REDEMPTIVE SUFFERING AND THE CIVIL RIGHTS MOVEMENT

1. Oates, *Let the Trumpets Sound*, p. 101.

2. Aung San Suu Kyi, *Voice of Hope*, p. 39. She is the Buddhist leader of Burma's nonviolent struggle for democracy.

3. My sources for this claim, as well as for much of the general information in this chapter, include: Oates, *Let the Trumpets Sound*; David J. Garrow, *Bearing the Cross: Martin Luther King, Jr., and the Southern Christian Leadership Conference* (New York: Quill, 1986); Taylor Branch, *Parting the Waters: America in the King Years, 1954–63* (New York: Touchstone, 1994) and *Pillar of Fire*.

4. I am necessarily simplifying the account by ignoring the contributions of whites, especially white college students who went south.

5. James Cone, *Martin and Malcolm and America* (Maryknoll, NY: Orbis Books, 1992), p. 143.

6. Frederick C. Harris, *Something Within: Religion in African-American Political Activism* (New York: Oxford University Press, 1999), pp. 64–65.

7. Cone, *Martin and Malcolm and America*, p. 147.

8. Lewis, *Walking with the Wind*, p. 47.

9. Stephen L. Carter, "The Black Church and Religious Freedom," in Dwight N. Hopkins, ed., *Black Faith and Public Talk: Critical Essay on James H. Cone's Black Theology and Black Power* (Maryknoll, NY: Orbis Books, 1999).

10. Marsh, *God's Long Summer*, p. 12.

11. Fowler, Hertzke, and Olson, *Religion and Politics in America*, p. 167.

12. David Halberstam, *The Children* (New York: Ballantine, 1998), p. 31.

13. Sources for Lawson's background include Branch, *Parting the Waters* and Halberstam, *Children*.

14. Lewis, *Walking with the Wind*, p. 189. My emphasis.

15. Ibid., p. 22.

16. The position runs throughout his writings. Perhaps the clearest statement is in Friedrich Nietzsche, *Genealogy of Morals* (New York: Vintage, 1989), pp. 46–48.

17. Oates, *Let the Trumpets Sound*, pp. 88–89; see also Garrow, *Bearing the Cross*, pp. 57–58.

18. Lewis, *Walking with the Wind*, p. 193.

19. Garrow, *Bearing the Cross*, p. 81. My emphasis.

20. Ibid., p. 140.

21. Ibid., pp. 47, 63.

22. James M. Washington, ed., *I Have a Dream: Writings and Speeches That Changed the World* (New York: HarperCollins, 1992), p. 172.

23. Ibid., p. 175.

24. Oates, *Let the Trumpets Sound*, p. 218.

25. Ibid., p. 236.

26. Halberstam, *Children*, pp. 139–140.

27. Lewis, *Walking with the Wind*, p. 75.

28. Søren Kierkegaard, *Fear and Trembling* (Princeton, NJ: Princeton University Press, 1988). I cannot recall the source of the Zen story, but I know I've been telling it for many years!

29. Nietzsche, *Geneaology*.

30. Lewis, *Walking with the Wind*, p. 52.

31. We must realize that this sense does not simply stem from mistaken beliefs. If others are richer, more powerful, and more respected and if those others can always set all the terms of social interactions—then one does experience social life as an inferior.

32. Halberstam, *Children*, pp. 76–79.

33. Eric Burner, *And Gently He Shall Lead Them: Robert Parris Moses and Civil Rights in Mississippi* (New York: New York University Press, 1994), pp. 17–18.

34. Garrow, *Bearing the Cross*, pp. 159–160.

35. Branch, *Parting the Waters*, p. 472.

36. Once infantile forms of communism or enlightenment theory are put behind us.

37. Charles Payne, *I've Got the Light of Freedom: The Organizing Tradition and the Mississippi Freedom Struggle* (Berkeley: University of California Press, 1996), p. 274.

38. *Washington Post*, January 2, 1960.

39. Jack M. Bloom, *Class, Race, and the Civil Rights Movement* (Bloomington: Indiana University Press, 1987), pp. 216–217.

40. Oates, *Let the Trumpets Sound*, p. 103; Garrow, *Bearing the Cross*, pp. 81–82.

41. Garrow, *Bearing the Cross*, p. 172.

42. Payne, *I've Got the Light*, p. 18.

43. Bloom, *Class, Race, and the Civil Rights Movement*.

44. Branch, *Pillar of Fire*, pp. 242, 494, 520.

45. Oates, *Let the Trumpets Sound*, p. 391.

46. Gottlieb, *History and Subjectivity*, chap. 12.

47. Of the many accounts of relations between capitalism and racism, see Bloom, *Class, Race, and the Civil Rights Movement*, especially chap. 8; Michael Reich, *Racial Inequality: A Political-Economic Analysis* (Princeton, NJ: Princeton University Press, 1980); Virginia Cyrus, ed., *Experiencing Race, Class, and Gender in the United States* (Mountain View, CA: Mayfield Publishing Company, 1993); as well as the journal *Race, Gender, and Class*.

48. Bruce Nelson, *Divided We Stand: American Workers and the Struggle for Black Equality* (Princeton, NJ: Princeton University Press, 2001), pp. 287–296.

49. Anthony Lukas, *Common Ground: A Turbulent Decade in the Lives of Three American Families* (New York: Knopf, 1985).

50. See Gottlieb, *History and Subjectivity*, chap. 16.

51. Wayne Washington, "For Black Politicians, Higher Office a Tall Order," *Boston Globe*, June 13, 2001.

52. William Julius Wilson, *The Truly Disadvantaged: The Inner City, the Underclass, and Public Policy* (Chicago: University of Chicago Press, 1987).

53. This account of the contemporary situation comes from Manuel Castells, *The Information Age: Economy, Society, and Culture*, vol. 2, *The Power of Identity* (Oxford: Blackwell, 1997), pp. 52–59.

54. Environmental racism will be discussed again in Chapter 7. One valuable source is Peter Wenz and Laura Westra, eds., *Facing Environmental Racism* (Lanham, MD: Rowman and Littlefield, 1995).

55. JoAnn Wypijewski, "Back to the Back of the Bus," *The Nation*, December 25, 2000.

56. For the importance of this encounter, see Gary Gerstle, *American Crucible: Race and Nation in the Twentieth Century* (Princeton, NJ: Princeton University Press, 2001); and Payne, *I've Got the Light*.

57. Oates, *Let The Trumpets Sound*, pp. 398–402.

58. Robert Weisbrot, *Freedom Bound: A History of America's Civil Rights Movement* (New York: Norton, 1990), p. 206.

59. Cornell West, "Black Strivings in a Twilight Civilization," in Henry Louis Gates and Cornell West, eds., *The Future of the Races* (New York: Knopf, 1996), p. 110.

60. Frances Fox Piven and Richard Cloward, *Poor People's Movements* (New York: Vintage, 1979).

61. Payne, *I've Got the Light*, pp. 340–362.

62. From 1979 to 1998, the top 1 percent of the nation had its income rise 106 percent. The other 80 percent ranged between a 15-percent increase and, for the bottom 20 percent, a 5-percent *decrease*. For a detailed presentation of the numbers, see Chuck Collins and Felice Yeskel, *Economic Apartheid in America: A Primer on Economic Inequality and Insecurity* (New York: New Press, 2000). The statistic given above is on p. 42.

63. See Stanley Wolpert, *Gandhi's Passion: The Life and Legacy of Mahatma Gandhi* (New York: Oxford University Press, 2001), pp. 257–263; Manfred Steger, *Gandhi's Dilemma: Nonviolent Principles and Nationalist Power* (New York: St. Martin's Press, 2000), pp. 181–194.

64. James Washington, *I Have a Dream*, p. 134.

65. Oates, *Let the Trumpets Sound*, p. 316; Washington, *I Have a Dream*, p. 156.

CHAPTER 6: AFTER PATRIARCHY

1. Rosemary Radford Ruether, *Sexism and God-Talk: Toward a Female Theology* (Boston: Beacon Press, 1983), p. 19.

2. Cynthia Ozick, "Notes Towards Finding the Right Question," in Susannah Heschel, ed., *On Being a Jewish Feminist: A Reader* (New York: Schocken, 1983), p. 150.

3. Sheila Rowbotham traces the origins of feminism in the Reformation. See her *Hidden from History* (London: Pluto Press, 1993).

4. *A Global Ethic: The Declaration of the Parliament of the World's Religions* (New York: Continuum, 1993).s

5. National Council of Churches, "Inclusive Language Lectionary," in Judith Plaskow and Carol Christ, eds., *Weaving the Visions: New Patterns in Feminist Spirituality* (San Francisco: Harper SanFrancisco, 1989), p. 165.

6. W.V.O. Quine, *From a Logical Point of View* (Cambridge: Harvard University Press, 1980), pp. 78–79.

7. Judith Plaskow, *Standing Again at Sinai: Judaism from a Feminist Perspective* (New York: Harper SanFrancisco, 1990), p. xii.

8. I will use Judaism for the most part and will rely less heavily on Christianity and Buddhism. This is partly for reasons of familiarity and partly because I believe many of the points made by Jewish feminists are transferable to other contexts.

9. Rabbi Elaine Zecher, personal interview, January 7, 2001.

10. Blu Greenberg, *On Women and Judaism* (Philadelphia: Jewish Publication Society, 1981), p. 3.

11. Ibid., p. 6. My emphasis.

12. Matthew 25:40.

13. Rachel Adler, *Engendering Judaism: An Inclusive Theology and Ethics* (Boston: Beacon Press, 1998), p. 134.

14. Ibid., p. 161.

15. David Blumenthal, *Facing the Abusing God: A Theology of Protest* (Louisville, KY: Westminster John Knox Press, 1993).

16. See Judith Ochshorn, *The Female Experience and the Nature of the Divine* (Bloomington: Indiana University Press, 1981), pp. 174–184; Joanne Brown and Carole Bohn, eds., *Christianity, Patriarchy, and Abuse*, 1990).

17. Exodus 19:14–15.

18. Arlie Hochschild, *Second Shift* (New York: Avon, 1997).

19. Max Weber, *The Protestant Ethic and the Spirit of Capitalism* (London: Routledge, 2001); R. H. Tawney, *Religion and the Rise of Capitalism* (New York: Transaction, 1998).

20. Of course, the question of women's equality—which for most writers and activists includes gay and lesbian rights as well—is in some ways an even deeper challenge than these other examples. Male-female relations have always been central to religion's self-understanding, in a way that many other attitudes or values are not. This will, of course, vary to some degree from one religion to another. However, insofar as gender is essential to social life and religions always exist within a social context, the general idea is broadly accurate.

21. Cobb, *Reclaiming the Church*, p. 65.

22. The documents of the American and French revolutions embody, if often imperfectly, this idea. Philosophically, they have no better original expression than in John Locke, *Second Treatise of Civil Government*.

23. Karl Marx, *The German Ideology* (Buffalo, NY: Prometheus Books, 1998).

24. Zecher, personal interview.

25. At least in the abstract, this position is also a cornerstone of science. For science to work, people must be free, for example, to do whatever research they think necessary and to criticize claims they think are false. We would not think much of a scientific community that forbade a whole category of people to be scientists—and claimed "scientific" reasons for doing so. This doesn't mean that we take a collective vote on each scientific—or theological—proposition. It means that no *group* is excluded from authority. This position is staked out well by the early work of Jurgen Habermas. See, for instance, his *Knowledge and Human Interests*.

26. Rosemary Radford Ruether, "Feminism in World Christianity," in Arvand Sharma and Katherine Young, eds., *Feminism and World Religions* (Albany: State University of New York Press, 1999), pp. 220–221. Ruether is summarizing the work of these other writers.

27. Rabbi Sandy Sasso, quoted in Laura Geller, "From Equality to Transformation: The Challenge of Women's Rabbinic Leadership," in T. M. Rudavsky, ed., *Gender and Judaism: The Transformation of Tradition* (New York: New York University Press, 1995), p. 247.

28. Plaskow, *Standing Again at Sinai*, pp. 60–65.

29. Carol Gilligan, *In a Different Voice: Psychological Theory and Women's Development* (Cambridge: Harvard University Press, 1993).

30. Nel Noddings, *Women and Evil* (Berkeley, CA: University of California Press, 1989), p. 20.

31. Plaskow, *Standing Again at Sinai*, pp. 166–167.

32. Carter Heyward, *Touching Our Strength: The Erotic as Power and the Love of God* (San Francisco: Harper and Row, 1989).

33. Adler, *Engendering Judaism*, p. 134.

34. Noddings, *Women and Evil*, p. 22.

35. Adler, *Engendering Judaism*, pp. 83–95.

36. See Stout, *Ethics After Babel*.

37. Rabbi David Edelman, interview in *What Is Enlightenment* 18 (Fall–Winter 2000), p. 78.

38. Adler, *Engendering Judaism*, p. 37.

39. Rochelle L. Millen: "An Analysis of Rabbinic Hermeneutics," in Rudavsky, *Gender and Judaism*.

40. There are analogies here to the way contemporary writers romanticize and distort the history of the family, representing the quite recent nuclear family as a long-term norm it in fact was not.

41. Elisabeth Schussler Fiorenze, "In Search of Women's Heritage," in Plaskow and Christ, *Weaving the Visions*, p. 34. See also Christin Lore Weber, *WomanChrist: A New Vision of Feminist Spirituality* (New York: Harper and Row, 1987), pp. 18–19, 30.

42. Tikva Frymer-Kensky, *In the Wake of the Goddesses: Women, Culture, and the Biblical Transformation of Pagan Myth* (New York: Fawcett, 1993).

43. Seymour Siegel, quoted in Susan Weidman Schneider, *Jewish and Female: Sourcebook for Today's Jewish Woman* (New York: Touchstone, 1984), p. 49. For a brief survey of women's active participation in Judaism, see Schneider, pp. 42–47.

44. The same position arises with the critique of religion's unself-conscious anthropocentrism.

45. Julie Greenberg, "Seeking a Feminist Judaism," in Melanie Kay Kantrowitz and Irena Klepfisz, eds., *The Tribe of Dina: A Jewish Women's Anthology* (Boston: Beacon Press, 1989).

46. Rita Gross, "Feminist Revalorization of Buddhism," in Sharma and Young, *Feminism and World Religions*, p. 79.

47. Alasdair MacIntyre, *After Virtue* (South Bend, IN: Notre Dame University Press), p. 222.

48. Elisabeth Schussler Fiorenza, *In Memory of Her: A Feminist Theological Reconstruction of Christian Origins* (New York: Crossroad, 1994).

49. Gross, "Feminist Revalorization of Buddhism," p. 84.

50. Plaskow, *Standing Again at Sinai*, p. 143.

51. Anne M. Clifford, *Introducing Feminist Theology* (Maryknoll, NY: Orbis Books, 2001).

52. For one example, consider the prickly exchange over the reality and importance of theories of prehistoric matriarchal societies and religion, in Charlene Spretnak, ed., *The Politics of Women's Spirituality: Essays on the Rise of Spiritual Power Within the Feminist Movement* (New York: Anchor, 1982), pp. 541–561.

53. Cynthia Eller, *Living in the Lap of the Goddess: The Feminist Spirituality Movement in America* (Boston: Beacon Press, 1995), pp. 204–205.

54. Judith Antonelli, "Feminist Spirituality: The Politics of the Psyche," in Spretnak, *Politics of Women's Spirituality*, p. 399.

55. See, for instance, Hallie Iglehart, "The Unnatural Divorce of Spirituality and Politics," *Quest: A Feminist Quarterly* 4 (3) (Summer 1978); Starhawk, *Dreaming the Dark* (Boston: Beacon Press, 1982).

56. Worse yet, there is something of a tendency to make the whole issue academic. When I recently asked a distinguished panel of Jewish feminists about the relation of Jewish feminism to the wider women's movement, the single answer I got was that "grassroots politics weren't really relevant anymore; and besides things are different now that we have the Internet"! (Panel on "Where Is Jewish Feminism Now?" American Academy of Religion, November 2000, Nashville).

57. Sandra Wilson, "'Which Me Will Survive All These Liberations . . . ' On Being a Black Woman Episcopal Priest," in Diana L. Eck and Devaki Jain, eds., *Speaking of Faith: Global Perspectives on Women, Religion, and Social Change* (Philadelphia: New Society Publishers, 1987), p. 131.

58. Spretnak, *Politics of Women's Spirituality*, p. 349.

59. See Susan Thistlethwaite, "Every Two Minutes: Battered Women and Feminist Interpretation," in Plaskow and Christ, *Weaving the Visions*; and the stories about sexual exploitation by Buddhist teachers in Sandy Boucher, *Turning the Wheel: American Women Creating the New Buddhism* (Boston: Beacon, 1993); Susan Brownmiller, *Against Our Will: Men, Women, and Rape* (New York: Fawcett, 1993).

60. The work of Mary Daly, which progressed from the attempt to reform Catholicism to a profound rejection of masculine bias in all of Western civilization, is an instructive example.

CHAPTER 7: SAVING THE WORLD

1. A Christian organization devoted to "love our neighbors as ourselves and to care for the earth," at www.targetearth.org.

2. Petra Kelly, *Thinking Green: Essays on Feminism, Environmentalism, and Nonviolence* (Berkeley, CA: Parallax Press, 1964), p. 37.

3. See http://www.biodev.org/index2.htm.

4. In Libby Bassett, ed., *Earth and Faith: A Book of Reflection for Action* (New York: United National Environmental Programme, 2000), p. 11.

5. Pope John Paul II, "The Ecological Crisis: A Common Responsibility," in Roger S. Gottlieb, ed., *This Sacred Earth* (New York: Routledge, 1995), p. 230. Emphasis in original.

6. Foreword to Allan Hunt Badiner, ed., *Dharma Gaia: A Harvest of Essays in Buddhism and Ecology* (Berkeley, CA: Parallax Press, 1990).

7. Bassett, *Earth and Faith*, p. 52.

8. Mark Wallace, *Fragments of the Spirit* (New York: Continuum, 1996), p. 141.

9. The antiglobalization literature is now very large. For informative recent treatments, see Jerry Mander, "Economic Globalization and the Environment," *Tikkun* (September October 2001); Mark Weisbrot, "Tricks of Free Trade," *Sierra* (September–October 2001); the International Foundation on Globalization, www.ifg.org; and Global Exchange, www.globalexchange.org.

10. See www.wcc-coe.org.

11. *Nation*, May 7, 2001.

12. For example, *Sierra* (November–December 1998).

13. Thomas Berry, "Ecology and the Future of Catholicism," in Albert P. LaChance and John E. Carroll, eds., *Embracing Earth: Catholic Approaches to Ecology* (Maryknoll, NY: Orbis Books, 1994), p. xi.

14. See www.elca.org.

15. A range of information and sources can be found in Gottlieb, *This Sacred Earth*.

16. Lynn White, "The Historical: Roots of Our Ecological Crisis," *Science* 155 (3767), March 10, 1967.

17. Wendell Berry, *The Gift of Good Land* (San Francisco: North Point Press, 1981), pp. 317–318.

18. Ellen Bernstein and Dan Fink, *Let the Earth Teach You Torah* (Philadelphia: Shomrei Adama, 1992).

19. Quoted in Gottlieb, *This Sacred Earth*, p. 449.

20. National Council of Churches web site, www.nccusa.org.

21. See www.umc.org.

22. American Baptist Churches, "Creation and the Covenant of Caring," in Gottlieb, *This Sacred Earth*, p. 239.

23. "Safety and Health in Workplace and Community," United Methodist Book of Resolutions, 1996, www.umc.org.

24. Justin Torres, "Religion and Environmentalism: Match Made in Heaven?" January 19, 2000, www.cns.com.

25. Seth Zuckerman, "Redwood Rabbis," *Sierra Magazine* (November–December 1998).

26. For a range of political activities of Buddhists see Christopher S. Queen, ed., *Engaged Buddhism in the West* (Boston: Wisdom, 2000).

27. For example, Theological Education to Meet the Environmental Challenge, www.webofcreation.org, has organized dozens of major conferences and offers resources to seminaries, divinity schools, and so on.

28. Of the now enormous literature on environmental racism and environmental justice, one might start with Robert D. Bullard, *Unequal Protection: Environmental Protection and*

Communities of Color (San Francisco: Sierra Club Books, 1994); and James Lester, David Allen, and Kelly Hill, *Environmental Injustice in the United States: Myths and Realities* (Boulder: Westview Press, 2001).

29. Deeohn Ferris and David Hahn-Baker, "Environmentalists and Environmental Justice Policy," in Bunyan Bryant, ed., *Environmental Justice: Issues, Policies, and Solutions* (Washington, DC: Island Press, 1995).

30. Commission for Racial Justice, *Toxic Wastes and Race in the United States* (New York: United Church of Christ, 1987).

31. Reprinted in Gottlieb, *This Sacred Earth*, p. 634.

32. See discussion in Peter Wenz, *Environmental Ethics Today* (New York: Oxford University Press, 2001), pp. 200–208. Also, Vandana Shiva, *The Violence of the Green Revolution* (Atlantic Highlands, NJ: Zed Books, 1991). For a useful overview of the by now large ecofeminist literature, see Victoria Dayton, "Ecofeminism," in Dale Jamieson, ed., *A Companion to Environmental Philosophy* (London: Blackwell, 2001).

33. See www.eco-justice.org.

34. See www.sai.ciriq.org.au/eco.

35. See www.sao.cirq.org.au/eco.

36. Daniel Faber, director of the coalition, personal communication, September 2, 2001.

37. See essays in Barbara Rose Johnston, ed., *Who Pays the Price: The Sociocultural Context of Environmental Crisis* (Washington, DC: Island Press, 1994); and Aubrey Wallace, ed., *Eco-Heroes: Twelve Tales of Environmental Victory* (San Francisco: Mercury House, 1993).

38. Paul Wapner, *Environmental Activism and World Civic Politics* (Albany: State University of New York Press, 1996), p. 41.

39. Ibid., p. 42.

40. Raymond Bonner, *At the Hand of Man: Peril and Hope for Africa's Wildlife* (New York: Knopf, 1993).

41. Macy, *World as Lover, World as Self*; Carolyn Merchant, *Earthcare: Women and the Environment* (New York: Routledge, 1999); Riane Eisler, *The Chalice and the Blade: Our History, Our Future* (San Francisco: Harper and Row, 1988).

42. Of many sources, see George Sessions, ed., *Deep Ecology for the Twenty-First Century* (Boston: Shambala, 1994). For connections with traditional religions, see David Barnhill and Roger S. Gottlieb, eds., *Deep Ecology and World Religions: New Essays on Common Ground* (Albany: State University of New York Press, 2001).

43. David Brower, *Let the Mountains Talk, Let the Rivers Run* (New York: HarperCollins, 1995), p. 176.

44. Christopher Childs, *The Spirit's Terrain: Creativity, Activism, and Transformation* (Boston: Beacon Press, 1999) p. 50.

45. Wapner, *Environmental Activism*, p. 50.

46. Sulak Sivaraksa, "The Religion of Consumerism," in Kenneth Kraft and Stephanie Kaza, eds., *Dharma Rain: Sources of Buddhist Environmentalism* (Boston: Shambhala, 2000), pp. 178–179.

47. Mary John Mananzan, "Globalization and the Perennial Question of Justice," in Mary Hembrow Snyder, ed., *Spiritual Question for the Twenty-First Century* (Maryknoll, NY: Orbis Books, 2001), p. 157.

48. David Kinsley, *Ecology and Religion: Ecological Spirituality in Cross-Cultural Perspective* (Englewood Cliffs, NJ: Prentice-Hall, 1995).

49. Charlene Spretnak, "The Spiritual Dimension of Green Politics," in Gottlieb, *This Sacred Earth*, pp. 532–535.

50. Kelly, *Thinking Green*, p. 37.

51. Bron Taylor, "Earth First! From Primal Spirituality to Ecological Resistance," in Gottlieb, *This Sacred Earth*, pp. 545–546.

52. Daniel Neal Graham, "The Theory of a Transformational Political Movement: Green Political Theory," in Stephen Wolpert, Christ Slaton, and E. W. Schwerin, eds. *Transformational Politics: Theory, Study, and Practice* (Albany: State University of New York Press, 1998), p. 75.

53. Theodore Roszak, Mary E. Gomes, and Allen D. Kanner, eds., *Ecopsychology: Restoring the Earth, Healing the Mind* (San Francisco: Sierra Club Books, 1995).

54. Manuel Castells, *The Information Age*, vol. 2, *The Power of Identity*, pp. 125–126.

55. Ibid., p. 126.

56. Aldo Leopold, *A Sand County Almanac* (New York: Oxford University Press, 1949), p. 258.

57. Mark Dowie, *Losing Ground: American Environmentalism at the Close of the Twentieth Century* (Cambridge: MIT Press, 1996), p. 226.

58. See McKibben, *Hope, Human and Wild*; Alan Richman, *Gaviotas: A Village to Invent the World* (Chelsea, VT: Chelsea Green Publishing, 1999).

59. Sue Hubbell, *Broadsides from the Other Orders: A Book of Bugs* (New York: Random House, 1993), pp. 74–89.

60. See accounts of this in Bruce Rich, *Mortgaging the Earth*, pp. 251–253; and Madhava Gadgil and Ramachandra Guha, "Ecological Conflicts and the Environmental Movement in India," in Dharam Gahi, ed., *Development and Environment: Sustaining People and Nature* (Oxford and Cambridge: Blackwell, 1994).

61. Heidi Hadsell, "Profits, Parrots, Peons: Ethical Perplexities in the Amazon," in Bron Taylor, ed., *Ecological Resistance Movements: The Global Emergence of Radical and Popular Environmentalism* (Albany: State University of New York Press, 1995), p. 77.

62. Vikram K. Akula, "Grassroots Environmental Resistance in India," in Taylor, *Ecological Resistance Movements*.

63. Bassett, *Earth and Faith*, p. 144.

64. Dorothy Soelle, *The Silent Cry: Mysticism and Resistance* (Minneapolis: Fortress Press, 2001), especially pp. 191–207.

65. For an accessible survey of nineteenth- and twentieth-century Marxism, see Gottlieb, *Marxism 1844–1990*. For some recent Marxist work on ecological issues, see the journal *Capitalism, Nature, Socialism*; James O'Connor, *Natural Causes: Essays in Ecological Marxism* (New York: Guilford Press, 1997). And, for an area study, see Daniel Faber, *Environment Under Fire: Imperialism and the Ecological Crisis in Central America* (New York: Monthly Review Press, 1993).

66. Among many treatments of this theme, see Shiva, *Violence of the Green Revolution*; Tom Athanasiou, *Divided Planet: The Ecology of Rich and Poor* (Athens: University of Georgia Press, 1998); and the journal *Ecologist*.

67. See Mike Jacobs, *The Green Economy: Environment, Sustainable Development, and the Politics of the Future* (London: Pluto Press, 1993).

68. See Andrew MacLaughlin, *Regarding Nature: Industrialism and Deep Ecology* (Albany: State University of New York Press, 1993); as well as the well-known Green self-description: "We're neither left nor right, but out in front."

69. Kelly, *Thinking Green*, p. 123.

70. For an inspiring account of individual leaders, see Catherine Ingram, *In the Footsteps of Gandhi: Conversations with Spiritual Social Activists* (Berkeley, CA: Parallax Press, 1990). For responses to current events, see publications such as *Fellowship Magazine*, *Tikkun*, and *Reconciliation*.

71. Thich Nhat Hanh, *Being Peace*, p. 91. See a commentary on these principles applied to environmental politics: Joan Halifax and Marty Peale, "Interbeing: Precepts and Practices of an Applied Ecology," in Darrell Posey, ed., *Cultural and Spiritual Values of Biodiversity* (London: United Nations Environment Programme, 1999), pp. 475–480.

72. See accounts in John McPhee, *Encounters with the Archdruid* (New York: Farrar, Straus, and Giroux, 1971); and David Brower, *For Earth's Sake: The Life and Times of David Brower* (Salt Lake City: Peregrine Smith Books, 1990).

73. For one brief but precise statement of these issues, see George Tinker, "The Full Circle of Liberation: An American Indian Theology of Place," in David G. Hallman, ed., *Ecotheology: Voices from South and North* (Maryknoll, NY: Orbis Books, 1994).

74. David Abram, *The Spell of the Sensuous: Language and Perception in a More Than Human World* (New York: Pantheon, 1997); Stephanie Kaza, *The Attentive Heart: Conversations with Trees* (New York: Fawcett Columbine, 1993).

75. Max Oelschlaeger, *Caring for Creation: An Ecumenical Approach to the Environmental Crisis* (New Haven: Yale University Press, 1994), pp. 57, 68.

76. Robert Paehlke, *Environmentalism and the Future of Progressive Politics* (New Haven: Yale University Press, 1988), p. 3.

77. I heard him say this during an interview on television, many years ago.

78. See www.webofcreation.org. Comparable groups exist in close to twenty other states.

79. Bassett, *Earth and Faith*, p. 8. My emphasis.

CHAPTER 8: BEYOND OUR PRIVATE SORROWS

1. Audre Lorde, *The Cancer Journals* (San Francisco: Aunt Lute Books, 1980), p. 60.

2. Nancy Mairs, *Waist-High in the World: A Life Among the Nondisabled* (Boston: Beacon Press, 1996), p. 14.

3. Charles A. Hart, "Life's Illusions," in Donald J. Meyer, ed., *Uncommon Fathers: Reflections on Raising a Child with a Disability* (Bethesda, MD: Woodbine House, 1995), p. 190.

4. Zillah Eisenstein, *Manmade Breast Cancers* (Ithaca, NY: Cornell University Press, 2001), p. 98.

5. Sandra Steingraber, *Living Downstream: An Ecologist Looks at Cancer and the Environment* (Reading, MA: Addison-Wesley, 1997), p. 251.

6. Robert Proctor, *Cancer Wars: How Politics Shapes What We Know and Don't Know About Cancer* (NY: Basic Books, 1995), pp. 54–75.

7. See www.breastcancerfund.org. For a brief recent statement about breast milk, see Dana Foley, "Moms and POPs: Nature Would Never Make Milk Like This," *On Earth* 23 (3) (Fall 2001):46.

8. Steingraber, *Living Downstream*, pp. 42–43.

9. Dan Fagin, Marianne Lavell, and the Center for Public Integrity, *Toxic Deception: How the Chemical Industry Manipulates Science, Bends the Law, and Endangers Your Health* (Secaucus, NJ: Birch Lane Press, 1996).

10. Ellen Leopold, *A Darker Ribbon: Breast Cancer, Women, and Their Doctors in the Twentieth Century* (Boston: Beacon Press, 1999), p. 272.

11. Janet D. Sherman, *Life's Delicate Balance: Causes and Prevention of Breast Cancer* (New York: Taylor and Francis, 2000), p. 149.

12. Ibid., p. 207.

13. Jane S. Zones, "Profits from Pain: The Political Economy of Breast Cancer," in Anne S. Kasper and Susan J. Ferguson, eds., *Breast Cancer: Society Shapes an Epidemic* (New York: St. Martin's Press, 2000), p. 144.

14. Proctor, *Cancer Wars*, pp. 256–257; Monte Paulson, "The Cancer Business," *Mother Jones* (June 1994).

15. Eisenstein, *Manmade Breast Cancers*, pp. 115–116.

16. Carol Weisman, "Breast Cancer Policymaking," in Kasper and Ferguson, *Breast Cancer*.

17. Proctor, *Cancer Wars*, p. 266; Peter Chowka, "The National Cancer Institute and the Fifty-Year Cover-Up," *East-West* (January 1978):22–27; Ralph Moss, *The Cancer Industry* (New York: Paragon House, 1991).

18. Proctor, *Cancer Wars*, p. 266. See also Sharon Batt and Liza Gross, "Cancer, Inc.," *Sierra* (September–October 1999).

19. Proctor, *Cancer Wars*, p. 268.

20. Steingraber, *Living Downstream*, p. 42.

21. Susan J. Ferguson and Anne S. Kasper, "Living with Breast Cancer," in Kasper and Ferguson, *Breast Cancer*, p. 1.

22. Proctor, *Cancer Wars*, p. 73.

23. Jerome Groopman, "The Thirty Years' War: Have We Been Fighting Cancer the Wrong Way?" *New Yorker*, June 4, 2001, p. 54.

24. Kenny Ausubel, "When Healing Becomes a Crime," *Tikkun* (May–June 2001):37.

25. Susan Love, *Dr. Susan Love's Breast Book* (New York: Perseus, 1999).

26. Zones, "Profits from Pain," p. 130.

27. Eisenstein, *Manmade Breast Cancers*, p. 66.

28. Lorde, *Journals*, pp. 59–60.

29. Rose Kushner, quoted in Barron H. Lerner, *The Breast Cancer Wars: Hope, Fear, and the Pursuit of a Cure in Twentieth-Century America* (New York: Oxford University Press, 2001), p. 178.

30. Barbara A. Brenner, "Sister Support: Women Create a Breast Cancer Movement," in Kasper and Ferguson, *Breast Cancer*, p. 326.

31. See a broad listing of these groups in Sherman, *Life's Delicate Balance*.

32. See www.breastcancerfund.org.

33. Statement of NOW President Patricia Ireland, October 27, 1999, from NOW web site, www.now.org.

34. See www.sierraclub.org.

35. Boston Women's Health Book Collective, *The New Our Bodies, Ourselves* (New York: Simon and Schuster, 1992), pp. 105–112.

36. Steingraber, *Living Downstream*; Theo Coburn, *Our Stolen Future: Are We Threatening Our Fertility, Intelligence, and Survival?—A Scientific Detective Story* (New York: Plume, 1997).

37. Lois Gibbs, foreword to Richard Hofrichter, ed., *Toxic Struggles: The Theory and Practice of Environmental Justice* (Philadelphia: New Society Publishers, 1993), p. ix.

38. For a highly readable account of such struggles, see Fred Setterberg and Lonny Shavelson, *Toxic Nation: The Fight to Save Our Communities from Chemical Contamination* (New York: Wiley and Sons, 1993).

39. Michael Oliver, *The Politics of Disablement* (London: Macmillan Education, 1990) p. 35.

40. Joseph P. Shapiro, *No Pity: People with Disabilities Forging a New Civil Rights Movement* (New York: Random House, 1994).

41. The Styrofoam story is from Bill McKibben, *The End of Nature* (New York: Anchor, 1999). On CFCs, see John Nance, *What Goes Up: The Global Assault on Our Atmosphere* (New York: Morrow, 1991).

42. Raised, variously (and among others), by Heidegger, the Frankfurt School, feminist theory, and recent works by Howard Gardener.

43. Martha Nussbaum, "Disabled Lives: Who Cares?" *New York Review of Books*, January 11, 2001.

44. For instance, the rights of individual restaurant owners to refuse service to African-Americans were overcome by an activist black movement seeking rights for an entire group.

45. This may remind us of issues about the differences between male and female rabbis discussed in Chapter 6.

46. Eva Kittay, *Love's Labor: Essays on Women, Equality, and Dependency* (New York: Routledge: 1999), p. 183. These last paragraphs owe much to Kittay's excellent book.

47. Alasdair MacIntyre, *Dependent Rational Animals: Why Human Beings Need the Virtues* (Chicago: Open Court, 1999).

48. Quoted in Mary Johnson, "A Test of Wills: Jerry Lewis, Jerry's Orphans, and the Telethon," in Barrett Shaw, ed., *The Ragged Edge: The Disability Experience from the Pages of the First Fifteen Years of the Disability Rag* (Louisville, KY: Advocado Press, 1994), p. 120.

49. Charlton, *Nothing About Us Without Us.*

50. See Richard K. Scotch, *From Good Will to Civil Rights: Transforming Federal Disability Policy* (Philadelphia: Temple University Press, 2001).

51. Ibid., p. 10.

52. Jean Stewart, *The Body's Memory: A Novel* (New York: St. Martin's Press, 1989), pp. 262–263.

53. Shapiro, *No Pity*, p. 185.

54. I do not mean to minimize the physical and emotional trauma that comes with the loss of one or both breasts to mastectomy.

55. Leo Tolstoy, *The Death of Ivan Ilych* (New York: Bantam Books, 1987); Elisabeth Kubler-Ross, *On Death and Dying* (New York: Macmillan, 1969).

56. Steven Levine, *Who Dies?* (New York: Doubleday, 1982), p. 157–175.

57. Susan Kenner, Carol Osborn, Linda Quigley, and Karen Stroup, *Speak the Language of Healing: Living with Breast Cancer Without Going to War* (Berkeley, CA: Conari Press, 1999), pp. 157–159.

58. Ibid., p. 40.

59. Ibid., pp. 165–67.

60. Ibid., pp. 97–99.

61. Kittay, *Love's Labor*, pp. 147–161.

62. Michael Berube, *Life as We Know It: A Father, a Family, and an Exceptional Child* (New York: Pantheon, 1996).

63. Stanley D. Klein and Kim Schive, eds., *You Will Dream New Dreams: Inspiring Personal Stories by Parents of Children with Disabilities* (New York: Kensington Books, 2001).

64. Greenspan, *Healing Through the Dark Emotions.*

65. Robert A. Naseef, "The Rudest Awakening," in Klein and Schive, *Dream New Dreams*, p. 209.

66. Jillian K. Welch, "The Journey," in Klein and Schive, *Dream New Dreams*, pp. 198–199.

67. C. S. Lewis, *A Grief Observed* (San Francisco: Harper SanFrancisco, 1994).

68. Susan Wendell, *The Rejected Body* (New York: Routledge, 1996), p. 63.

69. Ibid., p. 175.

70. The discussion of the church and disability, as well as this particular example, comes from the excellent book by Nancy L. Eiesland, *The Disabled God: Toward a Liberatory Theology of Disability* (Nashville, TN: Abingdon, 1994).

71. This is the theme voiced in Mairs, *Waist-High in the World*, as well as in countless other memoirs by people with disabilities.

72. Greenspan, *Healing Through the Dark Emotions.*

CHAPTER 9: TOWARD HOPE, TOGETHER

1. Ron Kovic, *Born on the Fourth of July* (New York: Pocket Books, 1976).

2. Ibid., p. 146.

3. Ibid., pp. 140–150.

4. This perspective is developed in Gottlieb, *Spirituality of Resistance.*

5. Joanna Macy, *Despair and Empowerment in the Nuclear Age* (Philadelphia: New Society Publishers, 1983), and *Widening Circles* (Gabriola Island, British Columbia: New Society Publishers, 2000).

6. Elie Wiesel, public lecture, National Catholic Center for Holocaust Education, 1989.

Index

West, Cornell, 125
Western Marxism, 91, 220(n41)
Westra, Laura, 226(n54)
Wexler, Philip, 45
White Violet Center for Eco-Justice, 161
White, Lynn, 157
Wiesel, Elie
Wiesel, Elie, 212
Williams, Roger, xix
Willimon, William, 52
Willis, Ellen, xxii-xxvii, 26
Wilson, Sandra, 148
Wilson, William Julius, 123
Wittig, Monique, 223(n46)
Women, 63
    and nature, 160

as rabbis, 132–134, 140
condition of, 130–131
equality of, 130–142, 227(n20)
in religious history, 143–144
Women's movement. *See* Feminism
Working class, 54, 121
World Bank 168
World Council of Churches (WCC),
    155–156
World Health Organization, 181, 190
World Making, 4–6, 9, 19–20, 21, 153,
    160
World Wide Fund for Nature, 177
Wuthnow, Robert, 35–36

Zecher, Rabbi Elaine, 132, 133, 138

DATE DUE

NOV 0 2 2007			
NOV 1 2 2010			
DEC 1 5 2010			
			Printed In USA